THE STORY OF INDIAN PHILOSOPHY

THE STORY OF INDIAN PHILOSOPHY

A journey across the ages
Through a modern day traveller

PRASANNA GAUTAM

MLBD PUBLICATIONS

Motilal Banarsidass Publications

MOTILAL BANARSIDASS
PUBLICATIONS
4741/23, Ansari Road, Daryaganj, New Delhi - 110002 (India)
Email: *mlbd@mlbd.com* | *sales@mlbd.com* | *exports@mlbd.com*
Website: *www.mlbd.com*

The Story of Indian Philosophy
by
Prasanna Gautam

First Edition Published in 2022

Published in India by Motilal Banarsidass Publications

ISBN : 978-93-91759-91-9 (HB)
ISBN : 978-93-91759-85-8 (PB)

Printed and bound in India

Dedicated to the readers.

"It does not matter how slowly you go
as long as you do not stop".

Confucius

"The journey of a thousand miles
begins with one step".

Lao Tzu

Acknowledgements

I am deeply grateful for the help and encouragement of my wife and children who allowed me to spend most of my time working on this manuscript during the enforced lockdown in 2020 due to the COVID-19 pandemic. In a strange way, keeping busy in this work helped me to focus on other things than becoming overwhelmed by the avalanche of tragedies all around us.

I am also thankful l to many friends and colleagues who have encouraged me to write this book. Professor Surya Subedi, Mrs Nandini Bahuguna, Mrs Hema Kamath and Mr Prakash Khanal helped a great deal with earlier drafts and their valuable suggestions. The proofreading and suggestions by Mr Lee Dickinson of the earlier drafts were very helpful. The in-depth review by Mr Clive Roberts and Dr Hemang Dixit with their frank comments and suggestions became useful in presentation of the text with clarity and coherence. The comparative overview by Professor Ramesh Adhikari became very encouraging. My special thanks are also due to Mr Nagesh Manay, the managing director of OPUS, Bangalore for personally desining the cover page.

Finally, I must express my deep gratitude to Professor Kashinath Nyaupane of Nepal Sanskrit University for perusing the manuscript and writing the foreword. I cannot thank him enough.

Epigraph.

"mā bhrātā bhrātaram

dwikshanmā swasāramuta swasā I

samyancah savratā bhūtwām

wācam wadata bhadrayā II"

Atharva Veda Book 3, Mantra xxx-3

Let no brother hate his brother,

No sister to sister be unkind.

Unanimous with one intent,

You speak your speech in friendliness.

Atharva Veda, Book 3, xxx3: Translation by Devi Chand

Foreword

Professor Prasanna Gautam is a serious scholar of ancient Sanskrit literature. He has been pursuing these studies in the tradition set by his grandfather, *Vidwatshiromani Sri Kulachandra Gautam*, who was a beacon of light for all of us. His exceptional original works are the pride of the Sanskrit literary world and make his presence felt amongst us even after his death so long ago. I have no hesitation in saying that Professor Gautam, too, has made an enormous contribution with his uniquely insightful *expose* of the Rig Veda, by his word for word translation of that ancient literature. Readers will remain forever indebted to him for this scholarly work.

I was also amazed to read his book *Reflections on Contemporary Values, Beliefs and Behaviours* (Cambridge Scholars Publishing, 2018) which prompts us to follow our own inherent inquisitive nature for the benefit of ourselves and humanity at large. This is a unique work for which no amount of praise will be sufficient.

I felt privileged to glance through the draft of this book on Indian philosophy. I found this to contain the core of the eastern philosophical concepts. This has the thoughts of the *Rishis* (sages) of the Vedic era and reflects their debates found in the Upanishads in a lucid manner. The secrets within *Mahabharata* and *Ramayana* have been clearly uncovered from the old dogmas over the centuries. This also has shaken our usual way of interpreting *Bhagavad Gita.* The gravitas of the teaching of *Buddha* has been well elucidated. In short, he has tried to fill a jar with all the waters of an ocean.

I find that the additional aspect of this work is to dig into the root cause of decadence that has developed into Indian thinking and behaviour. The book makes us realise that we have been unjust to the entire esoteric concepts by miring them into superstitious customs and traditional caste system. He has done this by explicitly presenting all the Vedic concepts in an analytical and logical manner as the proof of this narration.

One can appreciate his methodical manner of introducing and expanding complex subjects. He begins by an introductory overview of the Indian philosophical spectrum in Chapter one. He then takes the readers step by step in subsequent chapters which explain the concepts in an objective and logical way, thus helping them to comprehend the complex issues and develop unique insight by themselves. The book has twenty-three chapters, each full of facts, gravitas, lucidity and logic. Beginning from the era of nature worship (paganism), the book covers chronologically and systematically the Vedic thoughts, Brahminism, *Tantra, Upanishads,* various philosophical concepts, the renaissance, *Purva Mimamsa, Vaiseshika, Nyaya, Samkhya, Yoga, Carbaka, Buddhist* and *Jaina* thoughts, *Vedanta, Bhagavad Gita,* economic and political theories, astrological and mathematical concepts, modern Indian thinking, and many others. The concluding chapter sums up the essence of Indian philosophy. Each chapter is important and provides clear pointers for further research in future. Although appearing easy to read at first, the book guides the reader to comprehend the seriousness of the concepts, thus making him want to learn more about this subject. This book is a must-read for understanding this ancient wisdom.

I congratulate Professor Gautam for this great accomplishment and wish him a long and healthy life. Although he has stated at the outset that this is an introductory work, I hope he will produce another detailed exposition of these concepts giving his scholarly commentary.

Dr. Kashinath Nyaupane
Professor of Buddhism and Sanskrit
Nepal Sanskrit University
Kathmandu.
Email: kashinathguru@gmail.com

There is a story of a religious teacher who used to talk every morning to his disciples. One morning he got on to the platform and was just about to begin when a little bird came and sat on the windowsill and began to sing and sang away with full heart. Then it stopped and flew away, and the teacher said "The sermon for this morning is over".

J. Krishnamurti

Preface

Why this book?

Large parts of 2020-21 have been the most horrific period in our memory. Our belief systems have received the greatest jolt and made us re-examine our values and faiths. In addition, the unprecedented coexistence of wealth and poverty, and struggles for survival have precipitated global disharmony and conflict. It is in this context of deaths, devastation of families, and food banks and hunger that have compelled us to evaluate our concepts of quality of life, including mental and spiritual needs. The 'quality of living' in terms of a blissful existence in peace, equanimity and contentment had been foremost in the minds of the ancient Indian philosophers. This is different from the modern concept of 'quality of life', which does depend upon physical amenities and comfort. A true understanding of the evolution of our thought processes from the earliest time to the present may help us in this hour of need.

Indian philosophy appears at first to be a bewildering plethora of concepts. It is this curious potpourri of faith and logic that has made Indian philosophy an enigma. Although the original works appear in simple, short phrases or sentences in Sanskrit, they do require some knowledge of the ancient culture and religion of that land to comprehend them. Many Indologists of great renown have tried to explain this philosophy and have produced many tomes of learned literature. They had become profoundly impressed to find that the Indian subcontinent had produced many great philosophers even earlier than the Greeks and Egyptians who had influenced their Christian world. These commentaries, while showing their reverence to the works of the great Indian philosophers, also indicate the insurmountable complexities of the diverse cultures and the prevailing conditions in that unknown era of that unknown land which they had to comprehend. This was realised by General Wellesley, who unilaterally established the 'Oxford of the East' in Calcutta but was not allowed to make this a great institution. A general reader cannot be certain to have grasped the actual message of the original philosophers by reading these commentaries, which mostly focus on single issues, suggestive of 'not seeing the wood for the trees.'

One needs to study the ancient literature from India in Sanskrit to try to truly comprehend the original philosophical thoughts, culture, and aspirations. Most words in Sanskrit can be used to mean many different things in different contexts. The key to their appreciation is grammar [or indeed the lack of it], the context and the prevalent cultural or social practices relevant to the subject. The accurate translation of an ancient work from Sanskrit into English is extremely difficult because of the brevity of the phrases, unavailability of equivalent words and corresponding grammatical equivalents. Even the transliteration in the Roman alphabet is difficult, and the diacritic marks do not always exactly depict the joined or compound letters. Hence there is ample scope for alternative interpretations, as seen by the contradicting opinions among the great scholars in Indology. I have found similar constraints in the works of modern Indian scholars too, who have been much influenced by their own cultural, caste and religious backgrounds, in addition to the Greek and latter European philosophies that invariably have been the foundations of their education. They too have continued the use of inaccurate terms, e.g., 'sacrifice' for *Yagńa,* 'religion' for *Dharma,* 'Brahman' *for Brahma,* 'Ātman' for *Ātmā*, etc., irrespective of the grammatical and original context. Equally perplexing is the continued usage of 'Āryan' to indicate an ethnic group or a race. There does not appear to be any appreciation of the fact the colloquial expressions of the ancient Sanskrit vernacular of terms like *Dasyu, Nāga, Dāsa, Paṇi* do not always indicate ethnicity and are choice words of verbal abuse, implying robber or thief, a deceiver who stings, a slave or one of no consequence, a cunning or cheating trader, etc.

Max Muller had also observed that the job of a historian of philosophy was "to winnow what is permanent from what is temporary and to discover, if possible, the vein of gold that runs through the quartz, to keep the gold and sweep away the rubbish." This 'winnowing' cannot be done by taking a cross-sectional view of the existing philosophical concepts. This needs a dynamic approach, i.e., a three-dimensional view of an idea at its beginning, after it took strong root, and eventually its modification as well as its influence on other ideas which appeared subsequently. This understanding of when and how an idea developed, how it influenced the thinking at that period and how it evolved over time and related to the newer concepts is essential to 'winnow' any philosophical concept. It was Pierre Hadot who said that philosophy was a way of life. Hadot goes further, saying that modern philosophers are 'artists of reason' while the ancient philosophers were 'artists of life'. Indeed, can we really justify any intellectual pursuit by ignoring our way of life which is evolving incessantly? It is undeniable that the process of evolution includes the whole of the organism, including its mind and not just the body. I have tried to producc this small work to demonstrate that philosophy is the reflection of thoughts evolved from the earliest to the present time.

I have deliberately resisted the temptation to compare and contrast with the European and Indian philosophical concepts. This is to prevent introducing personal bias in the understanding of these important issues. I freely admit that I am not 'a historian of philosophy trying to discover the vein of gold' but merely an enthusiast, although readers may notice that I have tried to dispel some commonly held beliefs which are not corroborated by facts. Most Indians do not dwell upon these concepts at all, merely choosing to follow their traditions which are steeped in the ancient ways of life and the recorded philosophical expressions, legends, and history. The parents and the schoolteachers normally do not teach or explain these philosophical issues to their children and pupils.

This short work has squeezed a period of several millennia and presented the evolution of concepts in a quasi-historical manner to demonstrate the dynamic nature of Indian philosophy. I hope this makes it different from the hitherto published scholarly books on the subject. The brevity of this presentation has been a deliberate attempt to make the contents of this book as reader friendly as possible, hoping it to be sufficiently informative to satisfy those who wish to know about it but have hardly any time to study the scholarly tomes in this subject. This is further facilitated by making the first few paragraphs give the essence of the full text in that chapter. Hence, a general reader need not go through the whole text in each chapter; the details may be left for students and researchers. Footnotes given appropriately are to facilitate clarity of some statements in the text. A bibliography has also been given to suggest further studies, if desired.

Your views are most welcome.

gautam5@hotmail.co.uk **Prasanna Gautam**

Aberdeen, 2021.

Guide to transliteration and pronunciation

The same accentuation marks are used for the Roman alphabet in both upper case and lower case.

अ	A *a* as in *son*
आ	*Â ā* as in *master*
इ	I i as in *if*
ई	E ee ī as in *feel*
उ	U *u* as in *full*
ऊ	*Oo ū* as in *boot*
ऋ	Ṛ *ṛ* as *ri* in *ritual*
ए	A *a* as in *evade*
ऐ	Y *y* as in *my*
ओ	O *o* as in *oh*
औ	*au* as in *how*
क	K *ka* pronounced as in *curse*
ख	*kha* as in *Khartum*
ग	G *ga* as in *got*
घ	*gha* as in *ghost*

ङ	*ṅ* as *ng* in *slang*
च	C *c̄* as in *cello*
छ	*cha* as in *Chatrapati*
ज	J *ja* as in *journey*
झ	*jha*
ञ	*ñ* as in *Yagña*
ट	T *ṭa* as in *Tom*
ठ	*ṭha*
ड	D *ḍa* as in *daily*
ढ	*ḍha*
ण	*ṇa*
त	T *ta* as in *top*
थ	*tha*
द	D *da,* nearest pronunciation as in *'then'*
ध	*dha* as in *Dhahra*
न	N *na* as in *nun*
प	P *pa* as in *pot*
फ	*pha* as in *pamphlet*
ब	B ba as in *bold*

भ	Bh *bha* as in *Bharat*
म	M *ma* as in *must*
य	Y *ya* as in *yes*
र	R *ra* as in *raw*
ल	L *la* as in *lost*
व	V *va* as in *word*
श	S *śa* as in *Champagne*
ष	Sh *ṣa*
स	S *sa* as in *some*
ह	H *ha* as in *hurt*
:	*h* as in *hey* (half h)
`	*ḿ* ng as in *Sankhya*

" Never accept anything except clear and distinct ideas. Divide each problem into as many parts as are needed to solve it. Order your thoughts from the simple to the complex Always check thoroughly for oversight".

Rene Descartes

Contents

"Madness is doing the same thing repeatedly and expecting different results".

Albert Einstein

CHAPTER 1

Introduction

Man has always deluded himself with all kinds of fanciful beliefs. Many bewildering concepts, several cult practices, plethora of religions and their subdivisions, dogmas of atheism, agnosticism, existentialism, and nihilism etc. which are postulated with authentic zeal support this observation. The quest for reality or the truth of these matters too began from an early age. This led the learned people of the east to debate between pseudo-knowledge, *Avidyā,* and the true knowledge, *Vidyā.* This has been the hallmark of Indian philosophy since ancient times. *Avidyā,* the false knowledge, was regarded as the source of all evil, misery and suffering, but true knowledge, *Vidyā,* brought 'true bliss', the *Brahma.* This quest for bliss and its acquisition was accepted as the sole purpose of human life.

The ancient Indian philosophers had also realised the need for proof of their statements or conclusions. They called this *Pramāṇa* which corresponds to the epistemological and ontological aspects of any concept. Although they maintained that "knowledge comes from inside the self, whereas information is obtained by studying", they had accepted the fact that all philosophical thoughts were theories which needed to be verified by acceptable means. 'Intuitive knowledge' alone was not sufficient. In other words, the concept that loosely corresponds to epistemology had been realised and accepted from the earliest times. Max Muller had observed, "Such an examination of the authorities of human knowledge *(Pramāṇas)* ought, of course, to form the introduction to every system of philosophy, and to have clearly seen this is, as it seems to me, a very high distinction of Indian philosophy. How much useless controversy would have been avoided, particularly among Jewish, Mohammedan, and Christian philosophers, if a proper place had been assigned *in limine* to the question of what constitutes our legitimate or our only possible channels of knowledge, whether perception, inference, revelation, or anything else!" [1] However, these ancient philosophers were also unable to be consistently objective and without fanciful imaginations.

Indian philosophical concepts are centered on three entities, known as *Jīva, Ātmā* and *Brahma* [*Jīva* = physical; *Ātmā* = metaphysical; *Brahma* = the Ultimate, the Eternal, the Primordial]. Strange as it may appear, the great philosophers based their reasoning on sleep. One has no physical sensation during sleep, or indeed during unconsciousness. The observation that a sleeping person undergoes all kinds of experiences in dream but has none during dreamless state and returns to wakefulness eventually must suggest that there is another entity within the body besides the life-breath. This they called the Soul, *Ātmā or the Jīvātmā.* They reckoned then that there must therefore be another entity which would control or regulate both the living body and *Ātmā*, the soul. This they called *Brahma.*[2 3]

The deliberations thereafter went deep into the natures of *Jīva*, the *Ātmā* and *Brahma* and the ways and means to comprehend, acquire and use them. They deduced that the universe was eternal – it was neither created nor would it ever be destroyed; it only underwent cyclical transformations periodically. Latterly, the *Brāhmin* priests proposed that a creator must have created this universe and they called him *Brahmā,* the Creator. This led to the concept that there must be a protector and a destroyer, thus completing the trinity, although they have not put forth credible *Pramāṇa* for these theories, relying on mythology, the *Purañas,* instead.

Another tenet of Indian philosophy is that human beings must suffer or accept their *karma* within the cycle of *Samsāra,* i.e., birth, death and rebirth again. *Karma* is the action whose fruit gets attached to the Soul, which induces the latter to seek another body repeatedly until the effects attached to it wear off. This is the reasoning for repeated rebirths. Eventually the soul becomes free of the fruits of *karma*, thus making it eligible to merge into the source - the ultimate bliss, i.e., *Brahma.*

These views are not rigidly held by all, and many new concepts have since developed. A minority view also exists which demands solid proofs for the validity of these concepts, rejecting all but direct perception as the only acceptable *Pramāṇa,* the proof. It posits that all creation is a spontaneous phenomenon; the present is all that there is, neither is there a creator nor a cycle of *Samsāra.*

However, the manifestations of this *Samsāra Cakra* include many other issues which are not covered by the esoteric and abstract thoughts. Many scholars who have commented upon the classical 'Indian philosophy' have ignored these aspects, such as interpersonal relations, social norms, political concepts, quality of life, sexual fulfilment, expressions through arts and crafts, music, drama and other important issues. These issues must have been as relevant then as they are now.

The Indian *Pramaṇa* accepts one or more of the following:*

i. Direct perception - *Pratyaksha;* the visible, the obvious or personally experienced.

ii. Inference - *Anumāna; e.g.* only the stars are seen, so it must be the night-time.

iii. The word - *Śabda,* also known as *Āpta vacana;* the mantras of The Vedas (latterly, of the *Brāhmaṇas, Āraṇyakas, Upaniṣads,* the testimony of the scriptures and the two epics).

iv. Similarity - *Upamāna;* e.g. it could be a snake because it is coiled like a snake.

v. Absence or non-availability - *Anupalabdhi* or *Abhāva;* example: 'there is no precedence because this is the first time'; 'just because it has never been there before, its existence cannot be denied'.

vi. Opinion or belief - *Arthapatti;* e.g. one can form a valid opinion that the food in the oven must be burning, if one gets the smell of burning food coming out of the stove.

There were umpteen numbers of schools of philosophical thoughts; many have become extinct. The first compendium of these schools of philosophy, *Sarvadarśanasamgraha,* was compiled by *Mādhwācārya.*[4] We find in them that Indian philosophy is intricately woven with religious connotations, and it is always possible to appear inadvertently as a

---

* Monier Williams in Sanskrit English Dictionary: Pramāṇa: root Pramā; means of acquiring Pramā or certain knowledge (6 in Vedanta). Oxford Dictionary: Epistemology: the theory of knowledge, especially regarding its methods, validity and scope and the distinction between justified belief and opinion.

challenger to one's faith during its detailed deliberation. This will be most unfortunate. However, if we believe in the purity of our purpose, which is to discern the truth, we must realise that philosophy and science are not fundamentally different in their quest for proof, reality and validity. It is essential to follow scientific methods of enquiry into a concept that can unequivocally enhance our spiritual awareness. It is for this purpose that this contribution has been designed and presented.

The philosophies of *Mimāmsā, Vedānta, Sāmkhya, Vaiśeṣika, Nyāya and Yoga* have been grouped as belonging to the theistic and the *Lokāyata, Jainā* and Buddhist doctrines to the atheistic schools.

This arbitrary division is open to question, as will be evident when each of these concepts will be analysed. Direct perception is the only proof accepted by *Lokāyata* and Buddhist schools of philosophy. Perception and inference are accepted by the *Vaiśeṣika* schools. The *Sāmkhya* acknowledges the direct perception, inference, and the trustworthy affirmation, *Āpta vacana,* the Word. *Nyāya* schools accept the additional *Upamāna* or precedence [similarity or comparison]. *Pūrva Mīmāmsā* acknowledges the Word, the *Anupalabdhi or Abhāva* [absence or lack of precedence] and *Arthapatti,* the faith or belief. *Uttar Mimāmsā* acknowledges all the above six kinds of proofs or *Pramāṇas.*

First of these philosophical records are the *Vedas.* They were the guiding force and building blocks of the ancient Indian civilisation. No one has produced convincing proof of the origin or ethnicity of the people who gave the *Vedas.* The *Veda* mantras covered the large Asian subcontinent, extending from the western shores and Afghanistan to the Himalayas in the north and the tip of the peninsula in the south, (*Dakṣiṇa*, corrupted to Deccan) in that ancient epoch; hence it would be unlikely that this was given by the seers (*Ṛṣis*) of any one single ethnic race. The population is more likely to have been a conglomeration of several sects with mixed ethnicity but having common values and practices. Like any evolving society, many external thoughts and cultures must also have influenced that ancient civilisation, wrongly known as the *Āryan* civilisation**. Attempts at establishing some congruence among these influences are seen in the *Vedic* Mantras and subsequent ancient literature. Equally, the state of economy, culture, times of peace and conflict, natural disasters, foreign occupation, geography, development of skills and knowledge and many other issues exerted direct influence on philosophical thoughts. The patronage by temporal powers brought a relatively little-known philosophy into wider dissemination, which gained a following and a hold over the masses. The main religions of today have become what they are by the patronage of powerful rulers. Indian philosophy has also been subjected to these influences. One must be prepared to analyse this very long chain of ideas and their effects before arriving at any conclusion.

Roy Perret[4] suggests the following chronological events to summarise Indian philosophy.

** Ārya means one who is civilised, noble, or righteous. It denotes the qualities of a person and not an ethnicity or race, which regrettably has come to mean a race of a superior people having many characteristics of Caucasian race, the white supremacists. This fell into further disrepute when Adolf Hitler used this term to denote the fascist group of 'super-men'.

1. The ancient period, 900 BCE–200 CE.
2. The classical period, 200 CE–1300 CE.
3. The medieval period, 1300 CE–1800 CE.
4. The modern period, 1800 CE–present.

His suggestion of 900 BCE as the beginning of the ancient period would prove to be mainly a conjecture if we were to seek a *Pramāṇa* for this premise. The classical period would indicate that the various schools of philosophy developed during this period, which is also definitely not the case. I do not find this a satisfactory chronology for Indian philosophy, for several other reasons too, which will become apparent in the following pages.

Rādhākṛṣṇan and Moore[5] have asserted four major periods of development of Indian philosophy. These are:

a. The *Vedic* period, between 2500–600 BCE.
b. The epic period, 600 BCE–200 CE.
c. *Sūtra* period, 200 CE–900 CE.
d. Scholastic period, 900 CE to present.

This classification is largely based upon the assumptions of Western Indologists, viz. Wilson, Colebrooke, Deussen, Max Muller, Macdonnel and others in their desperate attempts to ascertain a precise chronology of events and thoughts according to the Western style of recording history and their opinions or conjectures. This division, too, is difficult to accept for the following reasons.

Deva Vāni, speech of the gentlemen, known as the earlier version of Sanskrit, was the language of the *Ṛg Veda*, the most ancient literature. This did not have a designated script, and writing was not the norm until the later years of the last millennium before the advent of the Common Era. The teachings and philosophical doctrines were passed on verbatim for several generations, as short aphorisms, or mnemonics, until writing became available.[6] It must be assumed that many of these would have been lost over the succeeding generations. Hence all the perceived developments in philosophical thinking of the ancient years cannot be assumed to belong merely to any one period, such as the *Vedic* era. The literature known as the *Vedas* had begun a minimum of three millennia earlier and must have been continuing for an awfully long time. Indeed, some Indian scholars and astronomers have attempted to calculate probable dates of the composition of the *Ṛg Veda* by the celestial configuration during the events mentioned in it. This places the *Vedas*, particularly the *Ṛg Veda,* as having begun around 4000 BC.[7]

The other reason is the unscientific grouping of all the very ancient literature as the *Vedic* literature. The *Vedic* mantras of the *Ṛg Veda,* known as *Rik*, had been accepted as revelations and heard, *Śruti,* by the *Ṛṣi* and accepted as 'not made by man', *Apauruyṣeya.* Only this *Ṣruti* is synonymous with the Mantras of the *Vedas*, not the subsequent literature which is man-made. The subsequent treatises, which appeared over the next few millennia, were memorised by the pupils, and are known as *Smritis,* or mnemonics. This voluminous literature, known as *Prātisākhya, Brāhmaṇa, Āraṇyaka, Upaniṣad, Anukramaṇi, Pariśiṣṭha, Smriti, Purāṇa,* and the literature known as *Vedāṅga,* were not the corpus of the four original *Vedas*. There has been an unquestioned and unjustified tendency to accept all these as *Ṣruti* – the *Vedic* literature, the unquestionable axioms. These had been produced much later, out of scriptural necessity. Historians[8] have grouped all this ancient literature, which spans several centuries and millennia, as contemporary. This is not a scientific method. Hence this confusion has arisen. All these later compilations can best be regarded as subsequent literary works; the majority of these have no reference to the original Mantras of the *Vedas*. The various *Smritis* and the *Sūtras* are later productions, and their contents cannot be taken as proof of the events that might have occurred hundreds or thousands of years earlier.

It is difficult to accept a distinct '*Sūtra* period', since most of the ancient texts, including many Mantras of the *Vedas,* is in brief cryptic phrases known as the *Sūtra* style of composition. This has no uniformity in its structure and ranges from being an obscure mnemonic as a record of questions and answers to a profound statement preserved in the shortest manner. This style of composition was a deliberate attempt at making it easy for pupils to memorise them. Many are so obscure as to be impossible to understand without the help of learned teachers, and even they at times might have given erroneous interpretations. Many of the *Smritis* are also in the *Sūtra* style of composition. The most quoted *Brahma Sūtra* is in a very cryptic question and answer form.

The period between 600 BCE and 200 CE has been presented as the epic period. I cannot understand the rationale for calling this 'the epic period', because only two epics are mentioned in ancient literature. The *Purāṇas* are not epics, although some of them might have been produced during this period. The well-known epics, *Rāmāyaṇa* and *Mahābhārata*, are mostly works of fiction, although the principal characters in them are largely based upon contemporary historical personalities. *Mahābhārata* appears to have originated in the western part of the Indo-Gangetic plain, and *Rāmāyaṇa* in the central and southern regions. There are sections in these epics where various philosophical discourses have been included, along with several juicy stories from the *Purāṇas* which have made the epics interesting to read. It is a fact that the stories in these two epics have been modified over many centuries by including much of the local folklore. Many variations in the stories within these epics were spoken aloud, and continued to be, even after writing and printing began to be freely available. Both describe the reincarnation of the god *Viśṇu*. They were preached as holy books by the traditional priests, most of whom are not really enlightened, being proficient only in their manuals for rituals. They concoct all kinds of symbolism to explain the fantasy. It is interesting to note that the name of Krishna as the Supreme God is not found in the Rig Veda. *Viśṇu* was a Vedic Rishi who was said to have been able to achieve divinity but there is no mention of his any reincarnations in the Vedas. There is no evidence in the Vedas of Ram being his incarnation.

It is certainly possible to attribute these two epics as being clever first attempts in trying to develop a framework in social philosophy. These could perhaps be regarded as heralding the rebellion of people against the atrocities committed in the guise of religion and monarchy. One must be aware of the ancient history of India to appreciate that this was a period of tremendous intellectual awakening in that subcontinent. Many works on epistemology, logic, and literary works, as well as novel religious sects, were developing. This was the early period of Indian renaissance which generated the most diverse philosophical thinking; this should not just be pushed aside to give prominence to the epics. This becomes apparent if we look at the content of these works.

A clue to *Mahābhārata* being a work of fiction is found in the original version. The narrative was described by a sage who had learned of the Great War from the chirping of two partridges. These birds had been hatched within the helmet of a fallen soldier in that war and were the only survivors left to tell that story. However, the epic describes how society at every level had degenerated from the Utopian society of the *Vedic* times. The need to save it from the atrocities being conducted by the two upper classes in society had been appreciated by *Lord Viśṇu*. He was born as the prince *Kṛṣṇa* to re-establish pious righteousness. He orchestrated a great war between the two feuding cousins in such a manner as to make the powerful ruling classes of the *Kshetriyas* fight among themselves and kill one another. The corrupt *Brāhmins* also perished. Be that as it may, the famous *Gītā* and the discourse by the dying patriarch *Bhīṣma* to the victorious *Yudhiṣṭhira* are certainly great philosophical works in this epic. This fiction was the work of a great genius, *Kṛśna Dwaipāyana,* who is also known as *Veda Vyāsa*. Many believe him to be the reincarnation of *Viśṇu.*

The villain in the second epic is *Rāvana*, a demon *(Rākshasa*). Can a demon - a mythological concoction of a huge human form with ten heads - ever qualify for serious philosophical deliberation? Evidence suggests that *Rāmāyaṇa* is a later, not an earlier, work than *Mahābhārata.* Sage *Vālmiki* is regarded as the original author of this epic. This epic describes the story of *Rāma* as the mortal incarnation Lord *Viśṇu,* the ultimate saviour. He took birth as a prince to an emperor of India to annihilate the demons who had become immensely powerful. The lesser gods and brave human beings had not been able defeat them. This epic too, true to the oral tradition of storytelling, has been modified over the millennia and several versions are available. *Rāvana* was the most powerful king of the demons, the *Rākshasas.* He ruled the world from the island of *Lanka.* He abducted *Sitā,* the wife of *Rāma,* from their hut in a forest. *Rāma* used this pretext to annihilate the entire clan of the *Rākshasas* by waging a war with *Rāvana.* He assembled an army of monkeys and was able to rescue his wife. This epic also has drawn freely from the *Purānas* to develop its principal characters. The main areas of philosophy are in the discourse of Rishi *Vaśisṭha* to *Rāma,* which is believed to be *Yogavāsisṭha,* a *Smriti.* The satellite pictures of the sunken archipelago between Sri Lanka and India are taken as proof of the bridge that was made by the monkey army of *Rāma* to attack *Rāvana. Vālmiki* had probably tried to project the essential attributes that the kings must have to rule their people. In addition, he projected *Rāma* to be the example of the ideal man, *Ādarśa puruṣa* – ideal in every respect, viz. as a son, a brother, prince, a king, a husband, and very brave person capable of supporting the scriptures and the teachers. *Sitā* has been portrayed as a silently suffering totally submissive wife, in contrast to the fiery *Draupadi* in *Mahābhārata.*

According to Rādhākrṣṇan, the scholastic period 200 BCE–1900 CE would imply that this was a period of education and modification of religious practices with little independent and original thought. This distinction is somewhat apt if we limit our understanding of this period to be the era of writing when the *Bhojpatra,* palmyra and home-made paper became available for this purpose. However, the printing machine reached India only in 1555 CE. But, far from being the focused insistence on theosophy, as scholasticism would imply, this period featured the most turbulent time in India, intellectually, socially, and culturally. This was also the most unstable period in Indian history. India was seen as a highly advanced nation economically and had repeatedly become the target for external attacks and pillaging. She was a highly developed nation in terms of the arts, industry, commerce, farming, mining, weaponry and practically in every field. The influence of Christianity and Islam was significant. Many secret cults and practices were developing. Parts of India on the eastern shores had been colonised – France and Portugal occupying large coastal areas in the east and west. The British had entered India in 1607 as traders and managed to colonise the peninsula within a hundred years. Internal and external influences had greatly affected traditional thinking and practices in India. The term 'scholastic period' thus does not appear to imply a comprehensive representation of the thoughts prevalent in that era.

It must be realised that there cannot be a clear chronological demarcation among the eras mentioned here. This may appear frustrating to pedantic scholars who wish to record accurate times. Indeed, Theodor Goldstücker[9] said that the vagueness of chronological events was "one of the most important problems of Sanskrit literature". The problem in reality lies in attempting to record ancient oriental history in the occidental system of recording, according to definite dates congruous with the lives of the persons identified with the subject. The ancient seers did not claim personal recognition or ownership of their aphorisms or teachings. This literature was preserved accurately by being short, pithy, mnemonic, and restricted. The tradition demanded of the pupils to memorise cryptic, short sentences or phrases known as the *Sūtras*. Hence, it is impossible to record the dates accurately for a 5000-year-old oriental literature. Writing had not been available freely until the advent of the Christian or Common Era. The literature written subsequently was usually the compilation of these *Sūtras,* both old and new, as seen in the varying styles of composition within the same collection. The later compilers attributed the *Sūtras* to a particular teacher or sage, who might have lived centuries earlier. There is no way of proving the authenticity of this claim of authorship. A well-known example is the *Vedānta Sūtra (Brahma Sūtra)* attributed to *Veda Vyāsa,* although the person compiling this called himself *Bādarāyaṇa.* Some believe both to be the same person. The scholars even to this date are not able to confirm or refute the identity of these two personalities. Hence it is best to appreciate the evolution of thoughts that had occurred steadily over the large subcontinent in the slow pace of ancient times. Any attempt to draw a clear demarcation line will not be a scientific exercise.

There is no doubt, however, that many philosophers and scholars in the first and early second millennium of the Common Era in India had begun to compile, edit and simplify the vast corpus of philosophical thinking and to add their own contributions as well. It is interesting to note that all philosophical systems that originated in India promise basically the same thing to their believers. This is bliss, variously known as *mukti, mokshya, kaivalya, amritatwa, apavarga, nirvāna.* A few have suggested the ending of *dukkha,* signifying suffering, misery, pain etc. This led *Haribhadra,* born a *Brāhmaṇa* who died a *Jaina* in 528 CE, to produce a short summary of Indian philosophy prevalent during his time: *Śaddarśana-samuchhayasūtram* (translation: a compendium of six philosophical thoughts). It is said he then saw the light and adopted *Jainism.* It is now accepted that there are two groups of philosophical thoughts - one atheistic and the other theistic. This distinction is illogical because the *Sāmkhya, Vaiśeşika* and *Nyāya* schools, which are included in the theistic group, do not propound any divine causes in their propositions. The theistic schools of philosophy are the *Pūrva mimāmsā, Vedānta, and Yoga.* The atheistic schools are *Jainism, Buddhism* and *Cārvāka.* The *Sāmkhya, Vaiśeşika* and *Nyāya* systems were included by *Śankarācārya* in his commentary of *Vedānta Sūtra* as the theistic philosophy. His logic has not been universally accepted. However, this has since been well established as the 'Six Philosophical Systems of India', and the orthodox view has been to refute the *Buddhism, Jainism* and *Carvāka* systems. These six and a few more were compiled and commented on by *Mādhvācārya* in *Sarvadarśana Samgraha* (translation: a collection of all philosophies). These two works appear to be the main resource books for most scholars. This book, however, is not a full compendium, as will be seen in subsequent chapters. Many commentaries have been produced subsequently without adding significant new ideas.

The commentaries refer to all the ancient literature, i.e., the *Vedas, Brāhmaṇas, Vedāṅgas, Śāstras,* the *Smritis, Purāṇas* and the epics such as the *Ŝruti* or the *Veda* or *Śāstra.* This has created great confusion and misinterpretation of Indian philosophy because they are all different, although related in many ways. Hence any credibility to a narrative must depend upon the reference to a specific book and not to the generic name such as *Vedas* or the *Śāstras.* For example, a mantra from an *Upaniṣad* cannot be said to have been sourced from a *Veda* if it is not there.

Indian philosophical concepts and their development therefore need to be understood according to the times of their presentation, perceived social structure, political and cultural events, external influence, and aspirations of the people who began as nomads seeking cultivable land to become the most wealthy, educated, highly civilised and structured nation over a period of more than 6000 years. The old ideas and the new concepts have remained side by side; just as in nature, where we see an evolved new species existing alongside the old from which it was transformed. It is unacceptable to consider a comment valid unless it has a reference to a context. Mohanty[10] has thankfully realised the need for a contextual rather than a rigid chronological appreciation of Indian philosophy. I find his inclusion of *Dhvani* and *Rasa* in the exposition of Indian philosophy is the most significant consideration in interpreting the *Sūtras* and the mantras. The essence of cognition depends upon how a word is pronounced and the context in which it is pronounced. The original mantras of the four *Vedas* need to be interpreted accordingly, and not just by simply stating them. The importance of the need to consider the *Chanda* and the *Nirukta* in the interpretation of *Vedic* mantras has not been strictly followed by many translators and commentators. The *Jainas*, the *Lokāyatas,* the *Buddha*, and several philosophers during the post *Brāhmaṇa* period were anti-ritualistic and not anti-*Vedic* in the esoteric sense of the four *Vedas.* The scriptural status given to the two works of fictions *Mahābhārata* and *Rāmāyaṇa* has been continued by many Indian scholars too. In addition, grouping the

Brāhmaṇa literature and several *Upaniṣads* also as the *Vedic* literature, propagates the original false claims made by the *Brāhmin* priests.

The way the facts are presented by modern scholars of Indian philosophy means we are unlikely to be sure of getting a relevant and true picture. They continue to use the erroneous words such as *Sacrifice, Brahman,* and all ancient literature as the *Vedas*. They consider the *Upaniṣads* as parts of the *Vedas,* rather than the revised versions of the priestly manuals called the *Āraṇyakas and* jump from one era to another in the blink of an eye. Regrettably, merely a superficial understanding of the *Vedas, Brāhmaṇas, Araṇyakas,* the *Upaniṣads,* the later *Sūtras,* and the epics, coupled with a similar understanding of ancient Greek philosophy, have generated many pundits of Indian philosophy. It appears that the system called the *'Adhyāsa'* has not been well appreciated by many of these scholars and dismissed as mere symbolism or imagination. This is a logical concept used in Indian philosophy; the nearest interpretation of this term in English being a 'system of superimposition or transference'. The interpretations, given by many curious colonialists of the past, without checking the authenticity of their own works first, are still being taken as acceptable for a scholarly monograph. This hardly inspires confidence.

Indian philosophy needs to be accepted as the evolution of thoughts, and not as a definitive historical narrative. This requires to be appreciated in a comprehensive, three-dimensional model inclusive of the society, culture, and prevailing circumstances, and not just in a cross-sectional overview. The timeline of this evolution could be as follows:

1. The earliest tribal period.
2. The *Vedas.*
3. The *Brāhmaṇas* and the *Āraṇyakas,* i.e., the establishment of *Brāhminism.*
4. The *Upaniṣads.*
5. The Renaissance.
6. *Buddhism.*
7. Scholarship in the early Common Era.
8. The middle Common Era.
9. 1500–2021 CE.

The last three periods have received less scholarly attention than they deserve. This may be largely by the fact that the Indian philosophy began to be introduced into Europe only in the 17th century. The contemporary Indologists were much influenced by the Greek philosophers, Christianity, and the prevailing imperialistic traditions, as influenced by Macaulay[11]. The colonial victors were selective to choose and give importance to those concepts which would also suit and strengthen the colonial rule and propagate their creed. This kind of quasi-historical and evolutionary appreciation will provide the essential background of the concepts and the reasons for the continued presence of those ideas which are no longer accepted, are wrong and others which have persisted and are profoundly affecting our current thinking.

References:

1. Muller, F. M. (1903). *The six systems of Indian Philosophy* (p. XIII). University Press of the Pacific.
2. Ṛg Veda. 1.1.64.
3. Mundaka Upaniṣad 3.1.
4. Perret, W. R. (2016). *Introduction to Indian*

Philosophy (p. 7). United Kingdom: Cambridge University Press.

5. Rādhākrishnan, S. R. Moore CA. ed. (1989) *A Source Book in Indian Philosophy* (pp. xvii–xxii).
6. Swāmi Cinmāyananda. (1954). Praśnopaniṣad. (p. 10). Central Chinmaya Mission Trust
7. Tilak, B. G. (1893). *Orion or the antiquities of the Vedas. Astronomical calculations based upon the planets, constellation, and the sun* (p. 199). Bombay: Radhabai Atmaram Sagoon.
8. Thapar, R. (1992). *Interpreting early India.* (pp. 63–64). *Oxford India Paperbacks.* Goldstucker, T. (1852). *en.wikipedia.org/wiki/Theodor_Goldst%C3%BCcker;* accessed on 20/11/2020.
9. Mohanty, J. N. (2000). *Classical Indian Philosophy (*pp. 133–137). Maryland, USA: Rowman and Littlefield.
10. Tharoor, S. (2016). An Era of Darkness. (pp.220-21). Alef Book Company, New Delhi.

There is a story of a religious teacher who used to talk every morning to his disciples. One morning he got on to the platform and was just about to begin when a little bird came and sat on the windowsill and began to sing and sang away with full heart. Then it stopped and flew away, and the teacher said 'the sermon for this morning is over'.

J. KRISHNAMURTI

CHAPTER 2
The Earliest Tribal Period

There is scant data regarding the earliest human settlers in India. There is some evidence to suggest the Indian population in very ancient times had people from African, Proto-Australoids, Mongoloid, Mediterranean, Alpine, Dinaric, Armenoid and Nordic origins. There has been much speculation regarding the original north Indian people who called themselves *Āryans*. A Nordic origin of the *Āryans* is mentioned by some historians. Others mention that they were from the Mediterranean region, and others call them a horde of horsemen who descended to north-west India from central Asia via Afghanistan. Little is known about them, but they are assumed to be nomadic in nature, continuously fighting on their travels with other chieftains and worshipping nature gods, viz. the sun, the moon, the earth, lightning, rain, wind, etc. They had a chieftain, usually chosen by the clan, whose duty was to protect and conquer anyone on their path toward lucrative fields.

Common beliefs are that the other ancient civilisations, e.g., Sumerian, Babylonian and Egyptian were also developing around the same period. Hence it is natural for us to assume that this prehistoric clan had similar norms and values as people of other ancient civilisations. But this is open to doubt because *Āryans* are recognised as neither belonging to any specific geographical region, like Egypt, Palestine, Syria, Greece, Turkey, etc. nor to any specific ethnicity or race[1]. One needs to wait for a few centuries, when we can glean definite information about these people who called themselves *Ārya* (civilised). However, the *Vedas*, regarded as a repository of the most profound philosophical ideas, could not possibly have begun at these earliest of times. The philosophy was just the thoughts for preservation of oneself and one's family. We find that they sought relief from supernatural phenomenona such as ghosts and wizardry. It is interesting to find that some ancient hymns of the *Ṛg Veda*, which do not have the sophistication of the composition of latter times, and which do not conform to the poetic metres, are simple prayers to nature gods*. The philosophers among them began to ask searching questions and astutely observe natural phenomena. It is quite possible that their civilisation began to develop once this wandering population had settled down in a fertile, lush region. Many think this to have been in the north-west of the Indian subcontinent – in the basins of the Narmadā and Sindhu rivers. These developments appear to have heralded the highly organised and accomplished *Vedic* era where primitive prayers also continued, as seen in abundance in the mantras, as shown. Indeed, it is even possible to surmise that subsequent folklore included some mention of their earlier wanderings and conquests. They were on the path to forming a well-organised society toward the end of this prehistoric period. This is seen among the Mantras of the *Puruṣa Sūkta*[2]. Appendix 1 gives important mantras from all the *Vedas*. These Mantras continue to be recited today, even though they are not as important or relevant anymore.

*The following mantras from the *Ṛg Veda* are given as illustrations of their earlier beliefs.

Ṛg 5.42.17. (O Gods!) May (we) remain in (happiness) without enormous obstacles.

Ṛg 6.64.11. *(O Āświns!* May I remain in the*)* superior happiness of you both, with the learned.

Ṛg 2.11.9. *Indra* slew the sorcerer sleeping in the wide river. Heaven and earth trembled in fear of *Vajra* of the powerful Indra, making thunderous noise.

Rg 2.11.12. When the benefactor of men (Indra) killed the unkind *Vritra,* then the *Vajra* of the powerful *Indra* roared. *Indra,* drinking the prepared *Soma,* destroyed the illusions of the demon sorcerer.

Rg 1.115.1. *Sūrya,* the face of the gods and the unique eyes of *Mitra, Varuṇa* and *Agni* arose. The soul of the ambulant beings and also of the static materials, *Sūrya,* pervaded the heaven, the earth and the Space.

References:

1. Majumdar, R C. (1964) *Ancient India. (*16-17) Motilal Banarsidass. Delhi.
2. Puruṣa Sūkta. *Ṛg Veda*. 10.90.

ONLY THOSE RETURN TO ETERNITY

WHO ON EARTH SEEK OUT ETERNITY.

KAHLIL GIBRAN

CHAPTER 3

The Vedas

Majumdar[1] has tried to summarise the opinions of former scholars to ascertain the dates of the *Vedas*. The span has been variously considered to be from 6000 BCE to 600 BCE, which is unhelpful. There are no clues to the times of the recording of these mantras. He also mentions that the earliest script for recording the mantras as written was by using the Brahmi script, with the probable date of circa 700 BCE. Again, there is no proof about these speculations. However, the fact remains that the names of the Rishis, the visionaries who saw these mantras, suggest several generations, indicating that this had occurred over a long time. This was the period of conception of many subtle and profound philosophical concepts which were later elaborated upon by the sages in the *Upaniṣads*. Literally, the *Vedas* are a body of obscure hymns in a language known as *Deva Vāṇi*, the precursor of Sanskrit. They contain stories, historical references, idle conversations, prayers, and philosophical enquiry into everything. There is much symbolism, innuendoes, and indirect reference to the intended subject matter. Hence many translators have chosen to impart whatever meaning they thought to be the hidden intent, which has made the *Vedas* either the most profound literature in the world or "a body of sacrificial hymns couched in a very ancient language which presents a number of almost insoluble difficulties of a nomadic people."[2]

It is widely believed that the Mantras of the *Vedas* were heard by the Ṛṣis. They were not the statements made by them. Indeed, these were regarded as *Apauruşeya,* meaning they were not man-made at all. *Kṛśna Dwipāyana Vyāsa,* a teacher in ancient times and thought to have lived circa 1200 BCE, asked his pupils to collect all the mantras, and divided them into four sections called the *Ṛg, Yajur, Sāma* and *Atharva Veda.* These became accepted by all as *swatah prāmāṇya,* the self-evident aphorisms.

Examples of the hidden symbolism:

An example of this is seen in the literal translation of the first and the last mantras of the *Ṛg Veda,* as follows:

> Ṛg 1.1.1. "I praise the leader of *Yagňa,* the performer of the *Yagňa,* the invoker of the gods, the giver of the superior wealth, the God *Agni*".
>
> Ṛg 10.191.4. "O performers of good deed! As your common actions can be performed, like that your resolve too may become similar, indeed. May your hearts and minds become similar!'!

Let us ask ourselves: why is this recorded as the first mantra in the *Ṛg Veda* out of 10,552 mantras? And why is the last mantra, the last? The symbolism indicated here is that conventionally one always begins by praying to God and wishing everybody well at the end. The Ṛşi begins therefore by invoking the god. He implies that the same one is the cause, the process, the effect, the arbiter, the supporter of all. The hidden meaning here is most probably the supreme reality, *the Puruşa.* This *Agni,* as the nature of the primordial energy, is represented by fire. The mantra enumerates the qualities attributed to the supreme entity. This is the definition of the god in modern parlance. Hence it begins by the prayer to God. The last mantra is the ultimate wish of an enlightened society, the aim for peace, comradery and goodwill. This is the message of goodwill expressed at the end, a message for universal harmony and peace.

These four *Vedas* are the bedrock of Indian civilisation and philosophy. The *Vedic* hymns are commonly known as *mantras*. According to Swāmi Ċinmāyananda, "till this time, every new edition of *Veda* was composed in the mouth of the guru and printed directly on the memory slabs of the pupils' hearts. *Veda Vyāsa* brought the first *Bhoja-Patram* and Palmyra editions".[3] The *Ṛg Veda* contains a veritable store of philosophical ideas, the early history of these people, knowledge and devotional hymns. This has most mantras covering the first three subjects. Most of its devotional components are added to *Yajur Veda,* which is mainly involved in ritualistic aspects. The *Atharva Veda* has technical or activity-based mantras, as well as many profound philosophical ideas. The *Sāma Veda* has mostly the devotional mantras, chants, and songs. There is considerable duplication of the mantras among the *Vedas*.

The authentic *Vedic* literature, known and revered as *Ṣruti*, consists of two broad components, ideas (*Gyānakānda*) and activities (*Karmakānda*). This division has been greatly misinterpreted and the fallacy thus accrued has been continuing for millennia. Each *Veda* has both components at varying levels. The *gyānakānda* refers to the parts of all the *Vedas* which include philosophy, knowledge, skills, ideals, nature and the environment, law, and order and so on. The *karmakānda* deals with prayers and the conduct of various ceremonies, life events, celebrations, special occasions and miscellaneous rituals, e.g., to ward off evil and demons, to bring prosperity and happiness, cause rainfall, prevent floods, quieten thunderstorms and damage by lightning, prevent shipwrecks, and innumerable other purposes. Thus, there has been separation of religion and spiritualism from exceedingly early times. These rituals eventually put the esoteric *gyānakānda* almost into oblivion through the production of many manuals [for conducting newer rituals which were called the *Brāhmaṇa* books], until it was resurrected at a later stage during the contemplation and their revision. The result was their revised production as the *Āraṇyaka,* from which the sections comprising the spiritual and philosophical enquiries were separated as the *Upaniṣads.*

It is not difficult to imagine that the tradition for conducting religious rituals started from this early period. This has persisted as the strict religious duties until today, particularly among the orthodox *Brāhmin* families. Young boys were taught in special academies called *Gurukula.* They lived within the household of the *guru* or the *Ācārya* (the preceptor) and memorised the mantras, as well as the epithets in the manuals. These *Vedic* mantras were maintained very strictly; the accents or phonation had to be identical and accurate throughout. This kind of strictness has preserved the mantras for several millennia.

A system of correct recitation and meaning of the words was produced for each *Veda*. Since there were as many *Brāhmaṇa* books as preceptors of the schools where the Brāhmin boys were being trained for priesthood, it became necessary to have uniformity among them. This was achieved by preparing a common reference manual, called *Prātisākhya,* which could perhaps be called 'a system of the *Vedas*'. All students were taught the same way. They had to remain celibate, demonstrate total submission to the guru, tend the cattle, gather firewood, and memorise the mantras. They were not necessarily expected to understand the mantras. After about sixteen years, the guru would declare them to have completed their education. They would then return home, get married and begin the life of a householder, according to the strict regulations as decreed in the *Manu Smriti.*

Society in the *Vedic* period:

They believed that society progressed through four phases: *Satya Yuga,* the era of the truth; *Tretā Yuga,* the era of three fires (rituals); *Dwāpara Yuga,* the era of doubts; and *Kali Yuga,* the era of conflicts. Vestiges of the traditional *Vedic* society have continued in the Indian subcontinent, although greatly modified. Additional *Vedic* mantras have not been recorded for the last three millennia. Society was based on *Varṇāśrama* with the lofty principles of *Varnadharma.* As mentioned earlier, philosophy has always been a way of life in the Indian subcontinent. Social norms and customs have been based on the ideals as propounded in the *Vedic* mantras: *dharma, artha, kāma* and *mokshya,* i.e., be charitable, prosperous, enjoy and then seek liberation from all were considered to be the purpose of one's life.

Varṇāśrama:

The early settlers had recognised the need of their society to have a structured framework for its myriad functions. This was accomplished by the design of *Varṇāśrama,* which assigned its members in four sectors, i.e., the learning, earning, reforming and renouncing sectors. The sectors were interdependent and of equal importance, lasting twenty-five years each. These are known as:

i. *Brahmacaryāshrama;* the learning phase.

ii. *Grihasthāshrama;* the householder phase.

iii. *Vānaprasthāśrama;* the retirement phase.

iv. *Sanyāsāśrama*; the phase of renunciation.

Brahmacaryāshrama, the learning phase, was considered extremely important. At birth, everyone was classed as *Śūdra.* During the learning phase, they entered appropriate groups according to their aptitudes and capabilities and learned the prescribed skills and knowledge. Experts in their profession taught their pupils as apprentices, usually in their homes. Celibacy for a pupil until the completion of education was mandatory. Some were called 'twice born' *Dwija* if they had become so learned as to have received enlightenment and had become a different personality. This was limited to the scholars who had become enlightened, after a much longer period of study and contemplation.

The Householder. This was regarded as the earning phase.

One entered this phase after learning the necessary skills to pursue the chosen line of work. One was obliged to get married, produce children, earn as much as possible for common good, support the community, the artisans, the weak, the vulnerable and disabled. Polygamy was common but polyandry was not, although practised. Sexual fidelity in marriage was desirable but not essential. The wife was the mistress in the home. She was skilled in domestic activities, fine arts, music, dance, arithmetic, and bookkeeping, and well read. She was the teacher of her children until the male children left home for their *Gurukuls,* and the daughters continued to learn from the mother. A child born out of another lover would belong to the husband and get his name.

Each household was required to pray three times a day - at dawn, midday, and sunset. It was a very personal activity done without any priest. This act varied widely from lighting a lamp, a fire, saying a small prayer to conducting special and elaborate rituals for specific purposes. One was obliged to earn, pay one sixth of the earnings as tax, help the poor and needy, enjoy all sensual pleasures and then aim for eventual freedom.

Vānaprasthāśrama:

The retirement, also known as the phase of contemplation, began after completing the duties as a householder. This phase absolved one from social obligations and allowed him to introspect, teach and practice the choice of austerities, or *sādhanā.* One often retreated to a small hut in a forest (*vana*).

Sanyāsaśrama:

The stage of renunciation was the final stage in life when one gave up home, cut off all relations with family, lived on nature and went into deep *sādhanas* and/or travelled widely.

Varṇadharma:

People were grouped into four categories or *Varṇa.* This was based on the *Puruṣa Sūkta*[4]. These were known as *Brāhmaṇa, Kshetriya, Vaiśya and Śūdra.*

i. *Brāhmaṇa:* This group of people had to be learned, clever and wise. These were the policymakers and guides, as well as the tutors and priests. [These are called the *Brahmins* in English.]

ii. *Kshetriya:* These were primarily the marshals or warriors providing security and defence. They had to maintain law and order. Their roles and responsibilities were clearly defined. They had to be good archers and swordsmen. As warriors, they would be required to wage just wars and defend their people and territory.

iii. Vaiśya: These were the craftsmen, artisans, traders, farmers. This group went far and wide, including distant shores, to trade and bring prosperity for all.

iv. Śūdra: These provided service and did unspecified, miscellaneous jobs. Their jobs and responsibilities were in no way considered unimportant or menial. Their status was respected.

A new-born male was at first unclassified. At birth, all were born as *Śūdra.* He was sent to the teacher at about eight years of age to be educated as appropriate to his aptitude, personality, and ability. It was the teacher who determined his category when he reached adulthood. This has been clearly stated in the *Atri Smriti* and *Parāśara Smriti.* This system was no different at its inception from the current social structure seen all over the world; every society has four classes of citizens – the policymakers, soldiers, traders, and the front-line workers. There was also an underclass, known as the *Mlecha*, who did not belong to their clan. These were people belonging to other ethnicity and the slaves captured after conquering a new territory. They were treated as the property of their masters.

Each phase had a set of rules and responsibilities within which every individual was obliged to function. This was the *Dharma* – to perform one's duty according to the assigned place in society.*

This has been translated as *religion,* which has been the most unfortunate act of ignorance over the last two millennia.**

The first governor:

The first person who was selected for overall supervision of their society was known as *Manu.* He gave a code of conduct known as the *Manusmriti*; parts of this are still in practice but the authenticity of many of its *Śūtras* is suspect, since many modern versions directly contradict the mantras of the *Vedas,* perhaps adapted later from of the codes of conduct given by Moses and Hammurabi circa 1500 BCE.

All men were created equal. Severe punishment was inflicted on anyone who violated the code of conduct. *Brahmā* was a Sanskrit term for a priest reciting a special prayer. It was not the Creator, as described several centuries later in mythological stories. A *Brāhmaṇa* was an enlightened teacher who was also a priest, reciting the mantras of the *Vedas,* and a guide on spiritual and ecclesiastical matters.

There were no temples; people meditated and worshipped in their own homes. The *Agnihotra*[5] was

* The characteristics of a *Brāhmaṇa* are truth, charity, forgiveness, good conduct, gentleness, austerity, mercy. As reminded by Vyasa in Mahābhārata, Vana Parva, 21.25-26.

** We have no evidence of there being a 'religion' in those days. The concept of organised religion based upon rituals to propitiate a god was a much later development. The *Brāhmin* priests named that cult as the *Sanātana Dharma,* and it made sense to the English translators to call it a religion. The real meaning of *Dharma* as the duty and responsibility has been ignored since then.

performed by the head of the house twice daily, at sunrise and sunset. Devout people performed *Yagńa**** (a selfless act, a religious ritual or ceremony; erroneously translated as sacrifice). These were known as *Pancamahāyagňa*. Rich and powerful people also performed specific rituals (elaborate religious ceremonies) to celebrate special national events, or accomplishments, and at times of hardship and natural disasters, for the benefit of all. The mantras of all the *Vedas* were recited by the designated priests of different orders and supervised or directed by an *Ācārya*, a title one received only after having learned all the *Vedas*, the prescribed studies and becoming enlightened.

Some of these enlightened *Ācāryas* gave further discourses which were recorded as *Smriti* by their pupils after carefully listening to and memorising them. *Smriti* means 'that which is remembered'. The most quoted *Smritis* are the *Manu Smriti, Atri Smriti, Parāśara Smriti, Yoga Vāshistha, Kaṇwa Smriti* and *Yāgňbalkya Smriti*. There was no hereditary caste system or kingship. Kings were elected by the elders and teachers in the society.

Crime was at a minimum. Justice was dispensed locally as far as possible, but the local sentencing could be challenged and taken to the higher authorities and, finally, to the king. This was done according to the codes of conduct, the

*** The names of Yagnas: *Agnihotra, Soma Yaga, Agnistoma, Pounderaka, Ashwamedha, Rajasuya, Vājapeya, Brahmayagńa.* The Pancamahāyagńa are: *Brahma* or *Veda Yagňa, Deva Yagňa, Pitri Yagňa, Bhuta Yagňa* and *Manuşya Yagňa*. The three fires are: *Āhavaniyāgni, Gārhapatyāgni, Dakshināgni*. These are the fires required to be lit for rituals, including worship at home. Fire worship by every householder was strictly followed.

opinions of the learned *Ācāryas,* precedence in history and finally by the king, whose decision could not be appealed. The region was rich and plentiful.

People were happy. The tribe must have been well organised but still unsettled. They were still somewhat nomadic and the quests for fertile lands were continuing. The concept of permanence of a settlement as a nation had not developed. It is important to know of a great historical event that occurred around this time. This was known as 'The War of 10 kings', *Dus Rajā Yuddha,* described in the next chapter. Subsequent developments must have brought tremendous changes to their ways of life.

The *Vedic* philosophy:

These *Śrutis* are accepted by the Indian philosophers as evidence or proof, but the *Ṛṣis* themselves question one another. Although the names of these *Ṛṣis* are quoted as the source of the mantras, they themselves do not claim their ownership. Moreover, the *Ṛṣis* in the *Vedas* state differing views and principles and vary greatly among themselves. There were many *Ṛṣis,* and many had been recognised as such within the same genealogy. This has significance which will be apparent when we deliberate on the next phase, i.e., the *Brāhmaṇa* period. The three mantras of the *Ṛg Veda, Ṛg* 1.1.1; *Ṛg* 1.164.46; *Ṛg* 3.62.3 (the translations given in Appendix 1) were the foundation of the original *Vedic* society.

The main philosophical issues covered in the *Vedas* are:

1. The guiding light for our life is knowledge.
2. Known by many names, It is One which is the Cause, the Process, and the Result.

3. The purpose of human life is to seek the ultimate happiness, living righteously for duty [*dharma*], wealth [*artha*], pleasure [*kāma*] and liberation [*mokshya*].
4. The life, synonym soul, goes to the original cause [the effulgent source] if the person has lived righteously, and falls somewhere in utter darkness otherwise, at death.
5. All are born equal. One gets assigned to a *Varṇa* (caste or colour or group) according to his aptitude, education and training.
6. Everyone must faithfully observe the norms *(Varnāśrama)*, as laid out by society.
7. The reality of the universe is debatable and subject to various theories.

Their constant prayers were:

i. May we never have to perform the last rites for our children!
ii. May we earn plenty to help the poor and the needy!
iii May we be able to perform our duty without blemish, as determined in *Varnadharma*!
iv. May we achieve the ultimate bliss by merging into the Eternal!
v. May we live a full and righteous life of a hundred years!
vi. May we kill our ignorance, greed, hatred, and lust!

The epistemology was the *Şruti*, or the *Āptavacana*. No other proof was accepted or required. There are 431 *Ṛşis* mentioned in the *Ṛg Veda*. However, the main *Ṛşis***** who

---

**** The names of the most illustrious *Ṛşis* in the *Vedic* period are: *Manu, Agastya; Atri; Bharadvāja, Gotama, Jamadagni, Vaśiştha, Viśvāmitra, Kaśyapa.*

gave shape and structure to the society during the Vedic period are known as the *mānāsputra* (mind-born sons).

The *Vedic* mantras were regarded as revealed as they were heard by the wise men of the past, known as the *Ṛṣis.* This is not dissimilar to the revelations in Christian philosophy, where John Locke opines, "the bare testimony of the Word is the highest certainty but must be judged by reason".[6]

References:

1. Majumdar, R. C. (1964). *Ancient India* (pp. 40–42). Delhi: Motilal Banarsidas.
2. Aurobindo, S. (1914–16). *The Secret of the Veda (*pp. 3–4). Sri Aurobindo Ashram, Pondicherry.
3. Chinmāyananda, S. (1954). *Praśopaniṣad* (p. 10). Mumbai: Central Chinmaya Mission Trust.
4. *Ṛg Veda,* 10.90.1-16.
5. *www.agnihotra.org ;* accessed on 27/11/2020.
6. Russel, B. (2004). *History of Western Philosophy* (pp. 553). New York: Routledge.

❖

Manu. He became the first governor and produced a manual, a code of conduct, known as *Manu Smriti.*

Viśvāmitra. He re-emphasised the need to learn. Knowledge was the path for enlightenment and happiness.

Atri. He gave *Atri Smriti,* elucidating law.

Parāśara. He gave the *Parāśara Smriti.*

Vaśiṣṭha. He gave the *Yoga Vāsistha.*

Brihaspati. He was the teacher and author of *Brihaspati Samhitā.*

'The mind is its own place, and in itself,

Can make a heaven of hell, a hell of heaven'.

Milton

CHAPTER 4

The *Brāhmaṇas*

The *Vedic* ways of life gradually and surreptitiously changed to a priest-led culture. The *Brāhmins* often performed as commanders of the army, as advisors and also as the teachers and priests. There was mutual dependence between the priests and the chieftain. They believed that society progressed through four phases: *Satya Yuga,* the era of the truth; *Tretā Yuga,* the era of three fires (rituals); *Dwāpara Yuga,* the era of doubts; and *Kali Yuga,* the era of conflicts.

The mantras in the *Ṛg Veda* have references to the fights of *Indra,* their king or leader, with many other kings. The mantras imply a fight for defence of the tribe, as well as offence for capture of additional lucrative land and other prizes, viz. women, slaves, cattle, gold, etc. It is not entirely speculative to assume that with the increasing population of the tribe, insufficiency of land for sustenance and growing ambitions and many victories, the imperialistic tendencies must have developed.

The people calling themselves 'superior and civilised', or *Ārya* (the Āryans), invaded and fought a bloody, protracted war in the valleys of the Indus in western India, as documented in the *Ṛg Veda*[1]. This *'Daśa Rāja Yuddha'* was probably the fiercest battle that they had to fight for supremacy in that region. The Great War had lasted for forty years. *Ṛṣi Vashisṭha* was the commander of the army of the invading king, *Sudāsa*. The mantras suggest that war took place around the river *Paruśṇī,* [current name, the Ravi]. The region of *Vikarṇa,* on either side of the river, was held by the local kings called *Turbaśa, Druhyu, Matsya, Kavaśa, Anu, Pūru, Tritsu, Devaka* and *Śambara* and *Yuddhamādh* respectively. Eight other chieftains or commanders whose names are not known were also slain or captured. *Pūru's army of 6066 troops* was slain, and ninety-nine palatial homes and seven cities were destroyed. The artefacts discovered by archaeological excavations suggest that the local inhabitants worshipped *Śiva* and *Śakti,* which are the non-*vedic* gods. These gods, as well as many of the customs of the vanquished people, were subsequently incorporated into the *Vedic* pantheon.

Three of the most exalted *Ṛśis* in the *Vedas* seem to have played major parts in making King *Sudāsa* victorious in that protracted war. *Ṛṣi Varadvāja, Ṛṣi Vaśiṣṭha* and *Ṛṣi Parāśara* were the advisors and commander of his army. Legend suggests that it was *Ṛṣi Varadvāja* who had masterminded the crossing of the river. They were richly rewarded by the victorious king, who celebrated this eventual victory by having a coronation. A new nation was established in western India in the fertile soil of the seven rivers, which subsequently extended eastwards to the Ganges and to the Himalayan range of mountains in the north. This progression into the era of supremacy of the Brāhmins, also known as the Brāhminism, is likely to have occurred around the middle of the third millennium BCE.

One can sense the struggle for power between the ruling classes and the teaching classes, both of whom had begun to exert their importance in society. Many clues to this kind of situation can be found latterly in mythological stories and epics. A symbiotic existence must have been established eventually which gave divine rights to the king and all scriptural authority to the priests, i.e., the *Brāhmins.* The hereditary system for both was thus established. Perhaps this could be thought of as the end of *Satya Yuga* and the beginning of the *Tretā Yuga.* A formalised religion was thus established.

The *Brāhmins* probably believed that the first era - the *Satya Yuga* - had ended by that time. It was now the era of the rituals, i.e., *Tretā Yuga*. The three fires are: *Ahavaniyāgni, Gārhapatyāgni, Dakṣiṇāgni.* These are the fires required to be lit for rituals, including worship at home*. Religion was strictly followed. *Brāhminism* had postulated that the conduct of religious ceremonies was one's *Dharma*, or duty, which led one to salvation. This could only be conducted by those who had the right to do so. This *adhikāri* concept, i.e., the decreed laws specifying who had and who did not have the right or the authority, became the greatest tool to subject everyone in the society to rigid customs and subservience. Many activities, known as religious ceremonies (*Yagńas*) which were initially designed to reveal the philosophical concepts inherent in them, became the monopoly of the priest class and began to be interpreted differently.

The *Brāhmaṇas* are the scriptural books designed and prepared by the *Brāhmins* for the conduct of the various religious and social ceremonies and life events. They were understood to have been based upon the *Vedas*. In reality, they are not so, as will be apparent to anyone who has also read the *Vedas*. But not many could read the *Vedas*, and fewer still understood the mantras. Hence the *Brāhmin* priests or teachers claimed their manuals also as *Śruti* - the revelations. These became as sacred as the *Vedas* and began to be quoted as *Śabda, Śāstra or Śruti* – the definitive source which could not be questioned or doubted. The specialists of each *Veda* produced several recensions of the *Brāhmaṇas* and ascribed them to the original *Veda*. There were as many *Brāhmaṇas* as the preceptors of the schools for the priests. The books written by the most powerful and revered *Brāhmins* have survived, and those produced by lesser-known teachers have been lost.

The contents of these *Brāhmaṇas* have many common features, although there are some procedural and recital variations. These specify the procedural steps of conducting several *Yagńa*, or celebrations, *Ākhyāna* (Illustrustrative stories), historical anecdotes and religious instructions, and methods for observing penance. Hence *Veda* began to be accepted as having two parts, i.e., *Gyānakāṇḍa* and *Karmakāṇḍa;* the latter had two parts, the *Vidhi* (the process) and *Upāsanā* (the method).

Many *Yagńas* were designed and created, viz. celebrate life events, ward off evil, invite good fortune, prevent bad things from happening, prevent drought, invite rain, prevent floods, enhance sexual prowess, impregnate wife, seduce a person, develop special psychic and or physical powers, etc.[2] These were added to the simplistic five daily *Yagńas*.*

This kind of supremacy by the *Brāhmins* required them to have some sort of similarity in practice among themselves.

---

* The five *Yagñas* every *Brahmin* householder was obliged to perform daily were: Teaching, *Brahma Yagña;* offering water oblation to ancestors, *Pitri Yagña;* offering into fire, *Deva Yagña;* offering food, *Bhūta Yagña*, and provide hospitality to a guest, *Manuṣya Yagña*.

Hence *Yaska* is said to have produced a compendium called the *Nirukta*: the etymological source of about 400 words in Sanskrit. This would allow the same interpretation of the controversial words in the *Sūtras*. All the symbols of natural phenomena and virtue represented in the mantras were given great prominence by depicting them to be the primary gods. This changed the original independent, monotheistic, or henotheistic philosophy of the *Vedas* to a priest-led, polytheistic religion. A cult began to be established with bizarre rituals, a hereditary caste system, and untouchability. This was supported by superstitions, mythology and the later *Smritis*.

They called this *Sanātana Dharma,* to project this as 'the eternal religion' as established by the *Vedas*. There had never been any organised system similar to a 'religion' in *Vedic* times. *Dharma* had signified one's duty, as prescribed by *Varṇadharma*, i.e., the responsibilities of every individual in that society. There is no mantra in the *Vedas* with a phrase *'Sanātana Dharma'*.[3]

In addition, the latterly incorporated *Śiva* and *Śakti* became important. There was no creator identified in the *Ṛg Veda*; *Brahmā* was the title of the highest priest who conducted special *Yagńya*, and *Brahma* was also a special mantra, although this name denoting The Ultimate was mentioned only once in the last mantra of *Śukla Yajurveda*, where it became *Brahmā*, the creator. Thus, a trinity of divinity was established – the creator *Brahmā*, the destroyer *Śiva* and the preserver *Viśnu.* Accordingly, the philosophy about the creation became totally changed. One could attain the ultimate by worshipping any of the three in this trinity or, indeed, even by following their subordinates. This also set in motion the beginnings of a number of sects or cults.

Once again, the uniformity of processes for conducting *Yagńas,* as appropriate for many gods, had to be established. This was done with the help of mythology, called *Purāṇas.* Moreover, the timings of these *Yagńas* had to be determined. This led to the development of astronomy and mathematics. However, these two developments have also been the greatest contribution of India to human civilisation. The concept of many galaxies, spherical planets, heliocentrism, relativity of time and mathematical calculations are the foundations of modern quantum theories, astrophysics, and the theories of evolution.

The society had grown much more complex, with larger areas to govern, dispense justice, collect revenue, taxes and establish standards of trade and barter and many other state activities, as well as religion. Hence a series of manuals were developed, collectively called *Śrauta Sūtra,* which was decreed to be sacrosanct. There is hardly any reference to the original *Vedic* mantras in these *Sūtras,* loosely termed *Śāstras,* which are in reality the protocols and procedural manuals for rituals. These are enforced rigidly as the scriptures. The impression among the uneducated *Vaiśya* and the *Śūdra* classes was that anything written in Sanskrit must be holy and reverential. These developments began to give enormous power to the *Brāhmins.* They began to claim that their blessings or curses would bear results. Ordinary folks believed in them. Although some educated *Kshetriyas,* particularly the kings, began to question this development, it took several centuries for the era of the *Upaniṣads* to come out in open revolt of *Brāhminism.*

This was the period when the original *Varṇāṣrama*

became inexorably modified. The *Brāhmaṇa* books sanctioned the modification of the ancient caste system by merit to the caste system by birth. The *Brāhmin* priests and the ruling *Kshetreyas* were able to exploit the two lower uneducated classes with impunity. The *Śūdra* caste was made untouchable and outcast, like the *Mlechha*, who did not belong to the *Āryan* pantheon. Only the *Brāhmins* were entitled to read the *Vedas*. Even *Brāhmin* women and persons of the lower two castes were not allowed to do so. The women became the possessions of their husbands, to keep, sell or present to anyone they wished.

Manu Smriti, the original code of conduct, was thus modified and many harsh and cruel punishments were added for trivial aberrations of the rigid norms. This became similar to the code of conduct given by Hammurabi, which was probably contemporary, *circa* 1400 BCE. Widows were required to immolate themselves into the funeral pyre of their husbands. They did not have individual rights to liberty anymore and were regarded as the property of their husbands. Children were regarded as the property of the father. Even bizarre rituals were being practised openly – these included animal and human sacrifice. The *Brāhmins* and the ruling classes had become extremely powerful by the 12th century BCE. The main concepts were as follows:

1. The kings were the divine representatives and had absolute temporal powers.
2. Priests were essential for every worship, or *Yagňa*; the prescribed rituals guaranteed the desired effect and a place in heaven only if administered by an authorised priest. One had the right to perform a ritual by oneself without the aid of a priest but could not expect

the desired outcome.

3. There was no need to understand the meaning of the mantras; one only memorised them by heart according to the strict guidelines. Knowledge of their contents came from within the person in due course, or a *guru* would find one if one had lived a life according to the *Brāhminical* scriptures.

4. The soul went to heaven after death if the person had lived a righteous life and would return eventually as a human being.

5. The soul of a person who had lived a sinful life would go to hell. The hells were several and graded according to increasing severity of torture required for the emancipation of the sinners. Eventually, they will be reborn as plants, insects, animals, etc. for a cycle of 8.4 million births and deaths. Only then will they be born again as human beings. This was known as *samsāra cakra* – the wheel of life and death.

6. Holy, enlightened, and extremely generous persons merged into God after death and would be liberated from the repeated cycle of death and rebirth. This is known as attaining the *Mokshya*, or the state of ultimate bliss.

The evidence of validity of these concepts, i.e., the *pramāna*, were the *Śāstras (scriptural texts), the Smritis, the Brāhmaṇas, Āraṇyakas* all produced by the Brāhmins themselves. In addition, it used to be commonly accepted that the words of a *guru* did not need any proof.

It is thus not difficult to appreciate how surreptitiously the ritualistic age – with a philosophy which gave credibility to the mythology, superstition, divine rights of the kings and supremacy to the *Brāhmins* in all religious matters - superseded the *Vedic* age. This led to subjugation or servitude for nearly half of society. Only a male *Brāhmin* had the birthright to become a teacher, advisor, commander of the army, priest, astronomer and also a physician, without having to prove the qualifications to do so. However, there were still the enlightened *Ācaryas,* who continued to observe and teach the original *Vedic* way of life. The concept of enlightenment was replaced by wearing a sacred thread, made of three, six or nine long strings of home-spun cotton. This was given at the time of initiation, known as *Upanayana.* The *Brāhmins* by birth and some *Kshetriyas* would be proclaimed to have become *Dwija* after wearing this sacred thread at their initiation into the caste by a priest.

The mantras of the *Ṛg Veda* and the *Atharva Veda* were found useful to develop medicine and surgery, collectively known as the 'knowledge of ageing' or *Āyurveda*; spells and magic began to develop as well and were practised widely. Medications were mostly herbal. There are several references to organ transplantations, cosmetic surgery and complicated surgical operations, including cataract operations, being performed. A whole new anatomy was proposed and accepted. Diseases were considered as having four sources - *Vāta, Pitta, Kafa* and evil spells, either singly or in combination. The external causes of diseases were divided into the visible and nonvisible agents. Science, mathematics, astronomy, science of warfare, metallurgy, legal systems, literature, art and crafts developed. Society became a rigid, inviolable edifice, and even minor deviation from the norm was severely punished. All this can be seen in the currently available *Manusmriti.*

The third phase of *Varṇāśrama,* the retirement phase, when one went to the forest to contemplate, had continued as before. These retirees, mostly belonging to the *Brāhmin* and the *Kshetriya* castes, lived in austerity in the forest, the *Bana* or *Araṇya*. They were exempt from observing the prescribed *Yagňa* and social obligations of a householder. They began to reflect and modify the *Brāhmaṇas,* producing their updated versions. These were called the *Āraṇyakas* [made in the forest]. The *Āraṇyakas,* however, contained additional debates on various aspects of life, death, values, and various rituals. The debates were mostly on philosophical issues and eventually became separated from the main texts. These are known as the *Upaniṣads.* In due course, the *Upaniṣads* too became regarded as the *Vedas,* as part of their *Gyānakaṇda.* Although the *Upaniṣad* era had begun along with the *Āraṇyakas, Brāhmaṇism* continued unabated.

Just as the *Prātiśākhyas* and *Nirukta* were indispensable, there arose the need for another agreed reference to produce similarity among the *Āraṇyakas* and other *Brāhmiṇical* texts. This was provided in several *Sūtras* and memorised as *Pūrva Mimāmsā,* compiled by *Ṛṣi Jaimini* in the 5th century BCE.

Notes:

1. The currently available *Brāhmaṇa* books are as follows:

   Aitereya Brāhmaṇa and *Kauśitaki Brāhmaṇa* are attributed to the *Ṛg Veda*; *Śatapatha Brāhmaṇa* and *Taitteriya Brāhmaṇa* to the *Yajur Veda*; *Tāndya Brāhmaṇa, Pancabimśa Brāhmaṇa* and *Śadbimśa Brāhmaṇa* to the *Sāma Veda*; and *Gopatha Brāhmaṇa* is attributed to the *Atharva Veda*.

1. *Śastras:*

   Śrauta Sūtra, Apastambha, Kalpa Sūtra, Grihya Sūtra, Dharma Sāśtra, Manusmriti.

2. *Puraṇas:*

   Śrimad Bhāgavat, Viśṇu, Agni, Śiva, Devī, Garuḍa, Vāyu, Nāradīya, Kurma, Liṅga, Skanda, Matsya, Brahmānḍa, Mārkandeya, Brahmavaivarta, Padma, Bhawisya.

3. *Araṇyakas*

4. *Vedāngas:*

   Sikshya, Nirukta, Jyotiśa, Vyakaraṇa and Chanda.

5. *Pratisakhyas:*

   Ṛgveda, Atharvaveda.

References:

1. *Ṛg* 7.18.1-25.
2. www.thehindu.com, accessed 7/7/20.
3. Vedic rituals and Sacrifices from *Śrauta Sastras* by Jayaram V', see *www.Hinduwebsite.com* accessed on 24/01/21.

❖

The reasonable man adapts himself to the world; the unreasonable one persists in trying to adapt the world to himself. Therefore, all progress depends on the unreasonable man.

George Bernard Shaw

CHAPTER 5

Tantra

Background:

Tantra has been present in northern India since very ancient times. The Indologists of the past had obviously failed to study this in depth and discarded it as crude, vulgar and unimportant – a potpourri of sorcery, magic, and bizarre violent rituals. This is an ill understood concept. I have chosen to include this here because the philosophy behind this has been extensively deliberated in the *Upaniṣads*, as well as by *Buddha* and *Mahāvīra*. Traditionally, *Tantra* has been deliberately kept under wraps and is known as *Rahasya Vidyā* – a secret doctrine. Part of this is included in *Brāminism* too, although the priests do not openly accept themselves to be its practitioners. The *Tantra* as a doctrine of human salvation in modern times was accepted according to the *Śiva* and *Devi Purānas*. The practitioner of *Tantra* is known as a *Tāntrik*.

There is a striking similarity between thc orthodox *Brāhminism* and *Tantra*. The main mantra of the *Tāntriks* is "*Om succeyko Brahma*" (*Om: aum; Sat:* the ultimate truth; *Cit:* eternal bliss; *Yekah:* only The One; *Brahma:* Brahma), which is the same for the *Brāhmins*. The *Brāhmins* forbade the study of the *Vedas* for all except boys who were born to pure *Brāhmin* parents. The teachers of *Tantra* continued to select their novitiates themselves, unrestricted by the caste system, and forbade them to talk about it, demanding total obedience and secrecy. *Brāhminism* took advantage of the mantras of

Yajurveda and reinforced the rituals by producing a corpus of *Pauranik Devi and Devatā* (mythological gods and goddesses), *Brāhmaṇa* books and mainly *Brihadāraṇyaka* and *Chāndogya Upaniṣads.* The *Tāntriks* also based their doctrines on the *Atharva Veda,* mythological gods and goddesses – mainly *Śiva* and *Pārvati* in their myriad forms and primarily two *Upaniṣads* known as *Śvetāśvatara and Jābāla.* The doctrines of *Sānkhya* and *Yoga* are freely adopted by both. The *Mahāyāna Buddhism* has adopted *Tantrik* rituals to a large extent and is an integral part of Tibetan *Buddhism.* The special powers as assured by the *Brāhmin* priests of curse, blessings, delivering the rainfall, a good crop, victory in battles for their hosts, etc. are similar to the *Siddhi* (achievements) of the *Tāntriks.* The five well-known gods and goddesses, i.e., *Śiva, Viśnu, Sūrya, Gaṇeśa,* and *Devi* as the various forms of *Śiva- Śakti,* are worshipped as gods by both cults. The special forms of *Śakti* are *Chinnamastā, Dhūmavatī, Bhairavī, Tripurasundari, Bhuvaneśvarī, Mātangī, Tārā, Kālī, Śodaṣī, Kamalā, Bangalāmukhī.* The principal gods like *Viśnu, Śiva* and *Devi* have been given at least a thousand names each – with each name signifying a particular trait, character, nature, purpose, or ritual in both cults.

There are some striking differences too. The *Brāhmins* believe that *Yagňa* (rituals plus penance plus austerity) is the method of achieving pleasure and wealth in this world, and the ultimate *Iśvara* after death. The *Tāntriks* believe that the *Siddhi* alone can lead one to the ultimate *Brahma* known as *Śiva-Śakti* in the present life itself. *Siddhi* is achieved after intense efforts for a considerable period of concentration, devotion, and practices, as prescribed by the teacher who has the demonstrable *Siddhi* himself or herself. Orthodox *Brāhminism* forbids meat eating, except the flesh of a slaughtered animal at special rituals. Meat obtained in this way was not forbidden. Sexual intercourse with a wife was strictly for procreation only; celibacy was mandatory until marriage, but polygamy was allowed. The *Tāntriks* believed sex to be a powerful tool to achieve *Siddhi* and it was one of the five offerings to *Śiva* or *Śakti*; these being wine, meat, fish, grains and sex (woman). The adherence to the caste system, i.e., *Varnadharma and Varnāşrama,* was essential in *Brāhminism*. The *Tāntriks* accepted novices from every walk of life without any other consideration such as gender, caste, creed, education, or social status, except the desire and determination to achieve the *Siddhi.*

Tantra also has two components - knowledge and action, similar to the *Vedic* Mantras, i.e., the knowledge and the rituals. The *Brāhmaṇa* books and certain rituals accepted by the *Brāhmin* priests are decidedly *Tāntrik* in nature. The *Purānas* such as *Śiva, Devi, Kālikā* and *Skanda* freely espouse the two aspects of The *Puruşa* as *Śiva* and *Śakti*. Indeed, the whole of *Tantra* is based on the questions and answers between *Śiva* and *Śakti*, who play this role alternately. The *Agamas* are the answers given by *Śiva* to *Pārvati (the pupil)* and the *Nigamas* are the answers given by *Pārvati* to *Śiva* (the pupil).

Pāśupata Śaiva Darśana (the Śaiva philosophy):

Background: This is regarded as the foundation of *Tantra*. Some background information is necessary before proceeding further.

This philosophy got formal recognition for the first time, probably by *Veda Vyāsa*, who presented this as taught by the Lord *Mahādeva* to his father-in-law, *Dakchya Prajāpati*, in the

Śāntiparva of *Mahābhārata*[1] and as the dialogue between *Bhīshma* and *Yudhiśṭhira*.[2]It is believed that this was called *Pāśupata Śāstra Pancārtha Darśana*. It was purported to have been composed in five chapters. The *Pāśupata Sūtra*, which is believed to be one of these chapters, was discovered in India in 1940. The rest have not surfaced as yet. A commentary on the original is said to have been given by Pandit Raşikara, circa 300–500 CE. *Abhinava Guptā* has mentioned this in his book *Tantraloka*, circa 1000 CE. India had many followers of this cult in the millennium before Christ, as witnessed by Megasthenes, the Greek ambassador of Alexander the Great. He called them *Śaivās* or *Śiveys*.

Śiva and its female form *Śakti* are really one and the same. This duality is the key for realising and achieving the Ultimate. This duality is achieved by dual efforts. *Madhwācārya* in his book, the *Sarvadarshan Samgraha*, described this philosophy as *'lakuliş pāśupata darśana'* and suggested it was prevalent in India, circa 200 BCE. This name was based on a mythological story in *Śiva Purāṇa* in which Lord *Śiva* entered the corpse of a *Brāhmin* known as *Lakuliş* and taught this philosophy. However, this philosophy was propounded very much earlier than that period, as has been explained.

This philosophy asserts that the entire universe itself is *Śiva-Śakti*. This Ultimate, known as *Śiva-Śakti*, manifests in duality as the male *Śiva* and the female *Śakti*. The *paśu* is the man, or indeed any animal or living entity. He/she is subjected to three major kinds of bondage: the physical or worldly, mental and the spiritual. One attains the Ultimate only after throwing away all these bondages. There are many ways to achieve release from these bondages, and *Tantra* is one of them. The evolution, maintenance and dissolution of the universe is done by *Paśupati* - the lord of all bondages. [*paśu,* signifies both living and non-living matter, and *pati,* the master or the lord.] There can be many *Tantras,* but one must follow the same two primary requisites - i.e. *Sādhanā* and *Pratigña,* effort and determination - for the accomplishment of power, the *Siddhi.*

The five reasons for following this philosophy are as follows:

1. *Kārana*: The cause. The cause of this entire universe is lord *Paśupati,* who sets the evolution, maintains, and destroys it.
2. *Kārya:* The action performed artfully (*kala*) and with knowledge (*vidya*).
3. *Yoga:* The merger. The ultimate aim is to integrate or merge the *Paśu,* the aspirant, into Him, the Pati.
4. *Vidhi:* The method that leads to the awakening of the *Kuṇḍalinī.*
5. *Dukhānta:* To end the tragic end (avoid tragedy).

The *sādhanā: (Kārya* plus *Yoga* plus *Vidhi).* This will awaken *the Kundalinī (Satchakraveda).*

The *Tāntriks* believe that there are six *Cakras,* or the neural centres of occult powers, in the human body. These are *Mūlādhāra, Swādiśsthāna, Maṇipura, Anāhata, Viśuddha* and *Agya.* These six need to be awakened from their dormant to conscious states. The various steps enumerated in the *Sādhana* are designed to bring these centres into conscious states. The ultimate power known as *Kundalinī* can manifest when these six centres become conscious. The awakened *Kundalinī* provides an aspirant with unlimited prowess to achieve anything. This power is popularly known as the 'Serpent Power' to denote the legendary thousand-headed serpent coiled and lying on the bottom of the Pacific Ocean, on whom rests the Lord *Viśnu*. In other words, the source or the basis of the Ultimate is this coiled, unlimited energy which is the eternal and original entity present in every living thing. Those who experience this state of realisation merge with *Śiva-Śakti*, and those who manage to awake only a few of these *Cakras* achieve limited specific powers.*

This *Sādhana* has two components.

1. *Vrata.* This is also known as penance *(tapasyā) or pratigyā* (the resolve).
   This requires the novitiate to smear the body with ashes (ash-bath) and sleep on a bed of ashes. Ash signifies fire, water, earth, sky, mind, eyes, emotions, and the Space.
   He/she is also required to fulfil the courses of instruction on singing, dancing, laughing, joining hands in obeisance *(namaskāra)*, grunting (*hunkāra*), repeating mantras *(japa)*, meditation (*tapa*) and circumambulation *(pradakshiṇā)*.
2. *Dwāra.* This is the gateway for release from sins and

---

* *Tantra* has been wrongly projected in the West as a means for achieving super-sexuality, ecstasy, and freedom from many social conventions. Naturally, this has attracted many westerners who believe in their spurious *Tāntrik* teachers and become their disciples. The internet is full of these advertisements, and an estimated several-billion-dollar enterprise has developed globally. Several cult practices and *Yogic* exercises too have been included, to give some semblance of authenticity to this *Tantra*. The display of erotic images during bizarre body contortions in the guise of *Yogic* exercises are offered for money. One needs to be as far away from these commercial concerns as possible.

to achieve the *siddhi.*

One is required to walk in sleep (*krathana*); shake the whole body (*spandana*); walk on one leg (*mandana,* a cripple), behave lewdly (*śringāraṇa*) and speak gibberish (*pralāpa or abhitad-bhāṣaṇa*).

The *Vāmana Purāna* mentions mainly four types of *Śaiva* cults, namely *Śaiva, Pāśupatā, Kāladamana (Kālamukha)* and *Kāpālika.* They sport a black mark on their foreheads and wear black loincloths. The extreme fundamentalists among the *Kāpalika* live in cremation grounds, are nude and eat unimaginable things. These are known as *Aghorī.* They carry a skullcap as a bowl for begging food. The purpose of these bizarre actions is for one to be shunned by society in order that the worldly or physical bond, i.e., one of the three fundamental bonds, is destroyed.

The *siddhi,* the power or accomplishment: The novitiate can desire the level of achievement of power, but it is the *guru* who determines his/her capacity or ability and provides instructions and guidance accordingly. No one is disallowed. Many *Tantras* of varying levels of accomplishment are designed and taught. According to the *Kulāsana Tantra,* the doctrines of *Tantras* are in three groups, namely *Viśnukrānta, Rathakrānta* and *Ashwakrānta.* Each group contains sixty-four *Tantras. Lalit Sahśranāma* enumerates 28 *Śaiva Tantras,* viz. *Vāmadeva, Aghorā, Tatpuruṣa* and *Īshāna,* each having five systems and eight representations (forms) of *Śiva.* It is thought that many invaluable manuscripts of *Tantra* are unavailable. It is hoped that these will resurface soon.

Pancarātra:

Similar to the concept of *Śiva and Śakti* in *Tantra Śāstra*, the worshippers of *Viśṇu* in the southern parts of India came up with the concept of *Viśṇu* and *Prakriti*. The philosopher *Nārāyaṇa* expanded the worship of *Viśnu* mentioned in *Taittirīa Samhitā*, which is a recension of the *Kṛśṇa Yajur Veda*. Legend has it that the sage *Nārāyaṇa* performed austerities for five nights and became enlightened. He taught that the soul *(ātmā)* and *brahma*, (the Supreme) were interrelated. He established a significant following known as *Vaiṣṇava Sampradāya*. This cult practice led to elaborate prayers, rituals and *Yogic* practices, and temple constructions were encouraged.

The literature on *Pancarātra* doctrine is vast. It is estimated that fifteen million *Slokas* were written, but many have been lost. Some rare manuscripts are preserved in *Viśnu* temples and are used as reference manuals for special occasions and temple constructions. These are also known as *Agama Sūtras* or *Vaiṣṇava agamas*. Nearly 100,000 *agamas* have been printed. The most quoted among these are *Aniruddha Samhitā, Pauṣkara Samhitā* and *Jayakhya Samhitā*. This cult progressed to be a pan-Indian movement in the second millennium CE, although *Śankarācārya* did not accept this as a true *Vaiṣnva* cult.

References:

1. *Mahābhārata* 1.121-124; 2. ibid 259. 7-9.

CHAPTER 6

The *Upanişads*

The *Upanişads* have profoundly influenced the Indian psyche over the last three millennia. The greatest contribution to Indian philosophy was made by the *Ŗşis* and some *Kshetriya* scholars, who had retired to the forest for reflection and contemplation. However, they had continued to teach and hand down their life's experiences to the younger generation of eager pupils. They reflected on the *Brāhmaṇas,* and the *Vedas* and the result was the production of a large number of *Āraṇyakas* which corresponded to the *Brāhmaṇas.* The parts of *Āraṇyakas* which dealt with esoteric spiritual knowledge and recorded the conversations between the teacher and pupil are the *Upanişads.* In Sanskrit, the term *Upanişad* means: *upa*, near; *nişad*, sit close; or *upa*, approach; *ni*, resolve; *şad*, destroy. A pupil approaches an enlightened *guru* and, sitting close to him, resolves to destroy his own innate ignorance. Indeed, all the *Upanişads* are in conversational style. The *Upanişads* are also known as the *Brahma Vidyā, Rahasya Vigyāna, Vedānta* and *Ātmagyāna.*

It appears to be true that some *Upanişads* are older than others. It is commonly accepted that the *Brihadāraṇyaka, Chāndogya, Taittirīya* and *Iśā Upanişads* are probably the oldest. It is not, however, possible to ascertain definite dates of origin of the *Upanişads,* although some scholars have suggested the probable 9th century BCE.[1] There are estimated to be more than 200 *Upanişads*; nearly 100 have been published so far. Every *Upanişad* conventionally begins with the loud chant of a prayer which is an aspiration for happiness and peace.

*"Om! Bhadram*karneyvi śruniyāma devā;*

bhadram paśyamākśviryajatrā...

Om! Śāntih, Śāntih, Śāntih."

Translation:

Aum! O Respected Ones! May we always hear with our ears only that which is blissful!

May we see with our eyes only that which is auspicious!

May peace prevail on the Earth, in the Sky and in the Space!

These philosophers believed that certain mental preparations were essential to understand the deep spiritual concepts and to experience them personally. This was called the preparatory phase, or *Upāsanā*. Equanimity of mind, objectivity in thinking, humility, faith in the *guru* and intense desire to learn were the minimum requirements expected of the pupil. These were achieved by observing the two disciplines called *Manana* (reflection) and *Nidhidhyāsana* (meditation).

Śankarācārya included only ten *Upaniṣads* in his commentary of *Brahma Sūtra,* commonly regarded as the essence of all the *Upaniṣads,* and hence these became known as the 'major' and the rest as the 'minor' *Upaniṣads.* These are *Brihadāraṇyaka, Isa, Chāndogya, Mundaka, Māṇḍukya,*

---

* *'bhadram'* has no equivalent single word in English; this may also mean well-being, graceful, prosperous, beneficial, benevolent, etc. Traditionally, the peace invocation is repeated three times for the three regions – the earth, sky, and the Space.

Aitereya, Taittiria, Praśna, Kena and *Katha*. The major ones are more like *Sūtras* than poems, although the *Praśna* is in prose and commonly regarded as the last in the series. The minor *Upanişads* may have been later productions but are not any less profound in their philosophical deliberations than the earlier ones. Samples of the contents of many Upanişads are given in Appendix 2.

The philosophy of the *Upanişads*:

They brought the concepts of *Brahma, Ātmā* and *Jivātmā* or *Self*, which included deliberations on bondage, liberation, life and soul, death and rebirth and their relevance and relationship with man. The main subject covered in most of these *Upanişads* is 'bliss', the achievement of which is the ultimate aim of human life. These philosophers introduced the concept of *'Brahma'* as being the Ultimate Reality and moved away from the concept of 'God' as postulated by the *Brāhmaṇa* scriptures, or *Puruşa* of the *Ṛg Veda*. This was a major departure from the priestly conventions claimed to have been derived from the *Puruşa*. Many also wished to equate *Brahma* to *Puruşa* and many others did not do so. This led to the debate on *'Vidyā and Avidyā'* which heralded the era of renaissance. There was a difference of opinion about the *Vidyā and Avidyā*, although all agreed that *Vidyā* was the true knowledge which led one to the ultimate reality. The *Brāhmaṇa* scriptures insisted on rituals being essential for the realisation of God and *Mokshya*, whereas the *Upanişads* insisted upon the non-ritualistic austerity to be the means of realising the *Brahma*. In essence, the difference was in the process, i.e., the *Vidyā* or *Upāsanā* vs *Yagńa* or the *Avidya* of the *Brāhmaṇas*. True knowledge, or *Vidyā*, has two parts:

i. *Parā vidyā, the* path of liberation, and

ii. *Aparā vidyā,* path of worship *(Upāsana)* of *Brahma*

One also finds references in the *Upaniṣads* to the advanced culture of people living in beautiful houses, palaces, gardens, enjoying music and dancing and partaking of different articles of food and drink. Several modes of transportation, agriculture, animal husbandry, archery, tools and implements, swordsmanship, astronomy, parties and celebrations, etc. are mentioned. Monarchical and republic states too are seen among the names like the Kuru, Pāncal, Kāshi, Mithila, Kekeya, Gāndhāra, Kośala, etc. Many ethical and moral concepts too are part of the deliberations.

A study of the *Upaniṣads* shows two types of doctrines - one in support of the orthodoxy, i.e., the ritualistic *Brāhminism,* but making allowances for *Brahma* of the philosophers as the *Puruṣa* described in the *Ṛg Veda*; the other unorthodox idea making their ultimate *Brahma* separate from the *Puruṣa* of the *Ṛg Veda.*

Max Muller thought that the *Upaniṣads* were "a system in which human speculation seems to have reached its acme."[2] It is easy to get baffled by the diversity of doctrines in the *Upaniṣads.* They do not present a systematised philosophical treatise. Radhakrishnan and Moore[3] assert "though remote in time from us, the *Upaniṣads* are not remote in thought. The ideal which haunted the thinkers of the *Upaniṣads* – the ideal of man's ultimate beatitude, the perfection of knowledge, the vision of the real in which the religious hunger of the mystic for direct vision and the philosopher's ceaseless quest for truth are both satisfied – is still our ideal."

The *Upaniṣads* take the manifested and the unmanifested

to be one whole. This one whole is divided into *Pinda* [the microcosm] and *Brahmānda* [the macrocosm] to facilitate the process of reasoning about phenomenal universe. Microcosm, though an infinitesimal portion of the macrocosm, is nothing but a prototype of the latter. Hence the study of microcosm in all its aspects enables one to study the whole of the cosmos. One can study the microcosm, i.e., the self, and ascertain what it is and what laws govern it.[4]

A relatively young treatise called *Sarvopaniṣad* probably represents most of the philosophy of all the *Upaniṣads* and is appropriately called by this title (*Sarvah,* All; *Upaniṣad, Upaniṣads*). This is presented here in part as a free translation.

Questions:

Aum! What is the bondage of the Soul? What is liberation? What is *Avidyā*? What is *Vidyā?*

What are the states of *Jāgrat* (awakened), *Svapna* (dream), *Śuṣupti* (dreamless sleep) and the fourth state, *Turia* (the Absolute Consciousness)?

What are *Annamaya, Prāṇamaya, Manomaya, Vigńānamaya* and *Ānandamaya Koṣa* (the five shrouds of the soul)?

What is the *Kartā* (the doer)? What is the *Jīva* (the individual)? What is *Kshetragńa* (the knower of the field, i.e., the body)?

What is *Sākshi* (the witness), the *Kutastha,* (that which exists in the non-existent); the *Antaryāmin* (the inner Controller)?

What is *Pratyagātma* (the core), the *Paramātmā* (the

Ultimate), the *Ātmā* (the Soul) and the *Māya* (the Illusion), too?

Answers:

The Controller of Soul looks upon the body as itself; this is ego and this is the cause of bondage of the soul. Liberation is the cessation of that Ego. *Avidyā,* nescience, is that which brings forth the egoism. That which turns away the egoism completely is *Vidyā,* the true knowledge.

The awakened state is that when the fourteen organs of perception such as the mind, influenced by the sun and the external environmental agents, perceive the gross entities such as sound etc., that is the awakened state.

When the self is not influenced by the external agents such as the sound but is still in possession of its passions and perceives by means of the four internal organs (mind, intelligence, memory, ego) the sound and the rest in the form of desires, then it is said to be in a state of dream.

When the fourteen organs are inactive and there is absence of perception, that is the state of dreamless sleep then the self is a witness of the absence of the three states but has no state of itself and remains as one and undifferentiated, then one is said to be in Absolute Consciousness. *Annamaya Koṣa,* the alimentary shroud, is said to be the composite of six kinds of food and nutrition. When the fourteen vital airs, including the one which causes the motion in the air, remain within the alimentary shroud, it is said to be the *Prāṇamaya Koṣa.* Endowed with these two shrouds, when the soul becomes active with the four sense organs for the desires of the mind, it is said to be in the *Manomaya Koṣa.* Being united with these three shrouds, when the soul glows with the knowledge of difference and non-difference, then it is said to be in *Vigyānamaya Koşa.* When the soul enveloped by these four shrouds exists for its own sake, like the hidden banyan tree within its own seed, it is said to be in the *Ānandamaya Koşa.*

This becomes the doer, when it dwells in the body as the knower of pleasure and pain; the desired is pleasure and the undesired is the pain. Their causes are the sound, touch, sight, taste and smell. According to the accumulated virtues and the sins, when it is seen to be connecting with a new body not yet received, it is said to be a *Jiva,* an individual self.

The ego consisting of the groups of five, each beginning with the mind, *Prāṇa, Sattva,* will and the merit, does not perish without realising and achieving the *Ātmā.*

Due to its closeness with *Ātmā,* that appears imperishable and is said to be a *Linga-sharira,* i.e., the subtle body, also known as the *Hridaya granthi,* the knot of the heart.

One who is aware of the knowledge of this body is called *Kshetrāgñya,* the knower of the body.

The philosophers in these *Upanişads* appear to suggest that the ritualistic *Brāhminism* was not the true path of liberation (*Vidyā*) or achieving *Brahma.* Hoping for the ultimate liberation from the cycle of birth and death by performing rituals, as advocated in the *Brāhmanas,* was called *Avidya,* 'the pseudo-knowledge or nescience'. There is evidence of each side claiming to be the proponent of *Vidyā.* The *Brahma* therefore is the main hypothesis of the *Upanişads;* this is not a *Vedic* concept which is the *Puruşa* and its lesser divine manifestations. The *Upanişads,* however, demand austerity and mental discipline as the prerequisites for understanding spiritual concepts. These also have been called *Vidyā* or the spiritual systems. About thirty-two spiritual practices are described; these can be classified into two primary systems. One teaches meditation upon certain *Vedic* rituals (*Yagńa*) by superimposing certain ideas on them, and the second implores the aspirant to meditate on mind *(manas),* speech *(vāk),* strength *(bala)* and name *(nāma).*

Historically, the *Upaniṣads* were the beginning of revolt, albeit subtle and discreet, against the excesses of *Brāhminism.* The truly enlightened sages were teaching their pupils the real knowledge, *Vidyā,* when some other successful *Brāhmin* priests were still propagating *Avidyā.* All of the ten *Upaniṣads* selected by *Śankarācārya* indicate this probability; this will be discussed again during the introduction on *Vedānta* or the *Uttar Mimāmsā.* Many of the teachers were of the *Kshetriya* caste also, and many of the *Brāhmin gurus* were poor because they were not as active as the professional priests and did not have the patronage of the rich and powerful. Caste was not considered a barrier to learning, although not openly challenged. [Nicely illustrated in the story of Raikya and the King Janaşruti; wealth helped, as always]. There are several lesser-known *Upaniṣads.* It is probably not essential to comment on them here. The gist of the *Upaniṣads* is commonly known as *Vedānta* – the end of the *Vedas.* This is a misnomer but has remained.

This heralded the era of renaissance. *Brāhminism,* however, continued unabated for the next millennium, although Jainism, Buddhism and subsequent philosophical deliberations affected its supremacy, probably from 700 BCE until 700 CE. Since then it has continued to this day as

Hinduism or *Sanātana Dharma.*

References:

1. Kumar, B. trans.ed. (2004). *Vaidik Vāngmamya Kā Itihās (p.* 307). Delhi: Parimal Publications.

2. Muller, M. (1903). *The Six Systems of Indian Philosophy* (p. 139). Honolulu: University Press of the Pacific. Honolulu.

3. Radhakrishnan, S. & Moore, C. (1973). *A Source Book in Indian Philosophy* (p. 37).

4. Taylor, J. trans. Mishra, K. (1893). *Prabodh Chandrodaya. Or the rise of the moon of the intellect.* (p.5) Kissinger Publishing.www.kessinger.net; accessed on 26/01/21.

5. Swami Harshananda. (1998). *The Ten Cardinal Upaniṣads.* Bangalore: Ramkrishna math.

A categorical imperative would be one which represented an action as objectively necessary in itself, without reference to any other purpose.

Immanuel Kant

CHAPTER 7

Philosophical expressions through Sound and Fine Arts

Concept of the *Om*: *(Aum)*

Sound is used in the physical and metaphysical context in Indian philosophy and religion. The correct pronunciation of words is considered as being of paramount importance. This has been illustrated with various legends in the *Vedas**. The loud chant of Aum has been the most common entity in Indian philosophical concepts. The *Atharva Veda* begins by invoking the god of Speech - *Vācaspati.* In the *Ṛg Veda,* the goddess of Speech *Vāgambhriṇī* declared that she created the universe.[1*]

The physical aspects of sound:

The obvious examples are spoken speech, prayers, musical instruments, signals in battles and for security, and noises of all kinds.

The spoken speech is said to have four components: *Parā, Pasyanti, Madhyamā* and *Vaikhari. Vaikhari* is the last stage when it becomes audible. The speech begins in the thought, which then travels down to the lowest *Cakra* at the base of the spine, when it is called *Parā. Parā* ascends up to the navel and becomes *Pasyanti.* When it travels up further, it becomes *Madhyamā* and when it travels through the lungs, trachea,

---

* The Bible and The Koran also believe the cosmic vibrations in their metaphysical sense to be similar to the *Vedic* concepts.

throat, tongue, mouth and teeth, it becomes *Vaikhari*, i.e., audible. When the sound expelled as *Vaikhari* expresses its intent, it becomes a word, or *Śabda.* This final stage is the word or the gesture which allows someone to understand the emotion or the intent of the speaker [*vide,* the gestures of the modern sign language]. This system of phonetics and semantics, known as *Chanda Śāstra,* has been given a great deal of importance as one of the six *Vedāngas.* This deals with the metre, phonetics and semantics of the *Vedic* mantras, besides having important metaphysical significance too.

The correct accent of the syllables is known as *Svara,* which is primarily of three kinds: *Udātta, Anudātta* and *Svarita.* This is done by controlling the expulsion of the breath as *Āyāma, Viśrambha* and *Ākshepa,* as determined by the *Prātiśakhya* of the *Ṛg Veda.* Later, Patanjali suggested seven kinds of *Svara.* This corresponds to the twenty-one vowels and their derivatives in the Sanskrit language. Correct pronunciation of the syllables is of paramount importance in Sanskrit because wrongly pronounced syllables can alter the meaning of the words, resulting in misrepresentation and wrongful actions.

Examples of vocalisation:

Udātta is long out breath, as in bravo.

Anudātta is short out breath, as in soft.

Svarita is neutral or balanced out breath, as in go.

The words which express emotions are known as *Rasa*; this implies the juice, taste, essence, sentiments, emotions expressed during speech, song, and/or dance. *Rasas* are of nine kinds, viz. anger, sorrow, delight, disgust, fear, laughter, heroism, wonder and serene. This *Rasa* became used in

Nyāya logic as well as in poetic composition when the written or spoken words could have three types of meanings – the obvious, the implied and the hidden. The visual and audible representation of *Rasa* led to the development of drama and dance, systematised by *Nātya Sāśtra*, which was probably an offshoot of *Chanda Śāstra*. This science was compiled by Bharata Muni, circa 200 BCE, and further expanded and explained by *Abhinava Gupta*, 1095 CE.[2]

Bharat Muni, circa 200 BCE, was an artist – an actor, dancer and singer. It is said that he wrote the book *Nātya Śāstra*, which is a comprehensive exposition of dance, drama, music, and the interrelation between the actor, the director, the art and the Ultimate. Another great Kāśmirī philosopher and a *Tāntrik*, a proponent of *Śiva* monism, Abhinava Gupta, wrote a commentary on this book, called *Abhinavabhārati*. This is not surprising because *Śiva* is revered as the greatest dancer, *Natarāja*, in all the cosmos.

He believed that human beings were like actors, expressing a variety of emotions, either to express themselves or to depict the world around them. He expanded the *Rasa* theory in this book. *Rasa* means the essence, the sap, the juice, which arises as a result of interaction between the cognition, experience and related factors, [*vibhāva*, *anubhāva* and *vyabhicāribhāva*]. All this eventually leads to the serenity of mind. Thus, is established an interrelation between metaphysics, semantics, religion, and aesthetics. He suggested that there were eight *Sthayi bhāvas*, permanent moods, eight *Vibhāvas* and eight *Rasas*.

The metaphysical aspects of sound:

Sound has great metaphysical significance in Indian

philosophy. The most well-known sound, the combination of the three letters – A, U and M, making OM – is well-known. The *Māṇḍukya Upaniṣad* is all about this *Aum*; a free translation is as follows.

1. Om is all the past, the present, the future and beyond.
2. Om is *Brahma*. It has four parts:
   i. The first part is waking, the *Vaiśvānara*, who has seven appendages and nineteen facets, and experiences external objects.
   ii. The second part, the *Taijasa*, is the dream state which recognises the internal entities; it also has seven appendages and nineteen facets.
   iii. The third part is the dreamless sleep. This is *Prajńa,* the pure mass of bliss, cognition and enjoyment. This is the beginning and the end of all – the master of all, the internal controller and knower of everything.
   iv. This is *Turia,* the fourth part. This is unique, indescribable, aware of all, and beyond knowledge. It needs to be realised.
3. *Ātmā is Aum – a, u, m.*
4. *A* is the first *Vaiśvanara,* the awake state; the knower of this achieves all his wishes.
5. *U* is *Taijasa,* the second syllable. Its knowers are all knowledgeable of *Brahma.*
6. M is the third syllable; the knower of this knows everything and gets merged with *Brahma.*
7. The fourth part is indescribable – it has no attributes; he who knows this knows *Brahma* and attains his own real self.

However, it has other connotations too. The sound in *Yoga* philosophy is the manifestation of the universal vibration, the *Aum*, which is also known as the cosmic vibration. There are varying pitched sounds heard by an aspirant practising *Yoga* at specific levels of accomplishment. *Veda Vyāsa* symbolically presented the *Yoga* concept of the cosmic vibrations by way of six kinds of sounds which emanate from the Conch shells of the five *Pandavas* and the Lord *Kṛśṇa*. This has been nicely explained by *Swāmi Yogānanda* as follows:

"The conch of Sahadeva, named Manipuśpaka, emanates Aum by a sound like that of a honey-mad bee. This represents the earth. This is related to the awakening of the sacral Mūlādhāra cakra. This is the first level of Yogic Samādhi, known as Sabitarka Sampragñata Samādhi.

The conch of Nakula is known as Sughoṣa; Aum is heard like a pleasant flute and corresponds to Savicāra Sampragñata Samādhi. This represents water and is the awakening of Svādisthāna cakra.

Arjuna's conch Devadutta emanates Aum as a joyous sound and corresponds to the fire element, the lumbar Maṇipura cakra, and Sānanda Sampragñata Samādhi.

Paundra is Bhīma's conch. It means that it disintegrates the various lower states and leads one to Sasmita Sampragñata Samādhi. It emanates a deep, long drawn-out bell like Aum. It represents Prāṇa, the life-breath and the awakening of Anāhata cakra.

Yudhiśṭhira's conch is named Ananta Vijaya, meaning which conquers the infinity, corresponds to Asampragñata Samādhi. This means that the four levels of mind, intelligence, perception and ego have been overcome. This is the awakening of Viśuḍha cakra. The aspirant hears Aum like the thunder or the roar of an ocean.

Kṛiśṇa's conch called Pancajanya, which generates the five elements, corresponds to Savikalpa Samādhi. The aspirant hears the undifferentiated cosmic sound Aum. This is the penultimate achievement of bliss or cosmic consciousness beyond which lies the ultimate state of Nirvikalpa Samādhi, attained by the awakening of Sahaşrāra, the final point in the cerebral cortex. The final act just before beginning the battle in Mahābharata when these conches were sounded as chorus signified the entire cosmos."

"The *Yogi* learns by the meditative activity of *Yoga* to listen to the cosmic sound of *Aum* and expands his consciousness with it into the cosmos."[3]

It is the cosmic vibrations which created the universe. This is affirmed by *Vāgambhriṇī* in the *Ṛg Veda.*[1] Indeed, the Speech or the Word is the source of creation which is neither existent nor non- existent, neither audible nor inaudible, the void which is not a void. As the *Chanda,* it envelops the universe within a protective shield. The *Aṭharva Veda* asserts that the entire universe is a prosody of divine creation. This is confirmed in the *Puruşa Sūkta,* where a number of *Chandas,* or metres, emanate from the *Puruşa.*[4] This is supported by physicists as well, e.g. Penelope Gouk: "the universe is filled with a vibrating ether that also serves as the connection of body and soul"[5] and Isaac Newton: "a medium filling the entire solar system that may also serve to function the actions of a rational will ... cosmic sound".[6]

References:

1. *Ṛg Veda.* 10.125.7.

2. Radhavallabh Tripathi, ed. Bharat Gupta. (2016). *In Bharatmuni in Chanda Sastra: Natya Sastra Revisited* (pp 89–121). New Delhi: BVB.

3. Yogananda, S. (2002). *God Talks with Arjuna. The Bhagavad Gita* (p.118, 119, 717). Kolkata: Yogoda Satsanga Society of India.

4. *Ṛg Veda* 10. 90. 1-16.

5. Gouk, P. Cosmic vibrations. (Sep.2017). Terrain. (p.26-45). www.terrain.org. accessed 15/11/2020.

6. Newton, I. (1704). *Opticks.* Part 4. The Royal Society. London.

The whole history of the world, as at present known, although of a length quite incomprehensible by us, will hereafter be recognised as a mere fragment of time, compared with ages which have elapsed since the first creature, the progenitor of innumerable extinct and living descendants, was created.

Charles Darwin

CHAPTER 8

The Renaissance. 1500 BCE to the Common Era.

This is the period of reawakening of philosophical thinking in India. Three mutually opposing concepts, i.e., the traditional ritualistic *Brāhmanism*, the newer cults and sects pertaining to the Holy Trinity and the mysticism of the *Upaniṣads*, were being rampantly followed. This period probably stretched from the middle of the second millennium BCE to the beginning of the Common Era. The winner in this period of turmoil was probably the cultism of *Śiva* and *Śakti* (*Tantra Śāstra*), which lured people into providing immediate gratification and possession of supernatural powers. This aspect is dealt with separately in the preceding chapter. The two other factors not identified by the earlier historians and philosophers are the influence of the ruling classes and the reformers.

The ruling classes had by then been accepted to be the temporal powers; the *Brāhmins* had established themselves as the religious authority. These two groups supported one another and thrived. As a result, their misdemeanours and crimes began to escalate in society. Many bloody battles and wars were fought purely to satisfy the ego and greed of these two classes. Much suffering ensued. The *Brāhmins* had decreed that the duty of a *Kshetriya* was indeed to wage war on other kings and get into a 'win-win' position which proposed that if one became victorious in battle, one got the riches and additional powers, and if one lost or died, his soul would reach heaven to enjoy the reward.[1] The sedate rules and regulations of the original *Varnāśrama* were being openly misinterpreted and flouted – as a result, society had begun to suffer. The people belonging to the *Śūdra* caste were mercilessly treated in the most inhuman way, which would have made the apartheid system in South Africa or the racial segregation in the USA a very welcome proposition.

There must have been many reformists in those times, but we have no record of them. However, we know of the four philosophers who tried to re-establish the *Vedic Varnadharma* during the beginning of this era. These reformers were *Kṛṣṇa Dwaipāyana, Vālmīki, Śaunaka and Yāska.*

Kriśṇa Dwaipāyana: *circa* 1200 BCE*

Kriśṇa Dwaipāyana was perhaps the greatest sage, scholar, social reformer and teacher ever to have been born in the Indian subcontinent. It is not established whether he lived at Badarinath or Damauli.[2] He noticed the decadence, distrust and destruction of the good utopian era (the *Satya Yuga*) of the *Ṛg Veda* and lamented his own helplessness at first.[3] Hence he decided to do something that would involve all strata of Indian society. First, he collated all the *Vedic* mantras and divided them into four categories, as previously described; hence he was known as *Veda Vyāsa*. This was primarily for the *Brāhmins*. He then produced the epic

---

* According to some scholars, *Vyāsa* is also identified to have some connection with Zaruthrustra, circa 1700–1000 BCE. This is proposed because of linguistic and cultural similarities, including some Hindu gods, found in the Avestan *Gāthās* and the *Ṛg Vedic* gods and Sanskrit. *en.m.wikipedia.org/wiki/Zoroaster*; accessed on 27/12/2020.

Mahābhārata to make people realise that society at that time had become full of violence, greed, ignorance, lust, and anti-*Vedic* practices. This story is well known and has many versions in many Indian languages. He projected himself as the lowest of the low by birth who had become the most revered sage of that time and created an incarnation of *Viśnu* as his own alter ego, the war- neutral charioteer *Kṛṣṇa*.[3] This epic was probably produced circa 1200 BCE, although some of the incidents described in the book reflect the much earlier history of the north-western region of India. The two sets of cousins who fought a bloody war of unimaginable carnage and destruction were made to be his own illegitimate grandchildren. This was all fiction, of course, since he was a very chaste and righteous human; it would be unthinkable that he would have stooped so low as to have sexual intercourse with the chaste widows of his own half-brothers and fathered their sons. This was perhaps to demonstrate that the wrong done by the earlier generation inevitably manifests with horrible consequences in due course. *Mahābhārata* has been presented as an eyewitness account by two partridges who had been covered and protected by the helmet of a fallen soldier in the Great War. Perhaps this was to mock the ritualistic *Brāhmin* priests who quote *Taittarīya Brāhmaṇa* to justify their practice;[4] all the knowledge of the *Kṛśṇa Yajurveda Samhitā* had been obtained from the partridges who had eaten a vomitus! The story of *Mahābhārata* was retold by *Ugraśravā* to *Saunaka* at the *Naimiṣa* forest.

One can get many good ideas from the book, viz:

- No war was a righteous war and contrary to their expectations, the victors had to go to hell instead.

This was to nullify the spurious teaching of the *Brāhmins* that the duty of a *Kśhetriya* was to wage righteous war and achieve *Mokśhya*.[5]

- Conflicts occur when duty is not observed. These lead to war. *'Dharmo rakshati rakshtah, nānṛtam* [duty protects them who protect duty] was his oft-quoted exclamation.[6] He portrayed the legendary Prince *Bhīṣma*, who in the mistaken belief of being devoted to his lecherous father, had chosen to break his vows of serving as a crown prince, and violated the code of conduct of *Varnāṣrama* – he was not a *Sanyāsī*, neither a householder nor an *Ācārya*.
- There were four ways to feel happy and be blessed, e.g., by doing the prescribed duty, having faith in the Supreme, gaining true knowledge and by controlling one's mind and body.[5]
- Man is a sub-microscopic miniature of the whole universe– this becomes apparent if one magnifies the body millions of times.[7]
- One cannot do a wrong action and hope for the right – i.e., the desirable – result. One must suffer from wrongdoings, even at the death bed. [*Bhīsma* suffered for six months, pierced on a bed of arrows, before he died].

The *Bhagavad Gita* is the best-known part of this great epic. He created a most dramatic episode by making the main Commander-In-Chief, Prince Arjuna, refuse to fight the war when the armies on both sides were ready to begin. The Lord *Kṛṣṇa*, the neutral charioteer of Arjuna, then encouraged him to fight. This book is discussed in a separate chapter.

CV Vaidya has summarised the main philosophy depicted

in *Mahābhārata* as follows:

"Give up not righteousness for greed or fear,

Or for desire or even life's dear sake.'

Eternal is virtue, pain and pleasure fleeting,

Fleeting is life, but not the soul divine."[8]

***Vālmīki:* circa 1100 BCE.**

Another great social reformer was *Vālmiki*, who wrote the *Rāmāyaṇa*. The *Puřanas* describe a *Ṛşi Paraşurama* who had gone on killing the Kshetriya Kings sixteen times round the earth because they had become wicked and immoral. He would have been like a modern self -styled vigilante. Society at that time had greatly deteriorated in its values, ideals, and function. Hence *Valmiki* proposed a practical philosophy, by describing the ideal qualities essential for each person. If individuals behaved ideally, the whole of society would flourish. This should begin with the king. This he called *Rāma Rājya*, meaning 'the ideal state'. He illustrated how an unkind act done even in jest by a prince can have devastating consequences. Like *Vyāsa*, he too had to create a reincarnation of *Viśṇu* as *Rāma*. Like the *Mahābhārata*, this also has anecdotes with historical reference to the central eastern Gangetic and southern regions of India.[9]

He wrote the *Rāmāyaṇa* to painstakingly illustrate the qualities of an ideal king, a son, a brother, a friend, a husband, and a good human being. He also demonstrated the need for personal sacrifice for the greater good of society. *Rama* was the eldest of the four sons of the king *Dasaratha* of Ayodhya. The second queen wished her son *Bharata* to inherit the throne, although *Rama* should have been the heir.

Hence *Rāma* was banished to a forest for fourteen years. His half-brother *Laxmaṇa* and wife *Sitā* accompanied him. They were living incognito as hermits in a small hut. One day, a demon Princess *Sūrpaṇakhā* innocently lusted after the princes. *Rāma* managed to extricate himself but sent her to *Laxmaṇa,* who was not amused, even though she was beautiful. He cut off her nose and ears in jest. The injured princess rushed to her brother *Rāvaṇa,* the great king of the demons (*the Rakshasas*) who ruled from Sri Lanka. *Rāvaṇa* exacted revenge by abducting *Sita*. *Rāma* then gathered an army of monkeys and bears and attacked Rāvaṇa. A horrible war ensued. *Rāma* became victorious in the end although *Laxmaṇa* would have died in the battle if it were not for the assistance of the servant *Hunumāna* and a physician. Millions of innocent monkeys and bears also died. The demons, too, were annihilated. *Rama* returned to Ayodhya after fourteen years and was crowned king. But he had to put his own wife *Sita* through a 'fire test' (*agni-parikchya*) first to demonstrate her chastity. He ruled well and ideally but had to deal with unhealthy rumours and emerging disorders in his kingdom. Eventually *Rāma* had to abandon *Sitā* for life despite her being pregnant with twins. He had to do these distressing acts of great personal sacrifice. He lived bereft of his family life until the end. His spiritual *guru* and the royal Priest *Ṛṣi Vaśistha* gave many philosophical sermons to *Rāma* which are compiled as *Yoga Vāsistha. (YV)*

Yoga Vāsistha has not received much accolade from Indian and western philosophers. This should not overlook the fact that this is a compilation of profound wisdom and subtle philosophical concepts which have been also illustrated by parables and legends. Often called the Science of Self Realisation, this makes remarkably interesting reading.

There is also some possibility that modern publications have been corrupted by additions of several slokas from *Patanjali Yoga Sutra* and *Gita*.

This is an elaborate work, written in 32,000 verses in 64,000 lines. This has six major sections:

1. Dispassion
2. Longing for freedom
3. Origin
4. Preservation
5. Quietitude of mind
6. Liberation.

Some examples are given below.

> YV 3.84. Serenity alone exists and all descriptions cease when the truth is realised.

> YV 3.111. Liberation is to be free from ideas and thoughts which are the bondage.

> YV 4.35. Bondage is the lust for pleasure, its cessation is liberation.

> YV 5.50. Consciousness is devoid of limitations or intelligence. It is that state which is the Reality, the omnisciensce.

Some scholars have tried to present the essence of this treatise as the doctrine of "*dristishristi- vada*" which asserts that the world exists only so long as it is possible to perceive it.

Vālmiki was probably born soon after *Vyāsa*. There are at least twenty-one different recensions of *Rāmāyana* in many Indian languages. These two epics are read, enacted, quoted, sung and debated until this day. Like *Mahābhārata*, this epic too has become a sacred scripture.

***Śaunaka*: circa 1000 BCE.**

There are several legends about this philosopher. He is variously known as a teacher of the *Vedic* rituals, a reincarnation of *Indra*, a *guru* of *Aśvalāyana* and the priest who officiated the great ritual of King Janmejaya at which the story of the *Mahābhārata* was told. Some believe that he was *Ṛṣi Gṛtsamāda* who has given most of the Mantras in the second Mandala of the *Ṛg Veda* and was adopted by *Ṛṣi Śunak*, hence called *Śaunaka. Śaunaka* was probably a title, like the *Vyasa*, signifying a teacher of the *Vedas*, rather than the *Ṛṣi* who gave the mantras. However, it is safe to believe that he was very particular about the truth and correctness in every aspect of life.

He must have noted their misinterpretations of the *Vedic* mantras. This was obviously causing conflicts and confusion among the people, pupils and the patrons. He must have felt that it was essential to have uniformity in the interpretation of the *Vedic* mantras to maintain society as envisaged in the *Vedas*. He produced the *Ṛg Veda Prātisākhya*, the *Ṛg Veda* being the oldest and most important of all the *Vedas*. He also composed *Brihaddevata*, the *Carana-Vyūha* and six *Anukramaṇīs* of the *Ṛg Veda*.

***Yāska*: circa 700 BCE[10].**

He was a grammarian who believed that the knowledge of the formation of a word in Sanskrit was essential to comprehend the knowledge in the *Vedas*. He produced the first ever treatise on etymology and semantics in Sanskrit, which is known as the *Nirukta*. This is probably the oldest lexicon ever produced. This explains nearly 400 words in Sanskrit which were being misinterpreted, and several non-

Vedic practices were being performed accordingly. The orthodox *Brahminism* did not reform their practices according to this treatise, although it was considered a *Vedānga.* The importance of specificity of the words in the growth of Indian philosophy is different in each of the different systems, as will be seen in subsequent chapters.

These philosophers were the foremost social reformers of those times. They had tried to demonstrate the non-*Vedic* activities of the *Brāhmin* priests and the ruling classes of the *Kshetriyas.* It is very unfortunate that their stories within the epics began to be interpreted instead as religious edicts; they are continuing to be believed as such by most Hindus. This is encouraged by the *Brāhmin* priests, for obvious reasons. This misrepresentation has been given credibility by Indologists from 1600–1800 CE as being religious documents of scriptural status. Indeed, they have called this era of renaissance the 'epic period'. This kind of endorsement by Western scholars has not helped to promote the social norms and the philosophical concepts.

It was during this period that several philosophical concepts were crystallised. The other great thinkers of those times, viz. *Maheśwara, Jaimini* and *Vardhamāna Mahāveera, Siddhārtha Gautama, Bārhaspatya Lokāyata, Kaṇada, Kapila, Gotama, Patanjali,* were well known before the advent of the Common Era. These great minds have given structured thoughts which have been subsequently grouped as the Indian philosophy. These are considered separately in subsequent chapters.

It is this era of renaissance which liberated 'Indian philosophy' from being a traditional theosophical potpourri of occultism, faith, superstition and haphazard debates. Although *Pūrva mimāmsā* had sowed the seeds of modern philosophical thinking, and the *Upanișadists* debated at length about *Vidyā* and *Avidyā* and began to question many of the prevalent theories, it took six great philosophers, as mentioned above, to produce systematic ways of conducting philosophical deliberations. This era continued until the colonisation of India by the British, which began in 1607 CE. The *Dwaper Yuga* is said to have followed by the Puranic *Kali Yuga.* Perhaps this began at the beginning of the first millennium BCE and could be called *the Era of Remodelling and Regeneration.*

References:

1. *Gītā*, 2.37.
2. http://vedicheritage.gov.in/samhita; accessed on 27/01/2021
3. *Srimadbhāgavata Mahāpurāṇa; 1.4.15-20.*
4. Gautam, P. C. (2018). *Reflections on contemporary values, beliefs and behaviours* (pp. 152–3). Newcastle Upon Tyne, UK: Cambridge Scholars Publishing.
5. Kashyap RL. (2005). *Krișṇa Yajurveda TaittiriyaSamhita*, Vol 1. (p.17) Sri Aurobindo Kapali Sastry Institute of *Vedic* Culture, Bangalore.
6. *Mahābhārata,* 18.15-40.
7. *Srimadbhāgavat.* 1.4.15-20.
8. Vaidya, C. V. (1907). *Epic India* (p. 413). Bombay: Asian Educational Services.
9. Avari B. India: The Ancient Past. (p117-18). Routledge. London.
10. https://www.britannica.com>Yaska accessed 21/01/21.

❖

CHAPTER 9

Jaimini

Brahminism had postulated that the conduct of religious ceremonies were one's *Dharma*, or duty, which led one to salvation. One needs to read the ancient literature in Sanskrit to understand the Indian philosophy. The nearest equivalent word for philosophy in Sanskrit is *Mimāmsā* (analysis and examination of a concept, a word, a content of a statement or a process or activity), although *Darśana* has been widely accepted in modern literature. *Darśana* denotes observation, appreciation, experience or cognition. These activities, known as religious ceremonies (*Yagňas*), were claimed to have been designed to reveal the philosophical concepts inherent in them.

It was *Ṛṣi Jaimini*, who began the process of systematically examining a concept and its associated effects or activities. He called this process *Mimāmsā*. It was a bold attempt to analyse these practices in a systematic manner and give opinions on them. He was a revered teacher and was successful in his efforts. His treatise known as *Pūrva Mimāmsā*, or *Jaimini Sūtra*, is well accepted as the final arbiter of the practice and philosophy of the *Brāhmins*. He was a pupil of *Kṛiśṇa Dwaipāyana*, the compiler and the classifier of the *Vedic* mantras in four major *Samhitās*, known as the *Ṛg*, *Yajur*, *Sāma* and *Atharva Vedas*. Like his guru, *Jaimini* systematised the prevalent *Yagńas*.

Pūrva Mimāmsā of *Jaimini*: *collated 500–400 BCE*

This is in twelve chapters. Its philosophy is the belief that the only way of eventual liberation is by doing one's *karma* – the religious rituals (*the Yagńas*) faithfully by adhering to the correct system and methodology. This is the meaning of *Dharma*, which is the only means of salvation.

A major part of this *Sūtra* is known as *karma mimāmsā.* It contains the exposition of the religious rituals by means of establishing the following four systems:

i. *Utpatti Vidhi* – the system of origin.
ii. *Biniyoga Vidhi* – the analytical methods.
iii. *Pryoga Vidhi* – the system of application; and
iv. *Adhikāra Vidhi* – the system of authority or entitlement.

This also helped to remove the doubts on interpretation of much related ancient literature. The last two chapters also cover *Tantra.*

This *Sūtra* was subsequently explained in a detailed commentary by *Śāwara Swāmi* in 600 CE, which led his pupil, another philosopher, *Kumārila Bhatta,* to propound the philosophy of existence. This has deliberation on true knowledge: *Vidyā* vs nescience, *Avidyā.* The theory of existence (*Bāhyarthavāda)* asserts that no knowledge is false knowledge or nescience. It exists but its interpretation is dependent upon the intellect. For example, a coiled rope may not be a snake, but it is a rope whose existence cannot be denied. This tradition of re-examining and redefining earlier concepts and aphorisms appears to have continued, as seen by the establishment of another school of *Pūrva Mimāmsā* by his pupil, *Prabhākara.*

Soteriology: The ultimate salvation is assured by the faithful adherence to duty which is to conduct *Yagńa.*

Epistemology: The only *pramāṇa or* proof that was quoted

by *Jaimini* was *Śabda,* the Word; these were the *Vedas* and the scriptural texts like the *Brāhmaṇas, Āranyakas* and *Upaniṣads,* as well as the *Kalpa Sūtras.* However, following *Śāwara Swāmi's* commentary, the *Śabda* was put into two categories, i.e. self-evident (*Swatah prāmāṇya),* and *Āptavacana* - given by the learned teachers. The former being, *Apauruṣeya (*not uttered by human), needed no proof, unlike the latter, which depended upon human cognition requiring a proof of authenticity. This was elaborated by *Kumārila* in the 700s CE. He and his disciple also added all the other *pramanas* as valid.

He reasserted that the universe was real and was made up of eight entities, namely matter *(dravya),* characteristics *(guṇa),* activities *(karma),* commonalities *(sāmānya),* order or mechanism *(paratantra),* energy or power *(śakti),* similarity *(sādriṣya)* and quantity *(sankhyā).* To these proofs, absence or non-availability (*abhāva*) was added later. This philosophy asserts that 'matter' has nine constituents, i.e., earth, water, air, fire, the Space, self, mind, time and quarters. To these, sound (*dhwani*) and darkness (*tamas*) were added later. [Matter here signifies a complex entity rather than a physical form].

Subsequently, *Uttar Mimāmsā* was produced to provide support for this treatise and also *Brāhminism,* from those *Upaniṣads* which mostly supported the *Brāhmaṇas.* It was then called the *Vedānta* [*ved,* Veda; *anta,* the end, i.e., the essence], as this would imply total vilification by the original *Vedas.* It is exceedingly difficult to comprehend. Most people understood this treatise by studying its commentary written by *Śankarācārya.* This is discussed in a later chapter.

❖

"If you cry because the sun has gone out of your life, your tears will prevent you from seeing the stars".

Rabindranath Tagore

CHAPTER 10

Vaiśeşika

Generally accepted as an elder sister to *Nyāya* philosophy, *Vaiśeşika* has its own special features. Some Indian scholars regard the concepts in *Vaiśeşika* as being earlier than those of *Nyāya. Kaṇāda,* circa first century CE, produced the treatise known as *Vaiśeşika Sutra*, which elaborates this philosophy. Since words like *Aṇu, Paramāṇu* and *Dravya* have been mentioned both in the *Atharva Veda* and in the *Upanişads*, it is quite possible that he was more of a compiler of the existing aphorisms than their original author.

There is a legend which suggests that the philosopher was poor and used to survive on thrown grains of rice, thus receiving the name *Kaṇāda,* although his own name was *Ulūka Kāśyapa*. It is more likely that he was gathering even the tiniest fragments of the aphorisms pertaining to this doctrine, rather than the discarded grains of rice. The word *Kaṇa* means a grain, *Kaṇāda* means an eater of grain [*Aṇu* and *Paramāṇu* mean a molecule or atom respectively]. This view may be supported by the fact some of the *Sūtras* are in brief, ambiguous phrases which are extremely difficult to comprehend. This does not specifically mention God but indicates some entity which he calls '*tat*', or 'That'. This prompts one toward guesswork, imagination, and fantasy, as seen in some interpretations.

This school proposes that the true knowledge of matter, its property and motion, leads one to the state of enlightenment where nothing else remains. This is called *niśreyaşa*, or the ultimate bliss. This school of philosophy has attempted to elucidate this concept by applying principles of physics as well as metaphysics, some of which are as follows:

a. Matter, property of matter and action exist together.

b. The matter in its minutest form is special and differs from other matter.

c. Action is dependent upon motion, and upon gravity in its absence.

d. Motion is impossible without cause.

e. Motion cannot generate motion.

f. Action is opposed by its effect.

g. Certain matters are eternal, and others are not.

h. Matters have similarity as a group but differ in their individuality.

i. Properties of matter are not eternal.

Subsequent commentators have elaborated the individuality or special characteristic of an atom and put forward the theory of the combination of two atoms making a dyad, three atoms, a triad and molecules with six sides which can exist independently.

Vaiśeşika Sūtra has 373 verses which are presented in ten books. The first two *Sūtras* assert that the *Dharma* (the natural law) needs to be fully explained because this knowledge produces enlightenment which leads to real happiness. Simply stated, this is a law of relationship between an object, its character, action, and effect. *Kaṇāda* sets about explaining this *dharma* or the law of the universe in his treatise, which remained unexplained until 400 CE, when *Praśastapāda* wrote a commentary in *Padārtha-*

dharma-samgraha. Many believe that he has deviated from the original texts, which is not surprising, as explained. Subsequently, *Jayanārāyana, Candrakānta* and *Śankara Mişra* have also produced differing points of view. Subāsh Kak[1] has tried to explain these *Sūtras* in terms of pure physics and quantum theory, making a comparison between *Kaṇāda* and Newton.

Kaṇāda postulates that this universe is composed of entities, *padārtha,* which is explained by Radhakrishnan as objects of experience,[2] which are in six categories, namely:

i. *Dravya* –matter, including the entities which exist physically as substance (corporeal) and in perception (non-corporeal).

ii. *Guṇa* - characteristic or quality.

iii. *Karma* - activity, action.

iv. *Sāmāny* - commonality or universality.

v. *Viśeşa* - the special entity that determines a *dravya.*

vi. *Samavāya* - inseparability.

1. The *dravya* are nine in number. These are earth, air, light, water, Space (ether), time, area or space, self or soul and mind.

2. *Guṇa*: There are seventeen characteristics. These are: colour, taste, smell, touch, number, quantity, individuality, integration, separation, proximity, distance, intelligence, pleasure, pain, desire, detestation, and action.

3. *Karma*: the principal activities which affect *drabya* are throwing upwards and downwards, shrinking, and stretching, and general movement.

4. *Sāmānya:* This refers to a class or species without a specific identity, e.g., utensil, book, weapon, etc.

5. *Viśeṣa:* Individuality, i.e., a special attribute which distinguishes it from everything else in the class. This has been interpreted by some scholars to mean the unique characteristic of an individual atom which cannot be divided further.

6. *Samavāya*: Existing in an object permanently as its characteristic, e.g., a pink rose. The pink colour here is a permanent and inseparable entity in that rose.

In addition to the above, some scholars have added *abhāva, i.e.,* absence or non-existence, as the seventh category of existence. This is a logical possibility. Example: 'David's pen is there'. This also signifies 'David is not there'. Thus, the statement cognises two realities; one, the pen is there and two, David, although not visible at this moment of observation, must be somewhere.

Similarly, *Prasastapāda* has also added the following:

Samskāra: inborn tendency; *Dravatwa:* liquidity; *Sneha:* adhesiveness, viscosity; *Gurutwa:* weight, gravity; *Dharma; Adharma; Śabda:* word, sound.

Conclusion:

The *Vaiśeṣika* school recognises four kinds of atoms: earth, air, water, and light. The rest of the objects, *Padārthas,* are a matter of perception. The existence of the Soul can only be inferred. Its activity, i.e., perception, can be recognised only in a body. Hence there must be many souls. Each soul therefore must have its own special individuality. Therefore, the body, with its myriad attributes, must understand the law of the universe to reach a state of enlightenment, which is the final state where nothing else remains - the *niśreyaśa or Kaivalya,* only The One. *Nyāya* and *Vaiśeşika* are similar in many respects.

References:

1. Kak, S. (2016). *Matter and Mind: The Vaiśeşika Sūtra of Kaṇāda (p.24,25).* Ontario, Canada: Mount Meru Publishing.

2. Radhakrishnan, S; Moore. (1973). *A Source Book on Indian Philosophy* (p. 386). New Jersey: Princeton University Press.

❖

No one created the universe, and no one directs our fate. This leads me to a profound realisation: there is probably no heaven and afterlife either. I think belief in afterlife is just wishful thinking. There is no reliable evidence for it, and it flies in the face of everything we know in science. I think that when we die, we return to dust. But there is a sense in which we live on, in our influence, and in our genes that we pass on to our children. We have this one life to appreciate the grand design of the universe, and for that I am extremely grateful.

Stephen Hawking

CHAPTER 11

Nyāya

Nyāya is ordinarily translated to mean 'a just or a right decision'. In its real sense, it denotes the method of demonstrating the correct knowledge, i.e., the science of reasoning and proof.

Gotama Akşapāda is regarded as the founder of this philosophy, although it is highly likely that he too was the compiler of the ancient *Sūtras* which had been in existence long before his time, circa 300 BCE. *Nyāya* is essentially a system of ascertaining the reality of any statement, idea, or object with the aim of reaching the most blissful state. This system of philosophy has been in practice since the early *Brāhmaṇa* period, as evidenced by its mention in *Pūrva Mimāmsā* and *Āpastamba Dharma Sūtra*.[1,3] This is also mentioned in *Mahābhārata Śantiparva*, where *Muni Nārada* is credited with being the most proficient in this system. This has a strong similarity with another school of philosophy, *Vaiśeşika.* Many scholars tend to regard them as complementary to one another. This is indeed a brilliant example of the great philosophical concepts of ancient times. This is as modern and contemporary thinking as anything a present-day philosopher or a quantum physicist may postulate.*

---

* School of *Nyaya* philosophy became substantially modified by the great Scholar *Gangeś* (circa 1289 CE) and his son *Vardhamān Upādhyāya*. It received a further boost from another great logician, *Raghunath Shiromani* (1475 CE). This modified and modernised doctrine is known as *Nabya-Nyāya*.

The epistemology accepts the following:

i. Direct perception – *pratyakśa;* the visible, the obvious or personally experienced.

ii. Inference - *anumāna;* e.g. only the stars are seen, so it must be night-time.

iii. The word – *Śabda*; the mantras of the *Vedas* (latterly, of the *Brāhmaṇas, Āraṇyakas, Upaniṣads,* the testimony of the scriptures and the two epics).

iv. Similarity – *Upamāna;* e.g. it could be a snake because it looks like a snake.

v. Absence or non-availability – *Anupalabdhi* or *abhāva;* e.g. there is no precedence because this is the first time; 'this is Hari's pen', implying that Hari may not be there but must be present somewhere.

vi. Opinion or belief – *arthapatti; e.g.* one can have a valid opinion that the food in the oven must be burning if one smells burning from the stove.

Nyāya proposes that supreme bliss can be achieved only by true knowledge of all subjective and objective entities, such as emotions, doubts, conflicts, matter, structures or forms, energy, etc. In other words, if one knows the reality of everything, that knowledge itself becomes the ultimate happiness or bliss. It does not propose any god or supernatural power. This is the purest form of logic as a tool for our understanding of everything. It is accepted that *Nyāya* identifies all the subjective and objective entities as *Padārtha,* which has been translated as 'matter'. This has caused confusion, since this word includes both matter and non-matter, as mentioned above. This *padārtha* is traditionally enumerated as follows:

1. Proof, validity: *Pramāṇa*.

2. Object, thing: *Prameya.*
3. Question, doubt: *Samşaya.*
4. The aim, purpose: *Prayojana.*
5. Example, instance: *Drişţānta.*
6. Principles, dogma: *Siddhānta.*
7. Components, premises, syllogism: *Avayava.*
8. Logic, reasoning: *Tarka.*
9. Conclusion, ascertainment: *Nirṇaya.*
10. Debate, reasoning: *Vāda.*
11. Deceitful, sophistry: *Galpa.*
12. Wrangling, hostility: *Vitanḍa.*
13. Fallacious, erratic: *Hetvābhāsa.*
14. Quibbles, dissent: *Khala.*
15. False analogy, disingenuous: *Gāti.*
16. Faulty syllogism, unfitness for argument: *Nighrasthāna.*

Gotama's Nyāya Sūtra is in five books. The first book provides the main principles of the *Nyāya* School. The second deals with the *Pramāna* in detail. The third and the fourth books deal with *Prameya* at length. The fifth deals with paralogism. Rādhākŗşṇan has eloquently explained this treatise based upon the works of SC Vidyābhuşaṇa and Gangānātha Jhā, which cannot be improved upon.[2] The following headings from the first chapter of Book One indicate the extensive scope of this philosophy:

A. *Statement of subject matter, purpose, and relation of the treatise.*

B. *Definition of the instruments of right cognition.*

C. *Definition of the prerequisites of a process of ratiocination or reasoning (Nyāya).*

D. *Definition of the tenet which is the basis of*

reasoning (Nyāya).

E. *Definition of reasoning (Nyāya).*

A short summary of *Gotama's Nyāya Sūtra* is given below.

Book 1, Chapter 1.

This deliberates on the scope of nine of the sixteen *Padārthas.* Each topic is considered in detail. He begins with a consideration of the proof of validity, i.e. the means of true knowledge which is essential for real identification of any entity. Then he goes on to identify and elaborate the essential objects of knowledge. The *Sūtras* also dissect and demonstrate the associated influence of the existing dogmas, doubts, examples, precedents and antecedents, as well as the hostility and resistance encountered in the path of enquiry.

1. *Pramāṇa:* proofs are of four kinds:

   a. *Pratyakśha,* Perception or experience, which is the acceptance of the reality as perceived by sense organs. This may be direct or a feeling, i.e., indirect.

   b. *Anumāna,* Inference. He postulates that there are three kinds of inference, i.e. as before (*pūrvavat);* following from what was before *(śeṣavat);* and commonly or constantly seen (*samānyatodriṣta*). In other words, inference is based upon the object, its character and association – the cause, its effect and corollary.

   c. *Upamāna,* Similarity. If an unknown object looks like a known object, it is likely to be of the same kind.

   d. *Śabda,* Word or testimony. This is the *Āptavacana* or the testimony of someone who is trusted. This may be the *Vedic* mantras or aphorism believed to have been given by any trusted person.

2. *Prameya:* objects or things. *Gotama* identifies the following to be the objects of right knowledge:

i. Soul: Desire, hatred, wish, pain, pleasure, and intelligence are the marks of soul (Self).

ii. Body: This is the centre of action, of the senses and their functions.

iii. Senses (organs of senses): Nose, smell; eyes, sight; skin, touch; ear, hearing; and tongue, taste.

iv. Objects of sense: The elements which produce the senses are earth, water, light, air and space.

v. Intellect: This is either *anubhava,* experience, or *smaraṇa,* memory.

vi. Mind *(manas):* This is the gatekeeper of intelligence. It only allows one Knowledge within the Self at any one time. It is infinitely small - an *Anu*, the atom.

vii. Activity: This is the collective operation of voice, mind, and body.

viii. Fault: These cause activity. These are attraction, rejection, and ignorance.

ix. Rebirth (transmigration) *Pretyabhāva*: Cycles of separation and integration of body and soul.

x. Result: The fruit of activity or fault which causes pleasure or pain or both.

xi. Pain: Everything is intermingled with pain. Nothing exists separate from pain.

xii. Release: This is the liberation from pain.

3. *Samsaya:* (Doubt). This is questioning the judgement upon an object. Five kinds of doubts are postulated:

a. Recognition of common properties.

b. Recognition of properties which are uncommon.

c. Conflicting testimony.

d. Irregularity of perception.

e. Non-perception.

4. *Prayojana:* Aim or purpose. This is the motive for any action or achievement.

5. *Driṣṭānta:* Example. This is what produces identical opinion between a philosopher and a common man.

6. *Siddhānta:* Principle, dogma. This is based upon the authority of an established source, a school or hypothesis.

7. *Avayava:* (Components, syllogism, premise). The components of syllogism are the following:

i. *Proposition*

ii. *Reason*

iii. *Example*

iv. *Application*

v. *Conclusion*

8. *Tarka:* Logic, reasoning. This is either refutation or reasoning from the appropriateness of the case.

9. *Nirṇaya:* Conclusion, ascertainment. This is the final judgement or declaration after full consideration of all the relevant sides.

Book 1. Chapter 2.

The remaining seven topics, 10–16, are considered in

detail in this chapter. The areas covered are the correct ways of reasoning, identifying false logic and hostility, dealing with dissent and inappropriate behaviour or situations. These are shown to be the path of enquiry to seek true knowledge. The ancient philosopher of the *Nyāya* School was known as an *Anwekshiki,* the enquirer.

10. *Vāda:* Discussion. The proponent and opponent both care for the truth but present opposing reasons and debate the issue according to established norms in order to reach a common understanding or conclusion.

11. *Galpa*: Deceitful, sophistry. This is a purposeful attempt at deception or fraud to attack an established concept or principle.

12. *Vitanḍa:* Wrangling, hostility. This is a hostile attempt at resisting and denying the proposition without making any effort to establish another opinion.

13. *Hetvābhāsa*: Fallacious, erratic. This is the proposition of erratic logic which superficially may appear sound but is wrong and deceitful. This is also known as sophistry. This leads to more than one conclusion which cannot be correct. Max Muller subdivides this topic into *savhyabichāra* - arguments that prove too much; *viruddh* - that prove the reverse; *prakaraṇasama* - equally applicable to both sides; *and kālātīta* - mistimed.

14. *Khala:* Quibbles, dissent. This is deliberate use of words in the wrong sense, i.e. fraudulent usage of words.

15. *Gāti*: Futility or going either way. Objection

based on inappropriate similarity or dissimilarity.

16. *Nighrasthāna:* Faulty syllogism, unfitness for proper debate. Rendering oneself liable for rebuke when one deliberately misunderstands or does not understand but continues to argue.

The second book deals with the *Pramāṇa* in detail. It differs a little from *Pūrva Mimāmsā* in accepting the word, *Śabda,* in its traditional sense as the *Vedic* mantra by discussing the association of a word with sound. He questions the other *Pramāṇa,* namely *Arthapatti, Sambhava* and *Abhāva.* The third and the fourth books deal with *Prameya* at length. He goes on to prove that both the senses from the sense organs and *Śaṛra,* the body, are different from Ā*tmā,* the soul. He has dealt with *Smriti,* memory in great detail. The fifth deals with paralogism or distorted logic. Covering aspects of knowledge, *Pramāna* and the scope, often explained as the five-membered form of exposition, he aims to avoid paralogism and arrive at the correct conclusion. These five members are: statement, reason, example, application and ascertainment.

In summary, *Nyāya* posits that wrong knowledge or nescience is the awareness that the soul is identified with the body, mind, and intellect. This awareness culminates in the cycle of *samsāra.* The means of liberation or ultimate bliss is to separate the soul successively from the body, the intellect, and the mind by ascertaining the reality of these things. This leads the soul, *Ātmā,* to the 'awareness-neutral' state known as *Apavarga,* similar to *Nişreyas – i.e.,* 'no remainder' of the *Vaiśeşika* School.

References:

1. Radhakrishnan, S; Moore. (1973). *A Source Book on Indian Philosophy* (p. 386). New Jersey: Princeton University Press.

2. Ibid, p. 356

3. Buhler. *Sacred Book of the East: Āpastamba Dharma Sūtra* 11.4-8.13.

❖

You can never step into the same river twice.

Heraclitus 500 BC

You cannot step in the same river even once.

Cratylus 400 BC

CHAPTER 12

Sāmkhya

The legend says that an incredibly sad person once approached the sage *Kapila* and asked him three questions: "What is most important? What is the truth? What do I have to do to save myself?" The sage answered that "the most important is *'Puruṣa'*. The universe evolves only when it encounters *Prakriti*. This is the Truth. It is this knowledge which discerns the difference between *Prakriti* and *Puruṣa* that is your saviour". The knowledge of this difference was called *'Pra-śakhyāna'*, from which *'Sāmkhya'* was coined. *Ṛṣi Kapila* elaborated this evolutionary doctrine in *Sāmkhya Pravacana Sūtra,* containing twenty-five aphorisms. Because of this number, some believe this to be called a *Sāmkhya* – a numerical.

This is a revolutionary philosophy propounded by the sage *Kapila,* although it is impossible to ascertain that he was indeed the original thinker of this doctrine. This was during the rampant orthodoxy of the *Brāhminism, Tāntrism, Śaivism* and *Vaiśṇavism* cults, when everything was considered to be thc divine will of one or the other god. However, one can find indirect reference to this doctrine in some of the *Upaniṣads* too. Many believe that *Buddha* had received this knowledge, along with that of *Yoga,* prior to formulating his own doctrine, which shows some similarity. It was *Iśwarkṛśṇa,* circa 400–300 BCE, who provided an explanation of this doctrine in *Sānkhya Kārikā.* It is said that *Ṛṣi Kapila* had taught this philosophy to his pupil *Asuri,* who in turn taught *Pancasikha,* and the latter modified and expanded it. Max

Muller thought that it had 6000 slokas.[1] This is mentioned in sloka seventy of *Iśwarakṛśṇa's Sāmkhya Kārika.* This treatise has now been universally accepted as the authentic commentary of *Sāmkhya* philosophy.

This philosophy states that man suffers from physical, mental and spiritual affectations. This realisation is due to the 'intelligence' which is inherent in living beings. The feelings of pleasure and pain are the interpretation of this intelligence. This concept does not attribute these states to any divine will.

These twenty-five principles are:

1. *Puruṣa.*
2. *Prakriti,* the unmanifest or inactive *(avyakta).*
3. *Mahat-tattva,* the great element – i.e., intelligence.
4. *Ahankāra,* the ego.
5. *Pancha Tanmātrā,* the five continuous particles or primal elements, i.e. word, *śabda;* touch, *sparśa;* form, *rupa*; juice, *rasa* and smell, *gandha.*
6. *Indriyas,* the ten organs of perception:

i. *Buddhi-indriya*: The five organs of sensation: *şrotra,* ear; *twachā,* skin; *rasa,* tongue; *ghrāna,* nose; and *kakşhu,* eye.

ii. *Karmeyindriya:* The five organs of function: *vāc,* of speech; *paṇi,* to grasp; *pāda, to* walk; *payu,* of excretion; and *upastha,* procreation.

7. *Panca mahābhūta:* The five gross elements: *ākāśa* (the Space*); vāyu,* air; *jala, water; priţhvi,* earth; *tejas, fire.*
8. *Mānas,* mind.

Puruşa:

This is from the *Puruşa Sūkta* of the Ṛg *Veda.*[2] This is also equated with *brahma* of the *Upaniśads.* This is also defined as the 'super consciousness' by the quantum physicists[3] and in *Śvetaśvatara Upaniśad.*[4] The logic is: if this by itself is all that is consciousness, then there is nothing remaining to be conscious of; in other words, the source of light itself is the light and hence it does not need any other light for illumination.

Prakriti:

The commonly used equivalent word in English, nature, does not explain *Prakriti* in this context. *Prakriti* is not what we normally mean as 'nature'; it is the cause of nature. This *Prakriti* denotes the *Mūla Prakriti* made of three constituent characteristics: *(guṇa*) which are *Satya guṇa* (the real), *Rajoguṇa* (the shiny and visible) and *Tamoguṇa* (the invisible and in darkness*)*. These three *Guṇa*s remain in equilibrium and dormant until evolution begins.

Mahat tattwa:

The great entity is also known as *buddhi*, the intelligent principle. This is the first to emanate from *Prakriti*. This *buddhi* is called the great entity because it is this which wishes to evolve into matter - both living and non-living. It is this which perceives pain, pleasure, suffering or happiness. But people think erroneously that these are felt by the living beings due to the *Puruṣa* within it. *Puruṣa* is inactive and does not feel anything. Because pain and pleasure do not exist singly, one needs to dissociate from both. This action leads to *Kaivalya*, i.e., the state of the supreme bliss, the *Puruṣa.* This is the ultimate liberation from all kinds of experience.

The process of formation, i.e., the evolution:

The universe is formed when *Puruṣa* encounters the

unmanifested *Prakriti*. *Puruṣa* is pure Consciousness; a catalyst (*Sākśhitam,* a witness), and aloof (*Kaivalya*) and multiple. Although *Puruṣa* is omnipresent, it is inactive and not the creator.

Unmanifest at first *(avyakta),* the primal *Prakriti,* known as *mūla prakriti,* has three constituent characteristics *(guṇas)* which are *Satya guṇa* (the real), *Rajoguṇa* (the shiny and visible) and *Tamoguṇa* (unseen and in darkness). These three *Guṇas* remain in equilibrium until they come into the proximity of *Puruṣa.* This makes them unstable or imbalanced, which sets off a chain reaction activating the unmanifested *Prakriti.* This imbalance makes *Prakriti* active and creative. The *mahat tattva,* the great entity, i.e. the 'intelligence', is first created. This is followed by the ego, *Ahankāra.*

The intelligence to manifest itself develops when the dormant *Prakriti* encounters the *Puruṣa* - which is neither existent nor non-existent, neither active nor inactive, neither with a form nor without a form - and becomes active. This leads to the ego, which sets creation in motion with the five primal elements, the main building materials known as the *Pancatanmātra.* Then the five gross elements, the *panca mahābhūta,* are formed. This produces the ten organs -each of the five organs of function and sensation. Lastly, the mind is formed. The *Puruṣa,* although just an inactive witness at first, becomes attached to this creation during this process and thus gets manifested in as many forms as are found in the universe. The reverse occurs at 'death'. This philosophy suggests that creation is the evolution of the original or primal *Prakriti,* called 'nature' in English, and destruction is its dissolution into the same primal *Prakriti.* Nothing new is ever created; all are transformations from the earlier existence.

The ultimate aim of man should be to separate the *Puruṣa* from himself, i.e. to release or regain the state of *Kaivalya* (isolation).

Epistemology:

Ṛṣi Kapila has asserted that perception (*Pratyakśya*), inference, *Anumāna* and the Word or testimony (*Śabda or Āpta -vacana*) are the basis of his knowledge of this philosophy. He asserts that the existence of *Prakriti* is obvious *(Pratyakśya)* from its effects.

References:

1. Muller, M. *The Six Systems of Indian Philosophy.*1903. (p. 241). Hawaii. University Press of the Pacific.
2. *Ṛg Veda.* 10.91.1-16.
3. Kaku, M. Cosmology today (3/5/16). 23/10/2017.
4. *Śvetāśvatara Upaniṣad,* 6.14.

"If you think you are too small to make a difference, try sleeping with a mosquito"

Dalai Lama

CHAPTER 13

Yoga

The word '*Yoga*' has been variously interpreted in the modern world. It is derived from the root *yuj*. Some suggest this to have been derived from *yujir*. In simple Sanskrit, *Yoga* is used in arithmetic, astronomy, metaphysics, Buddhism, Jainism, *Pancarātra, Pāśupata* and in general as addition, fusion, contemplation, concentration, and the probability of an event. This is used as a prefix, e.g., *Yoga-Darşana, Sāmkhya-Yoga. Patanjali,* circa 200 BCE, is credited as the founder of this philosophy, though this too is a much older concept than 200 BCE.

This word means making an effort, harnessing, or striving to achieve the objective of human existence, which is perfect happiness. It is important to remember that the idea of fusion of one's mind or soul with the Ultimate has been known since earlier millennia. This kind of union is not the aim of *Yoga*; instead, it is of *Viyoga*, separation of *Prakriti* and *Puruşa*, as decreed in the *Gītā,* and postulated in *Nyāya* and *Vaiśeşika* schools. *Patanjali* himself appears to have realised the multiplicity in the meaning of the word *Yoga*, and begins with the statement, "therefore we begin with the exposition of *Yoga*" (*Sūtra* 1)[1]. Hence, he should be recognised as the person who systematically compiled the *Sūtras,* or aphorisms, and produced *Patanjali Yoga Sūtra*. He has used this word to mean that it is through the harnessing of body and the occult faculties in a rigorous manner that one can achieve total control of oneself. The cause of the avoidable suffering is the union of the *Puruşa* with the *Prakriti*. He proposes that the fusion of the physical planes of existence with metaphysical entities results in a state of *Samādhi;* its highest level is the state of pure bliss and nothing else, known as *Kaivalya*.

The first authoritative commentary of this work was produced by *Kṛśṇa Dwaipāyana Vyāsa.* A subsequent commentary was produced by *Vācaspati Miṣra,* circa 850 CE. In *Sarvadarshana Samgraha, Madhwācārya* concludes "the *Yoga-Śāstra* consists of four divisions, as those in medicine treat disease, its cause, health and therapy, so the *Yoga-Śāstra* also treats of phenomenal existence, its cause, and liberation and its cause".

Although included as one of the six systems of Indian philosophy, *Yoga* hardly qualifies as an original doctrine. It is almost identical to *Sāmkhya* philosophy, except it proposes *Citta* instead of *mahat* and adds God, *Iśwara,* as the 26th entity. This is reiterated in *Gītā* [2] that "only the children find the difference between *Yoga* and *Sāmkhya.* He who is deeply involved with either attains the fruits of both".

Yoga is more of a practical method of controlling mind and body to reach the state of perfect happiness than dealing with metaphysical knowledge of human existence. We must remember that every Indian philosophical system has a practice component, be it the *Upāsana* of the *Upaniṣads,* the rituals of *Vedānta, Sādhanā* of the Jains and Buddhists and the meditation and contemplation in *Nyāya and Vaiśeṣika* and the *Vidhi* of *Tantra.* One can attain supernatural powers through *Yoga* too, as in *Tantra.* Indeed, *Śiva* is considered by the *Yogis* and the *Tāntriks* as the Supreme *Yogi.* But, unlike the *Tāntriks,* the *Yogis* do not aspire for magical prowess, but concentrate instead on attaining spiritual calm and moral virtues.

As a philosophy, it accepts *Pratyakśha, Anumāna* and *Āptavacana* as the proofs for its concepts.

Patanjali Yoga Sutra is in four chapters. Its mnemonics are as complex and difficult to interpret as those of the *Vedānta Sūtra*. The first chapter explains the concept, its scope, its methodology and the conclusion. Most of the work is a detailed exposition of the first two *Sūtras* at the beginning* [Note: The *Sūtras* given as references are examples of the aphorisms].

Book 1: *Samādhi Pāda*

The passionlessness

The first chapter has 51 *Sūtras*. *Patanjali* begins by declaring that "now we begin the discipline of *Yoga*". This would imply that some preparatory steps needed to be accomplished before the aspirant would be entitled to take up *Yoga*. He confirms the same minimum attributes to be necessary in the aspirant who wishes to become a *Yogi*: *Satya,* truthfulness; *Asteya,* not stealing; *Brahmacarya,* celibacy or avoidance of promiscuity; *Ahimsā,* non-violence, including vegetarianism; *Aparigraha,* not hoarding; and *Swādhyāya,* study of scriptures or any moral treatise, as by any pupil en route to learning. There must be a firm resolve and that must not be interrupted.

Patanjali defines *Yoga* as "the method of restricting the *britti* i.e. the behaviour of *chitta",* which is commonly translated as 'mind' or 'intelligence', but it is a word that expresses

---

* The *Sūtras* given as references are some illustrative examples from the text.

comprehensively all that we can possibly mean by a combination of mind, intelligence, thought, memory and fantasy, (the 'mind-stuff'). According to *Sāmkhya,* the mind perceives pleasure, pain and delusion. *Chitta* is the *Mahat* which is the basis of intelligence, *Buddhi.* Hence the total control of mind is the demand of *Yoga.* Since the mind has a direct relationship with body, one needs to restrict both in order to control either one. The rest of the chapter deals at length with different thought forms, different ways to control them, and experience different kinds of conscious experiences that are loosely translated as trance, *Samādhi.*

Samādhi is the main activity of a *Yogi. Dhyāna* leads to contemplation. This is done on the object of concentration or a thought or upon itself. If a *Samādhi* is focused on an idea or object or thought, it is called *Sabija Samādhi.* This denotes that there is a seed of something for contemplation. This state is described as *Sabitarka Samādhi or Nibirtarka Samādhi,* and eventually the highest or final stage of memoryless supra-conscious trance is known as *Nirbija Samādhi.* It is this state where differentiation does not exist between the knower, the knowable and the knowledge. He outlines all the prerequisites to be able to reach the *Nirbija Samādhi.* This is further elaborated in the next chapter.

Book 2: *Sādhana Pāda*

The Techniques

In *Sutra* 1–3, the sage begins by instructing the aspirant to purify his body and mind by *tāpas, (*heat, signifying pain), *swādhyāya, (*reading moral literature) and surrendering to *Iśwara (Puruṣa).* He goes on next to explain that these three means help to minimise misery or afflictions and assist one to perform *Sādhanā,* the contemplation. The source of afflictions is nescience, hatred, desire to live long and one's egoism or superiority complex. He reminds all the aspirants that this endeavour must be firmly grounded and regularly practised with all honesty and austerity.

This is called *Kriyā Yoga,* which has eight components, and hence is known as *Aṣtānga Yoga.*

Like any discipline, one needs to observe all requisites prior to beginning the practice of *Yoga*. This preparatory phase has the following steps:

i. Resolve or vow of becoming a *Yogi*. This is essential. This cannot be broken.

ii. Then one must accept pain as a means of purification. Pain is associated with austerity, which means self-discipline.

iii. Austerity is of three types - verbal, physical and mental. Speaking only the truth, performing non-violent actions, and not thinking negative, bad or lustful thoughts are all signs of austere living.

iv. One must read something that is uplifting, be it scripture of one's choice, any aphorism, or whatever may inspire the mind toward sublime thoughts.

v. It is essential to have utmost faith in *Puruṣa*, known here as *Iṣwara*.

vi. Identify the obstacles that will surely get in the way. These are ignorance, pride, infatuation, hatred and fear of death. One has to overcome this. This is reinforcement of *Mundaka Upaniṣad*:[3] " ... is not reached by the weak or careless or those who practise wrong austerity; but the wise who strive in the right way lead their soul into the dwelling of *Brahma*". *Patanjali* suggests using a technique of substitution of one with its opposite number, e.g., hate with love, anger with calm in order to control negative thoughts or feelings. He describes proper techniques to achieve this by practising *Aṣtānga Yoga* or an eightfold technique.

The eightfold techniques are *Yama,* regulations; *Nīyama,* discipline; *Āsana,* posture; *Prāṇāyāma,* withdrawal or inward flow of senses (breath); *Dhārana,* fixation; *Dhyāna,* concentration and contemplation; *Samādhi,* contemplation and meditation and *Samyama.*

Yama and Nīyama: These are the regulations placed on the aspirants. The aspirant is not allowed to do as he or she pleases. There are certain standards and norms which must be followed. These restrictive practices are essential to control the influence of the outer world for an aspiring *Yogi.* These have been enumerated earlier in the introductory paragraph of chapter 1.

Āsana: These are the postures to be adopted for the purification of the physical body. The text does not deal with these exercises in detail but expects the teacher will help the aspirant to perform these often arduous and difficult exercises. This practice is known as *Hatha Yoga.* The postures or physical exercises are specifically targeted for each individual organ and its function in the body. For example, exercises targeted for the nervous system will be for activating the neural centres in the spine and elsewhere. The well-known are the *Mulādhar Cakra* and *Kundalini Cakra.* The lotus position for meditation is well known.

Max Muller made a remark on the practice of *Hatha Yoga,* "This was the simple beginning of *Yoga,* and in that sense it was meant to be a useful addition to *Sāmkhya,* because even a convinced *Sāmkhya* philosopher who had obtained *Gyāna Yoga* or knowledge-yoga would inevitably suffer from disturbances caused by external circumstances and the continual inroads of the outer world upon him, i.e. upon his *Manas,* unless strengthened to resist by *Karma Yoga* or work yoga the ever present enemy of his *peace of mind.*"[4]

Prāṇāyāma: Commonly translated as breath control, this is a particularly important technique to regulate the entire physical and mental processes in the individual. *Prāṇa* is the life-breath which pervades and infuses every cell in the body. *Sūtra* 49 states that the posture must be correct and steady before practising *Prāṇāyāma.* The normal respiratory pattern is modified by deep and shallow breathing and exhaling, as well as holding breath for a specified duration in phase, number of times and the context of the *Āsana (Sūtra* 50*).* The *Sūtras* 52 and 53 state, "this dissolves the shroud over the light of truth and enables the mind for *Dhyāna,* concentration".

Dhāraṇā: This is fixation or concentration. This is the first step. One needs to look at an object or thought and concentrate on it without letting the mind wander, bringing it back to the object when the attention has drifted. Staring without blinking is known as *Trādaka* when the mind begins to explore the reality of that object or the idea that is being focused.

Dhyāna: This is meditation. This is the second step. This is the continuous flow of the awareness or cognition toward the subject of concentration. Meditation is an effort to understand the real nature of what is concentrated upon. One needs to meditate on an object or thought, trying to understand its real nature. The true nature of what is seen is apparently the nature or *Prakriti,* but this is made of constantly changing qualities known as the *Satya, Raja* and *Tama Guṇas.* This seen *Prakriti* is joined with the *Puruṣa* who sees (the seer). It is this *Samyoga,* the amalgam of the visible and the viewer, which manifests as the Creation and all the actions. *Sūtra* 14 asserts that actions result in pleasure and pain depending upon their merit and demerit. The true knowledge is that which separates the *Puruṣa,* the inner entity, (the Self) from the *Prakriti,* the outer world. At its successful state, this becomes the trance-like state of contemplation, the *Samādhi.*

Samādhi: Dhāraṇa leads to *Dhyāna*, which culminates in *Samādhi*, where the object of concentration, and the concentrator, i.e., the aspirant, become one. At lower levels, thoughts, place, pride, and joy manifest at first. These are *Sabija Samādhi.*

Samyama: The amalgamation of the above results in *Samyama* which is the transcendental knowledge of the object of contemplation, the penultimate step before reaching the *Nirbija Samādhi.*

Book 3: Vibhuti Pāda

Achievements of extraordinary prowess

Patanjali asserts in this chapter that it is possible for an aspirant to be what one wishes to be, get what one wants or achieve whatever one wants to accomplish. The requirements were enumerated in the preceding chapters. He elaborates the techniques to identify the inner world and the outer world. The inner world is the mind, consciousness, and the soul. This deals with *Citta,* which is a conglomerate of many metaphysical entities, as already explained. *Rāja Yoga* teaches the techniques of accomplishing control over the inner world.

The outer world is the body, the environment, and the actions. *Hatha Yoga* has the techniques for mastery over the body. *Prāṇāyāma* deals with the vital breath, the *Prāṇa. Pratyāhāra* deals with the senses. Both need to be brought under control.

The accomplishments begin to manifest in an aspirant after the practice of the final three limbs of *Rāja Yoga.* This level of *Samādhi* leads one to have many kinds of abilities:

Animā, become tiny or like an atom.

Laghimā, become as light as anything.

Garimā, become as heavy as desired.

Prāpti, access anywhere, reach anywhere.

Prākāmya, achieve all desires.

Iṣtva, able to create anything.

Vaśitwa, able to control anyone.

Thus, the *Yogis* can levitate, hold breath, remain dormant or appear as one or many, or at different places at the same time. But this ability must not be used for selfish gains, because the purpose of *Samādhi* is to get that transcendental awareness or knowledge, i.e., becoming the ultimate - the actor, the spectator and action, all as one. [*Prakriti, Puruṣa* and the universe]. This is the final aim of *Samādhi.*

Real achievement is the freedom of spirit and dispassion even with the lesser abilities, as outlined. *Sutra 3.36 states:* "The intellect and the *Puruṣa* are totally different: the intellect exists for the sake of *Puruṣa,* while the *Puruṣa* exists for its own sake. Not distinguishing this is the cause of all experiences." *Samyama (i.e., by Nirbija Sādhana)* accesses this distinction and thus is gained the knowledge of *Puruṣa.* The *Sūtras* 51-56 suggest: "By *Samyama,* discriminative knowledge comes on single moments in sequence. This enables the *Yogi* to discern the uniqueness of one despite similarity in characteristic marks, species, and positions. The discriminatory knowledge that simultaneously comprehends all objects in all conditions is known as the intuitive knowledge which heralds liberation. When the calm mind achieves the pure consciousness of the soul or the Self, the ultimate is achieved."

Book 4: *Kaivalya Pāda*

The ultimate bliss or absolute freedom

This begins by suggesting that extraordinary abilities may accrue from drugs, repetition of mantras, *samaadhi* or because of the past life. (*Sūtra* 1). *Patanjali* asserts that there is always a past, a present and a future birth, and the results of our actions, *karma,* also continue in the same manner. He denotes this as *Sanjita karma,* the inevitable one from before manifesting at present; *Prārabdha karma,* the current actions; and *Agāmi karma,* the ones to come. The past and future exist in the real forms of objects which manifest due to differences in their characteristics (*Sūtra* 12). The reality of objects is the characteristically changing gunas (*Sūtra* 14). This causes changes in *Citta,* which is always known to the eternality of the *Puruṣa,* the master. He who remains in a permanent state of discrimination, known as the *Dharmamegha samādhi,* is totally disinterested in his achievements (*Sūtra 29*). All the suffering and the effects of *karma* cease to exist in that state. Nothing remains to be known when all the shrouds of knowledge disappear. All the *Guṇas* get reabsorbed in *Prakriti* and the ultimate liberation ensues (*Sūtra* 36).

We can see that *Patanjali* does not deviate much from the general acceptance of the Indians that the subliminal impressions, *Samskāra,* attached to the Self in the past births, remain until the chain is broken. It is this *Samskāra* that plays a vital part in preventing the Self from gaining the absolute freedom. The aim of *Yogi* is to obtain freedom from this *Samskāra* and attain *Kaivalya* - the state of ultimate bliss, the absolute liberation.

References:

1. *Patanjali Yoga Sutra: #, 1, 2, 3, 12, 14, 29, 36, 49-56.*

2. *Gītā*.5. 4, 5.

3. Mascaro, H. (1965). *The Upanishads* (p. 81). London: Penguin Classics.

4. Muller, M. (1903). *The Six Systems of Indian Philosophy* (p. 311). Honolulu: University Press of the Pacific.

❖

For great men, religion is a way of making friends;

Small people make religion a fighting tool.

APJ Abdul Kalam

CHAPTER 14

Bārhaspatya or Cārvāka

This philosophy proposes that the only reality is this world. Nothing exists beyond this world. This is also known as the *Cārvāka* or *Lokāyata* School and is one of the three traditionally accepted atheistic philosophies, the other two being *Buddhism* and *Jainism*. Strangely, this has been attributed to *Ṛṣi Brihaspati*, who has contributed to all three *Vedas*. He is regarded as a great teacher; the planet Jupiter is named after him in Indian astronomy. The *Ṛg Veda* also mentions that he was a priest to Indra.[1] He has also contributed to *Pancarātra Agama* and to *Tantra*. He is the son of *Ṛṣi Angirasa* and his wife, *Surūpā*. He has been given divine status in the *Vedas*. His name has become synonymous as *Guru* - the teacher. It appears illogical to me to identify *Ṛṣi Brihaspati* as the proponent of a philosophy which is against his own identity and beliefs. The alternate explanation may be as follows.

There are several questions in the *Vedic* mantras, *Brāhmaṇas* and the *Upaniṣads* which indicate genuine doubts in the accepted theories regarding *Puruṣa, Brahma,* origin of the universe, morality, pursuit of happiness, austerity and renunciation of worldly pleasures and belongings. For example:

1. *Bṛhadāraṇyaka Upaniṣad*, 2.4,10 - "springing forth from these elements, itself solid knowledge, it is destroyed when they are destroyed; after death no intelligence remains".[2]

2. And repeated as, 4.5.13, 14 – "arising out of elements, into them it returns again: there is no consciousness after death".[3]

There are several sages with the surname *Bārahaspatya*, which denotes their genealogy as the descendants or the pupils of *Brihaspati.*

Indeed, *Brihaspati* is said to have had two wives, eight daughters and nine sons. It is therefore highly likely that one of his own descendants or an ancient philosopher who might have been a pupil of the great *Ṛṣi,* and hence qualified to call himself *Bārhaspatya* and who did not believe in the extant doctrines, called himself a 'teacher of the worldly people', i.e., *Barhaspatya Lokāyata,* as opposed to *Brihaspati Āngirasa,* and produced this doctrine. The great *Sāyaṇācārya* has tried to refute this probability by identifying him as definitely the son of *Ṛṣi Angirasa,* no doubt influenced by *Maitrāyanī Upaniṣad* where he is substituted for *Prajāpati,* to give credibility to the notion that he deliberately taught this false knowledge to the group of pupils who were the *Asura,* the demons, to prevent them from attaining the Ultimate Liberation, *Mokshya.* This was done so as to prevent the *Asura* from becoming equal to the gods[4] , and also to prevent others from following this doctrine. This is also indicated in *Kaṭhopaniṣad,* when *Yama* praises *Nāciketas* by declaring "even many pleasures do not tempt him away".[5] However, these appear to be mere mythological stories, probably told to safeguard the priestly livelihood.

Brihaspati Samhitā is the exposition of this philosophy. This is thought to have been compiled circa 600 BCE. The original texts have not yet been discovered, but there is no doubt of its existence, since this has been mentioned in very ancient literature and subsequently, in both the pre- and post-Common Era. This school proposes that sensual perception alone is the authority of knowledge. By refuting all other *Pramāṇas,* viz. *anumāna, āptavacana, upamāna, arthapatti* and *abhāva* accepted by the other philosophical concepts described earlier, and accepting only perception, i.e., *Pratyaksha* as the valid proof, this doctrine discards all other schools of philosophy. It asserts that this cognition arises from a combination of the elements which are earth, water, fire and wind. It asserts that the goal of human existence is to become happy and that the pleasures which give us the happiness must not be shunned just because they may be associated with pain. *Śankarācārya,* in 900 CE, begins his book *Sarvasiddhānta Samgraha* by commenting on this philosophy. This was translated by Professor M. *Rangācārya* in 1908 into English on the orders of the Government of Madras and is freely available for download. This is reproduced below.

1. According to *Lokāyatika* doctrine, the four elements alone are the ultimate principles - earth, water, fire and air; there is none other.

2. Only the perceived exists; the unperceivable does not exist, by reason of its never having been perceived; even the believers in the invisible never say that the invisible has been perceived.

3. If the rarely perceived be taken for the unperceived, how can they call it the unperceived? How can the ever-unperceived, things such as the horns of a hare, be an existent?

4. Others should not here postulate [the existence of] merit and demerit from happiness and misery. A person is happy or miserable through [the

laws of] nature; there is no other cause.

5. Who paints the peacocks or who makes the cuckoos sing? There exists here no cause excepting nature.

6. The soul is but the body characterised by the attributes signified in the expressions, "I am stout", "I am youthful", "I am grown-up", "I am old", etc. It is not something other than that [body].

7. The consciousness that is found in the modifications of non-intelligent elements [i.e. in organisms formed out of matter] is produced in the manner of a red colour out of the combination of betel, areca nut and lime.

8. There is no world other than this; there is no heaven and no hell; the realm of *Śiva* and like regions are invented by stupid imposters of other schools of thought.

9. The enjoyment of heaven lies in eating delicious food, keeping company of young women, using fine clothes, perfumes, garlands, sandal paste, etc.

10. The pain of hell lies in the troubles that arise from enemies, weapons, and diseases; while liberation *[mokshya]* is death which is the cessation of life-breath.

11. The wise therefore ought not to take pains on account of that [liberation, *mokshya]*.

12. Chastity and other such ordinances are laid down by clever weaklings. Gifts of gold and land, the pleasures of invitation to dinner, are devised by indigent people with stomachs lean with hunger.

13. The constructions of temples, houses for water supply, tanks, wells, resting places, and the like, is praised only by the travellers, not by others.

14. The *Agnihotra* ritual, the three *Vedas*, the triple staff, the ash-smearing, are the ways of gaining a livelihood for those who are lacking in intellect and energy - so thinks *Brihaspati.*

15. The wise should enjoy the pleasures of the world through the proper visible means of agriculture, keeping cattle, trade, political administration, etc.

We find reference to *Brihaspati Samhitā* in *Tattovapaplavashimha* in 700 CE; *Prabodh Candrodaya* and *Saddarşana Samuccaya of Haribhadra. Mādhvācārya* has commented on several passages from the original manuscript in *Sarvadarśansamgraha.* These have been quoted by most authors and make interesting reading. A few examples where the philosopher mocks the orthodoxy of the *Brāhmins* are quoted below from the translation of Professors E. B. Cowell and Gough.[6]

"If a beast slain in *Jyotiştoma** rite will itself go to heaven, why then does not the sacrificer forthwith offer his own father?"

"If beings in heaven are gratified by our offering the *Shrāddha*** here, then why not give the food down below to those who are standing on the house-top?".

He advises: "While life remains, let a man live happily; let

---

* This is a generic name for seven elaborate religious events conducted with sacrificing animal(s) as offerings to God. It is believed that the soul of the slain animal will go to heaven and be liberated.

** *Shrāddha* is a religious ritual conducted to offer food, water (also, at special events, clothes and jewellery) to the soul of the dead parents, usually three times a year. It is the priest who takes away all those offerings.

him feed on *ghee**** even though he runs in debt".

References:

1. *Ṛg Veda* 8.96.15.
2. *Brihadāraṇyaka Upaniṣad*, 2.4,10.
3. Ibid 4.5.13,14.
4. *Maitrāyani Upaniṣad 7.9.*
5. *Chāndogya Upaniṣad 8.8.*
6. Cowell, E. B; Gough, A. E. (1874–78).The-*Sarva-Darsana-Samgraha* Or Review Of The Different Systems Of Hindu Philosophy (1904). (p. 2–8). London: Keegan Paul Trench and Trubner & Co.

❖

*** *Ghee*, clarified butter, which is regarded a luxury item of food.

CHAPTER 15

Jainism

Prince *Vardhamāna**, 599–527 BCE was the second son of King *Siddhārtha* and Queen *Trişala* of Vaishali, India, who were the disciples of a *Jain* ascetic, *Paraśvanātha. The Jainas* were a sect of people who believed in non-violence and simple living, unlike the *Brāhmins* with their animal sacrifices and rich and colourful rituals. The prince renounced his wife, daughter, and princely lifestyle at the age of twenty and left home in search of the true knowledge. He attained *Kevala gyāna* or omniscience after rigorous penance, austerity, travels, and meditations for twenty-two years. He became a *Jina. Jina* translates as "the very brave", i.e., the one who has been able to overcome all worldly desires, vices and virtues, too. It was believed that there had been many *Jinas* born in India before his time, and they had preached good values to their disciples. He is known as *Mahāvīra* – the Great Brave.

He had attained enlightenment on the 10th day of the fortnight of the rising moon in the month of *Vaisākh,* 557 BCE, and became known as *Bhagavāna Mahāvīra* – the 24th *Tirthānkara* in the *Jain* pantheon. His first disciples were eleven *Brāhmins* who were most impressed by his second sermon. He established the *Jain Sangha* – which is a broad church of men and women from all socioeconomic classes and castes or creeds. Prior to the establishment of this formal

---

* These dates are approximate, but widely believed to be correct. No written record exists.

Sangha, the *Jain* followers used to call themselves *Swetāmbers* (wearing clothes). The male followers of *Mahāvīra* became *Digambaras*, i.e. the nudes, indicating total renunciation of all possessions, including even a loin cloth. He preached until death at seventy-two years. His teachings are known as the *Agamas.* There are some major differences between the two sects, but the guiding principles for both are the teachings of the *Bhagavāna Mahāvīra.* His first group of followers numbered 4400 – each of the eleven disciples brought along 400 of their own followers, who were known as *shramanas.* He had ordained 318,000 women *(Shrāvikā)* and 36,000 nuns *(Aryika).* He had a very large following; some estimated this to have been nearly 600,000 around the time of his death. Several kings in that region had accepted his teaching – notable among them were King *Bimbisāra* and *Ajātaśatru.*

Many millions of Indians, mainly in Gujarat, Rajasthan and adjoining parts of India, follow *Jainism.* They keep a low profile and do not have flamboyant monasteries or innumerable places of pilgrimage.

Philosophy of *Bhagavāna Mahāvīra*:

1. All human beings suffer from the bondage of their *karma* (which signifies the results of one's actions). Souls seek gratifications which generate greed, selfishness, anger, and violence. All these experiences result in *karma,* which binds the soul and causes it to be born repeatedly for suffering.
2. Purpose of life is to seek liberation, *Mokshya,* from the cycle of rebirth.
3. The means to achieve this liberation is by adopting the following three principles:

i. The right knowledge - *Samyaka gyāna.*
ii. Having the right faith - *Samyaka darśana.*
iii. Having the right character - *Samyaka caritra.*

These principles were elaborated by the first eleven disciples and recorded as the twelve *Āgamas. Bhagavāna Mahāvīra* did not personally systematise his own teachings. The earliest compendium is believed to be the *Kalpasūtra* and the next literature is *Tattvārtha Sūtra,* circa 300–400 CE.

Samyaka gyāna:

All living beings have an innate omniscience or the absolute awareness which exists in a dormant state within them. This knowledge remains covered under the layers of *karma,* which are material acquired over previous existences. This knowledge is of two types: direct knowledge (*Pratyaksha*) and indirect knowledge (*Parokshya*).

Direct knowledge is acquired through inference and the scriptures. One infers by memory, perception, and logic. The scriptures are the teachings of the *Tirthānkara.* Indirect knowledge has three forms, viz. intuition, extrasensory perception, and enlightenment.

To make his disciples understand these concepts, he taught a theory of *anekāntavāda,* i.e., the 'theory of plurality of existence' or 'the principle of many realities' *(syn. Syādavāda).* This is illustrated as follows:

Anything can be perceived from many angles, and to insist that any one perception is the only reality is erroneous. As explained by 'the seven may be' theory *(Saptabhangi Naya),* nothing can be 'the ultimate reality'. This refuted the existence of God, or *Brahma,* as being the Ultimate Reality or the Ultimate Truth.

For example:

This object is a spoon.

This object may look like a spoon, but it may be something else.

This object may be both – a spoon and something else.

This object is truly indescribable.

This object is something else which is also indescribable.

This something else is a spoon and is indescribable.

This is a spoon, and not a spoon, and both are indescribable.

Another example to illustrate this concept was given by a recent Indian philosopher, Mr Sukhalal Sanghvi.[1] He observed that as a forest did not imply an individual tree, shrub or a plant, the latter did not imply a forest. Both the tree and the vegetation are real and must be taken as such. This is the theory of plurality of existence. In other words, one object can have many ends. This is in total contrast to the *Vedic* and the *Upaniṣadic* theories, which affirm that the true essence of any living or non-living thing is God or *Brahma*.

The *Jains* affirm that everything has two properties; one is the inherent and the other is its changing nature. For example, a piece of gold is a metal, but it can be converted into many forms, e.g. jewellery, artefacts, gold plating etc., but its essence remains the same gold.

Samyaka darśana:

The *Jains* believe that this universe is real and eternal; it has not been created and cannot be destroyed. It exists in many forms. It has five principle independent components, viz. souls, atoms, Space, motion and stillness (*Jīva, Pudgala, Ākāśa, Dharma and Adharma,* respectively). *Karma* is the sum of life's experiences which the soul takes up independently and is regarded as (*pudgala, syn. Dravya, anu*) matter. Time or *Kāla* is also considered by the *Digambaras* as the sixth independent variable of this universe. These six independent variables transform independently and variably to create the myriad living and non-living forms.

Samyaka caritra:

Bhagavāna Mahāvīra taught that all our actions and behaviours should lead towards stopping and disassociating *Karma* and its influence on our souls. He called this the processes of *Samvara* (stopping) and *Nirjara* (disassociation). This required the following practices in daily lives:[2]

- *Ahimsa* (non-violence).
- *Satya* (truthfulness).
- *Asteya* (not stealing or coveting what belongs to others).
- *Brahmacarya* (celibacy or avoiding illicit sexual practice).
- *Aparigraha* (not hoarding or having the minimum of possessions).

We find that many of the Western Indologists have not given due credence to *Jain* philosophy. This was probably due to the small number of followers and the low profile kept by the *Jains* in that vast country. *Buddhism,* with its grand displays of statues of *Buddha* and the *Vihāras,* the monasteries, must have impressed Western scholars, who had not realised that many of the ideas later propounded by

Buddha were already being followed by the *Jains*.

It is said that by the time of the birth of *Buddha*, there were nearly sixty-two sects of people believing in a variety of philosophies based upon the *Vedas*, the *Brāhmaṇas*, the *Upaniṣads*, the *Jainas* and the *Tāntric* doctrines. The political philosophy was also taking different forms. The state structures too were varied, from a ruthless autocracy to a benevolent democracy.[3] The culture in the Indian subcontinent continues to go through intense debates on philosophical issues to this day.

References:

1. Sastri, D. N. (1953). *Bharatiya Darshan Shastra* (p. 352). Delhi. Motilal Banarsidass Publishers.
2. Ibid, p 46.
3. Avari, B. (2016). *India: The Ancient Past* (p. 100). London: Routledge.

❖

CHAPTER 16

Buddhism

It is difficult to define this philosophy, which is vast in its scope. One cannot improve the introduction of *Buddhism* given by Christmas Humphreys: "In its earliest form, it included the finest moral philosophy then known to man, with a range of mind development and pioneer psychology, second to none. In its developed form, it includes religion, advanced philosophy, mysticism, metaphysics, psychology, magic and ritual; the triple Yoga of India - intellectual, devotional, and the way of action - and its own contribution to human achievement, *Zen*".[1]

***Buddha*:**

We have no historical evidence about the dates of birth and death of *Buddha*. It is commonly believed that he was prince *Siddhārtha* of Kapilavastu, the capital of a small kingdom situated in western Nepal. He was born there in a garden at Lumbini on the day of full moon in May 563 BCE, *Baisākh Śukla Pūrnimā,* according to traditional Indian astrology. He had renounced everything and become a seeker of truth at the age of twenty-nine. He received his enlightenment at Bodh Gayā and gave his first sermon at Sāranath, near Vārānasi, 2600 years ago. He died at the age of eighty. He had established a moral order of his disciples opposing the traditional ritualistic *Brahminism*. His teaching, although greatly modified since, has been known as *Buddhism*.

Buddha did not leave any writing. Nothing of what he said

was written until 400 years after his death. The first written document is the Pali Canon of Sri Lanka, circa 100 BCE. *Buddha* attained his *Mahāparinirvāna* (death) at Vaishali, where he had inducted women and also his foster mother into his order along with, as the legend says, 84,000 men. Considering the scanty population of that period, this figure is obviously suspect. However, there is no doubt that he had a large following during his lifetime, mostly in northern India. His influence continued to grow and became global.

Buddha chose to speak and teach in *Pāli,* the language of common people, including the lowest in society. Sanskrit was the court language and spoken all over India during his time. The first *Buddhist* canonical book to be compiled in *Pāli* in Ceylon is called *Tipitāka*. This is in three parts – *Suttapitāka* contains the sermons of *Buddha*; *Vinnayapitāka* contains rules and regulations for a *Vikshu*, a *Buddhist* monk, and *Abhidhamma pitāka* contains philosophical deliberations on *Suttapitaka*.

It is accepted that *Buddha* taught three principles:

1. *Sarwamanityam,* i.e., all are transitory or impermanent.
2. *Sarwamanātmam*, i.e., all are without *Ātmā* or Self (soul).
3. *Nirvānaśāntam, i.e.,* total stillness is the state, or achievement, of *Nirvāna*. This is variously interpreted as The Absolute, The Bliss, The Liberation, *Buddhatwa, Bodhisatwa, Arhat,* etc.

His final message to his followers, given through his cousin, was: "After my death, the *Dharma* shall be your teacher. Follow the *Dharma* and you will be true to me. During the last forty years of my life, I have withheld nothing from my teachings. There is no secret teaching, no hidden meaning; everything has been taught openly and clearly. Take the Self as your refuge. Hold fast as a refuge to the truth. Look not for refuge to anyone besides yourselves".[2]

His sermons from *Suttapitāka,* however, have been variously interpreted, discussed and elaborated in *Abhidhammapitāka.* This caused significant differences among his following, resulting in the establishment of two different sects of *Buddhism, Hinayaana* and *Mahāyāna. Yāna* means a vehicle; *hina* is small and *mahā* is great; *Yāna* being the vehicle or the means to reach Buddhahood or *Buddhatwa.* This division became established among the followers soon after the death of *Buddha.* Tibetan *Buddhism* incorporates *Tantra* and has several fascinating subsects. The current Dalai Lama is the titular head of one such sect known as *Gelugit;* the other four - the Nyingma, Kaggu, Sakyait and Dugpa - are also well established. The followers are differentiated by the colour of their robes and headdress.

His followers had begun to debate the nature of Buddhahood, i.e., on the exact nature of *Buddha.* Was he a teacher, a law personified, a *Saguna Brahma* of the *Upaniṣads,* the *Nirguna Brahma* of the *Vedas,* an incarnation of a god? Was he a *Buddha* or a *Bodhisatwa*? The followers of the *Hinayāna* School believed that Buddhahood was the ultimate state reached after the observance of strict codes of conduct and penance. The followers of *Mahāyāna* believed that there was already a *Buddha* lying dormant within one and it needed only to be developed. They believed in *Bodhisatwa,* the enlightened teacher, the pre-*Buddha* state, who helped all mankind. An individual who seeks *Buddhatwa* seeks that for himself alone. The ultimate aim was to achieve the *Nirvāna*, the attainment of *Buddhatwa*, and not the annihilation of all external forces and merger into the *Brahma*, as postulated in the *Upaniṣads.*

Over the years, *Buddhism* became more complex as it began to expand all over Asia. It began to absorb some cults and *Tāntric* practices as well, particularly in Tibet, Sikkim, Bhutan, and Nepal. A third major school of *Buddhist* philosophy is also well established as the *Vajrayāna School.* This has had further divisions among its followers in the countries in the Himalayan belt, Mongolia, China, Korea and Japan. In Japan, it has taken a meditative form and is known as *Zen, Dhyān.* According to Stcherbatski, present-day *Buddhism* has the following subdivisions:[3]

1. *Theravāda* – in Pāli, i.e., the Doctrine of the Elders (*Thera*), as the main part of *Hinayāna* philosophy.

2. *Sarwastivāda* – under *Hinayāna,* as propounded by *Vasubandu* in his book *Abhidharmkosha.*

3. *Śūnyavāda* – propounded by *Nāgārjuna* as the *Mādhyamic darśana,* i.e. the philosophy of nihilism or relativism.

4. *Yogācāra* – propounded by *Asanga* and *Vasubandhu,* as idealism.

5. *Buddhist* logic – as proposed by *Diṅnāga.* This is also known as *Sautrāntric or Sautantātic Yogācāra.*

The latter three belong to the *Mahāyāna* School of *Buddhism.*

Buddhist practices:

All *Buddhists* believe in three concepts:

- *Buddham Śaranam Gacchami;* I seek refuge in Buddha.
- *Dhammam Śaranam Gacchami;* I seek refuge in (his) teaching.
- *Sangham Śaranam Gacchami;* I seek refuge in his Order. (commune).

Buddhism is unique in many respects. It is a religion without God. It has no priest. *Buddha* did not nominate any successor. It has no set rituals. There are no compulsory and universal rules except those followed in individual *Vihāras.* It is very individualistic. One need not become a monk (*Bhikshu*) to practise this philosophy. Anyone can join this at any time in his or her life. There is no supreme authority like the pope, God, archangel, saint or an ayatollah to follow.

Although the three fundamental concepts are explained in the *Theravāda* philosophy, the development and further thoughts on these principles are found in the large volumes of newer *Buddhist* literature of the *Mahāyāna* School of philosophy. It is not intended to provide in-depth information here. Interested readers are expected to study the original literature, given in the bibliography.

Buddha's sermons:

Buddha's first sermon, given to his five disciples, had four components. He had called this the Four Noble Truths.

The First Noble Truth is that this life is all *Dukkha* - the suffering.

The Second Noble Truth is the manifestation of *Dukkha* - the suffering.

The Third Noble Truth is that the causes of *Dukkha* are

known.

The Fourth Noble Truth is that this *Dukkha* can be avoided.

"This life is all *Dukkha,* the suffering. All its constituents are misery. All the beings and their constituents are transitory and lacking in an ego or substance".

Explanation: One suffers from *Dukkha, i.e.,* misery (sorrow, suffering) due to disease and ageing. The reason for this is one's birth. The birth is dependent upon the former existence (*Vawa*), which is dependent upon *upādāna,* i.e., attachment. Attachment happens due to *Trişnā,* the craving. The cause of craving is *Vedanā,* i.e., pain and pleasure, the experience. The cause of this is the *Sparśa,* the touch. The cause of this touch is *Şaḍayātana,* i.e., the six organs of perception. The cause of these sense organs is *Nāmarupa,* i.e., name and form. The reason for the name and form is the knowledge or awareness. The reason for this is *Samskāra,* the impression of acts done in former existence, the reason for which is *Avidya,* i.e., nescience. If nescience is destroyed, the wheel of this world will perish. This is the *Āryasatya,* i.e., the ultimate Truth.

In summary, this is the sequence: Past consciousness > Birth > Attachment > Craving > Experience > Touch > Sense organs > Name and form > Awareness > Impression > Nescience; thus completing the Wheel of Life.

The Noble Eightfold Path: the noble truth of cessation of suffering.

These are:

1. The right views; to know of suffering, its causes and means of amelioration.

2. The right intention; to renounce the world and to do no harm.

3. Right speech; to abstain from lies and slander, idle gossip.

4. Right action; not killing, not stealing, and not lusting after anyone or anything.

5. Right livelihood; supporting oneself with right action.

6. Right effort; striving to promote noble qualities and to suppress bad thoughts.

7. Right mindfulness; realisation of mind in freedom from want and discontentment.

8. Right concentration; to attain ecstasy which leads to further levels of ecstasy.

The Middle way:

Buddha taught the Middle way, where duality merges into unity. This concept of universal oneness is *Śūnyatā,* which signifies that everything in its essential nature has nil identity (existence). Even the enlightenment disappears, just like the light which exists only because of darkness and cannot shine without it.

- *Nirvāna* is achieved by the 'Middle way', which is neither the life of luxury nor the life of severe asceticism. This consists of the Noble Eightfold Path, as above.

- All things appear and disappear due to a long chain of their causes. Those who do not know this see life as it is, either an existence or a non-existence. But the wise men see beyond these two extremes. Hence avoid being entangled in any extreme.

- If people insist all things are empty and transitory, it is just as great a mistake as to think that all things are real and do not change. If a person becomes attached to himself, it is a mistake which will not save him from suffering. But if he does not believe in himself, it will also be futile for him to tread on the Noble Path.

No soul theory:

It is this which has made *Buddhism* fundamentally different from the *Vedic* philosophy. He asserts that everything, whether living or non-living, is without a soul, or *Ātmā.* According to *Buddha,* there is continuous change in nature, and nothing is stable or permanent in time. A soul is supposed to be eternal or permanent, but nothing is everlasting or all-pervading. There is nothing that pervades the Space; everything is but one point in Space. Hence a point cannot be said to have any substance. Therefore this 'no soul' theory is really a 'no substance' theory. This second principle has been richly debated. Some followers of the *Mahāyāna* School still believe that there is 'Soul', and this debate has continued to this day.

Buddhist literature of *Theravāda* School (the School of the Elders).

It is commonly believed that the first *Tipitāka,* the Buddhist canon, was compiled in Ceylon during the reign of the Sinhalese King Vattagamini during 29–17 BCE. This was in *Pāli* and subsequently composed in Sanskrit as *Tripitāka.* This translates as 'the three baskets'.

Several original sections from this treatise were lost

during the earlier years. However, early Chinese translations of the 4th century CE throw some light on their original purport.

Suttapitāka, containing *Buddha*'s teachings, were further divided into five sections by the third century BCE. These are the following:

Digha Nikāya; The long *Sūtras.*

Majjhima Nikāya; The medium-length *Sūtras.*

Samyutta Nikāya; The grouped or joined *Sūtras.*

Anguttara Nikāya; The numerically arranged *Sūtras.*

Khuddaka Nikāya; The unclassified or ungrouped *Sūtras.*

Dhammapada.[4] This is in twenty-six chapters arranged according to the ethical topics of the sermons given by the *Buddha*. It has 423 stanzas. The well-known parable of the blind men and the elephant is found in this book. Some excerpts are given in Appendix 4.

Khudduka Nikāya, the *Udāna*, the *Ittivuttāka*, the *Sutta Nipāta*, etc. are the other literature of renown in *Theravāda*. The *Mahāyana* School calls its literature *Agamas* or *Sūtras*, although most of them appear to have their roots in the *Hinayāna* literature.

Pragyānparimita is the most important book said to have been given by *Buddha* himself for safe keeping to the *Nāgas*, who gave that to *Nāgarjuna*. This is thought to have led to the foundation of the *Mādhyamika* school by him. Other important books are *Mūlamādhyamikakārika* by *Nāgarjuna*, *Abhidharmakoṣa* by *Vasubandhu* and *Pramāṇasamuccaya* by *Diṅnāga*.

Tibetan *Buddhism*.

Buddhist literature arrived in Tibet in the 5th century CE. It was a form of *Mahāyāna Buddhism* superimposed on the local ancient religion known as *Bon*, a form of nature worship with a curious mixture of demonolatry, occult cultism and mysticism. A *Buddhist* monk is known as *Lāmā, Gelong, Gestul* or *Gesnen*, depending upon status. The most exalted and famous *Lāmā* today is the *Dalai Lāmā*.

King Srongsten Gampo in the 7th century CE was converted into *Buddhism* by his two *Buddhist* wives. He became an ardent follower and began to build temples and promote *Buddhism*. The local sorcery and nature worshipping cult of *Bon* was unable to stop the spread of *Buddhism*. A *Tāntrik* sage known as *Padma Sambhava* was invited to Tibet by the king in 747 CE from Nālandā, in India. He was able to displace the *Bon* and establish *Tāntrism* within the corpus of *Buddhism*. His Tibetan name was *Guru Rimpoce,* and also 'the Lotus Born'. He established the order of *Nyingmāpa*. Subsequently another monk, *Atiśa,* arrived from India and established a new order of *Tāntrik Buddhism* known as *Kahdampā* Order. His pupil, *Mārpa*, founded another order, the *Kargyupta* School, in the 11th century CE. Another *Buddhist* monk, *Tsong Ka Pa*, from north-west China, arrived in Tibet in the 14th century CE and reconstructed the scattered order *Gelgupa,* building upon the *Vinaya* doctrine of *Theravāda,* although *Tāntrism* in its subtler forms is still very much a part of this order. He is venerated as the second *Buddha*.

The reformed *Buddhists* (the *Gelgupa*) in Tibet wear yellow hats; the unreformed (the *Nyingmapa*) wear red and the ancient *Bons* wear black hats. The *Gelgupa* School has become the most famous, with *Panchen Lāmā* and the *Dalai Lāmā*. The Tibetan *Buddhists* believe that many have attained the *Buddhatwa*, i.e., become the *Bodhisatwas*. The *Bodhisatwa* do not die in the normal sense, but their consciousness continues to live in successive bodies. Thus developed the Doctrine of The Two Paths, i.e., the Doctrine of the Eye (for the external and non-existing) and the Doctrine of the Heart (for the elected, the exalted *Bodhisatwa*).

Mahāyāna Buddhists in Tibet believe in a complex pantheon of *Buddhas*. The primal, the Omnipresent Universal Spirit or *the Padmapāṇi*, is the *Ādi Buddha*. The seven *Dhyāni Buddhas* emanate from Him in each *Kalpa*. These are the *Bodhisatwas*, or the named *Buddhas*. The last, i.e., *Siddhartha Gautama* – also known as the 4th *Dhyāni Buddha*, *Avalokiteśwara*, *Amitāva Buddha*, or *Amida* – was the founder of the present *Buddhism*. The next *Buddha* to come after a few hundred thousand years will be known as *Maitreya*. The omnipresent *Buddhist* prayer *'Om Maṇi Padme Hum'*, recited with every rosary bead, is for this eternal, the primal *Adi Buddha*.

The *Dalai Lāmā*: The nephew of the *Lāmā TSong Ka* Pa was the first Grand *Lāmā*. The title *Dalai*, meaning the Great Ocean, was given in the 17th century. He built the Potala Palace in Lhasa. He exerted full temporal and spiritual powers over his people spread far and wide from Mongolia to Kamchatka to Tibet. The current, most famous, yellow-hatted Lama is believed to be the 14th *Dalai Lāmā*. Born in a farming family in north-east Tibet, he was known as *Lhamo Dhondup*. At two years of age, he was recognised by the monks as the incarnation of the 13th *Dalai Lāmā*, *Thubten Ghyatso*. He was then educated until the age of twenty-three and subjected to the highest examination. He assumed the office of the *Dalai Lāmā* in 1954. Panchen *Lāmā* is also venerated as a spiritual leader by the people of Tibet, but he does not hold temporal powers. He lives in China and is revered by the Chinese.

Zen Buddhism

This is a unique form of *Buddhism* which is mostly a system of meditation. However, a great *Zen* master says that "all the *Buddhist* teachings as propounded in the *Sūtras* and the *Śāstras* are mere wastepaper whose utility consists in wiping the dirt off intellect and nothing more".[5] *Zen* aims at achieving a new viewpoint, 'the *satori*', which is the intuitive realisation of inner workings of our beings. *Zen* is supposed to do so in the most direct way possible, without recourse to any agency. It teaches concentration on the mind wordlessly to understand the true self. But this also has many temples, teachers and rituals which appear incompatible with its stated concept.

Buddhism has transformed itself over the years from being a simple eightfold path of life to an elaborate religion with rituals, scriptures and pantheons which is second to none. This is followed by 535 million people worldwide. We can see the parallel in the simple ancient *Vedic* philosophy which became transformed beyond recognition into *Brāhminism*, with numerous pantheons, rituals, sorcery, and superstition. Indeed, similar transformations are seen in other religions, e.g., Christianity, Islam, Judaism, and the rest. Perhaps it is the nature of man to seek power and position over other men that prompts us to develop ways and means to get a large following. *Buddha* had rejected his kingdom, wealth, and wife, but his followers enjoy the privileges of being the *Buddha (Bodhisatwa),* receiving awards and accolades and being both the temporal and spiritual leader of the followers.

References:

1. Humphreys, C. *Buddhism. 1951. An Introduction and Guide* (p. 12). London. Penguin Books Ltd.

2. Kyokai BD.1993.*The Teaching of Buddha. (p13-14)*. Tokyo. Society for the Promotion of Buddhism.

3. Sastri, D. N. (1953). *Bharatiya Darshan Shastra* (p. 352). Delhi. Motilal Banarsidass Publishers.

4. Easwaran, E. *The Dhammapada.*2007. (p. 223). California.The Blue Mountain centre Of Meditation.

5. Suzuki, D. T. 2018. *An Introduction to Zen Buddhism*. (p. 88). Dead Authors Society. Online books.

❖

Life is like riding a bicycle. To keep your balance, you must keep moving.

Albert Einstein

CHAPTER 17

Uttar Mimāmsā or Vedānta Sūtra

Uttara Mimāmsā is said to have been compiled by the philosopher *Bādarāyana,* circa 200–500 BCE. *Bādarāyana* refers to someone who lived at *Badrinath Dham,* the holy place of pilgrimage for the Hindus, at the lower Himalayan range of mountains in north-west India. Some claim him to be *Krisņa Dwaipāyana Vyāsa,* the author of the *Mahābhārata* and the divider of the *Vedic* mantras into four categories.*

Uttar Mimāmsā is in two parts. The first part with four chapters deals with the gods of the *Brāhminical* pantheon and their worship or rituals. This is called The *Devatā Kānda.* The second part is also in four chapters and deals with the knowledge, believed to be the gist of all knowledge of the *Upanişads,* the distillate of the *Vedas.* Hence this part is called *Gyāna Kānda* or *Vedānta.* These aphorisms or revelations by the sages, the *Ŗşis,* were regarded as *Śruti,* and the opinions and teachings by other learned scholars and sages were regarded as *Smriti, or the Āptavacana.* This distinction is important. *Śruti* is not regarded as given by any man (*apauruşeya)* but revealed as divine aphorism. Hence these have traditionally been considered to be beyond doubt or question and are taken as evidence. *Smritis* did not have the same status at first but, with the establishment of the orthodoxy of *Brāhmanism* as a 'religion', the powerful priests

* In my opinion, *Bādarāyana* is very unlikely to be *Vyāsa. The* timeline suggests that this treatise was a much later compilation. *Gitā* has also been quoted as proof or *Pramāņa* in its assertions. *Gitā* too has mention of *Brahma Sūtra.*

decreed these ancient literary works too as *Śruti,* and hence unchallengeable.

The text of *Brahma Sūtra* is made up of short phrases which are regarded as aphorisms. These aphorisms have a unique style of composition called *Sūtra*. Each *Sūtra* contains a doubt, question, or enquiry, and in most cases its answer or explanation as well. These phrases have no full sentence, no grammar and no clear separation between the subject and object of the statement. Significant symbolism is also abundant among these phrases. *Sūtra* in Sanskrit means a string or thread. Perhaps the title *Brahma Sūtra* was meant to indicate that this was a loosely strung collection of *Brahmas* (profound words or phrases). The first *Sūtra* gives the purpose of this treatise, which is to deliberate upon *Brahma.*

This is the first phrase: *athāto brahmagigńasā;*

Translation: *atha* = now, *atah* = therefore; *Brahma* = Brahma, *jigńāsā* = enquiry.

There has been much speculation on 'therefore' *(atah)* by the commentators. *Śankarācārya,* who wrote its commentary, comments this is a "sequence for deliberation". We might care to remember that the pupils had to memorise all the *Sūtras* without first understanding their meanings. The *Sūtras* were not usually explained to the pupils until they embarked on higher studies. The author might have been telling his students that it was time to learn their meanings. Max Muller says that since *Pūrva Mimāmsā* had been studied, the *Uttar Mimāmsā* could now be studied (*Uttara = subsequent*). Deussen thinks it wise to concur with *Śankarācārya.* However, if the scriptures had been studied already, there would be no need to reflect or speculate on

Brahma. The first *Sūtra* becomes clearer in the following three *Sūtras*:

1. *Janmādyasya yatah*; *yatah* = for this; *janmādi* = birth, etc.; *yasya* = its.
2. *Śāstrayonitwāt*; *śāstra* = scriptures; *yonitwāt* = because of womb.
3. *Tattu samannavat*; *tu* = but; *tat* = that; *samannavat* = due to similarity.

The translation combining all these four *Sūtras* would be this: *"Its conception, birth etc. occurs in the womb of the scriptures. This has that similarity. Therefore, we should now reflect on Brahma"*. It is presented in four sections (*adhyāya*). Each section has four chapters. Each chapter has a number of topics (*adhikāraṇa*) within it. The brevity of these *Sūtras* therefore needs deep and scholarly research, or a teacher for correct interpretation. This difficulty in its interpretation is reflected in various commentaries presented as *vākya, vritti, kārikā, bhāṣya,* etc. This is the most annoying aspect of this literature.

It appears to me that *Bādarāyaṇa* is accepting the challenge from the doubters and is inviting a debate on *Brahma*. It is likely that there had been several schools of *Vedānta* during this period. This is suggested by the names of great philosophers of that period found within the text of *Brahma Sūtra.* These are *Audololomi, Kāshakrtşna, Bādari, Jaimini, Aśmarāyathya* and others. *Jaimini* was indeed the pupil of *Vyāsa.*

The first section is called *Samanwaya*, or similarity. This tries to bring together various words or phrases as meaning or implying the same one, i.e., *Brahma*. The second chapter is called *Avirodha* – no opposition or conflict. This aims to suggest that all the subsequent schools of philosophy – *Sāmkhya, Nyāya, Vaiśeşica, Yoga, Buddhism* – do not really have any conflict with *Brahminism*. The third is *Sadhanā* – the spiritual practice. This aims to prove that the *Brāhmaṇic* rituals, or *Yagńas,* are indeed no different in essence to the *Sādhanā* suggested in other schools of philosophy. Finally, the fourth section is called *Phala*, or the outcome. This section reinforces the concept of the authorised and unauthorised persons to conduct rituals, which is not a concept stipulated in the *Ṛg Veda*. This refutes the so-called atheist philosophies of *Cārvāka, Buddha* and *Mahāvīra*, as well as *Sāmkhya, Vaiśeşika* and other schools of philosophy.

This is an extremely complex and difficult treatise. Further examples of word-for-word translation are given in Appendix 3. Although widely regarded as the distillate of the philosophical concepts indicated in the *Vedas*, this appears to be a misconception which has persisted to this day. There can be no doubt that this is a composition of the post-*Buddhist* period, presented as the distillate of the *Vedas*. Also, it is very unlikely that *Veda Vyāsa* would have written *Uttara Mimāmsā*, because he was a great social reformer and did his utmost to present the *Vedic* knowledge in a systematic manner, illustrating that with the *Srimadbhāgavat Mahāpurāṇa*. Not being satisfied with just these two, he had written the *Mahābhārata*. This *Brahma Sūtra* is designed to reinforce the *Brahminism*, and hence is best regarded as a supplementary to the *Pūrva Mimāmsā*, compiled by *Jaiminī*. A meticulous search for *Vedic* references shows that *Brahma Sūtra* has heavily drawn upon *Brihadāraṇyaka* and *Chāndogya Upanişads*. I have noticed the following references: *Taittaria Samhitā* x 13; *Ṛg Veda Mantras* x 11, *Satpatha Brāhmaṇa* x 3; *Garuda Purāṇa* x 2; *Gītā* x 5;

Mahābhārata x 2; *Manusmriti* x 3; *Chāndogya U* x 97; *Brih.U* x 64; *Katha U* x 11; *Aitariya U* x 2; *Mundaka U* x 8; *Kauşitaki U* x 7; *Narāyanīa U* x 1; *Patanjali Yoga Sūtra* x 1, *Śwetāśwatara U* x 2, *Jabala U* x 1.

Brahma Sūtra did not have an authoritative commentary until the 8th century CE, when the exceptionally gifted ascetic of great stature, *Śankarācārya (Śankara),* wrote the *Śānkarbhāşya.* His aim was to bring together various schools of philosophy prevalent at that time under the umbrella of *Brahminism* in the guise of '*Vedic*' doctrines. He successfully reinforced this by his commentary.

❖

By all means, marry. If you get a good husband, you will be happy. If you get a bad one, you will be a philosopher.

Socrates

CHAPTER 18

The *Bhagavad Gītā*

Gītā (BG), the song divine, has 700 melodious verses in *Sanskrit* presented in 18 chapters. This has intrigued great scholars like *Ādi Śankarācārya, Mādhvacārya, Rāmanuja, Swāmi Yogānanda, Sarvepalli Rādhākṛṣṇan, Jayadayāl Goendakā, Swāmi Chinmāyananda,* and many others. This is considered by many in India to be the *Pancam Veda*, the fifth *Veda*. Innumerable commentaries and translations of *Gītā* are found in established Indian languages. There is hardly any guru or scholar of Sanskrit who has not tried to devoutly interpret *BG* in his or her own way in a native language in India and abroad. Famous persons, e.g., Bertrand Russell, Aldous Huxley, R. W. Emerson, Roth, Max Mueller, Mahātmā Gāndhi and many others, have been greatly impressed by BG. Swāmi Yogānanda differs from all others when he believes this to be an exposition of sublime spiritual concepts in a psychological-metaphysical battlefield and the intuition of a confused individual who must battle out his internal conflicts.[1]

Background:

This is commonly believed to be a sermon given by *Kṛśṇa*, the mortal incarnation of God *Viśṇu,* to his favourite cousin Prince Arjuna, in the battlefield in the great war of *Mahābhārata.*

Arjuna clearly explained the reasons for his unwillingness to fight the war, in verses 28–46 of Chapter 1, but *Kṛśṇa* urged him to fight. He explained the philosophies of *Sāmkhya*

Yoga imploring Arjuna to fight. Arjuna was not convinced and asked more questions. Subsequently, the sermon on *Karmayoga* and *Bhakti Yoga* also did not convince him to pick up arms again. Arjuna still refused to fight, despite having been given the special powers to see the vision of God, the *Viśworūpa.* Thereafter, *Kṛśṇa* taught him the characteristics of the *Guṇa* and implored him to follow the *Varna Dharma* as established by the scriptures, e.g., eating recommended foods, performing rituals and other specified duties. Arjuna remained unconvinced. Eventually, *Kṛśṇa* ordered him to fight. Arjuna then realised that it was his duty to fight the war and he became willing to do so.

Vyāsa is commonly believed to be the author or the historian who dictated the *Jaya*, the precursor of the epic *Mahābhārata.* Sanjaya, who had been empowered to visualise the whole war and describe that to the blind emperor Dhritarāśtra, says, "through the grace of *Vyāsa* I have been imparted with this supremely important secret directly into my consciousness by *Kṛśṇa,* the god of *Yoga*".[2] This suggests that *Kṛśna* was the alter ego of *Vyāsa* who had created a metaphysical and psychological scenario. *Vyāsa* had projected himself as *Kṛśṇa* of *Srimad Bhāgavat Mahāpurāṇa*, whose authorship is also alluded to him.

There are several conflicting verses in *BG* which indicate that the original has been modified over the millennia. This modified version was probably compiled by *Bādarāyana*, who had also compiled the *Brahmasūtra*. This would explain how these are quoted in both the books. Perhaps this is referred to by *Rādhakṛṣṇan* when he writes, "the *Bhagavad-gītā* takes up the *Upaniṣadic* conception of Brahman (*Brahma*) as absolute reality and points out that the impersonality of the Absolute is not its whole significance".[3] Hence this should be regarded as a repository of the essence of all the traditional orthodox philosophies and refutations of non-orthodox doctrines, as well as the rituals and religious commands prescribed by *Brāhmiṇism*. In addition, it incorporates the *Bhakti* cults. Basically, one can summarise the contents of *BG* as the essence of Philosophy of Knowledge (*Sāmkhya Yoga*), Philosophy of Action (*Karma Yoga*), Philosophy of Faith (*Bhakti Yoga*) and the concept of the Universal Form, the *Viśvarūpa*, the *Puruṣa* of the *Ṛg Veda*. This treatise does not find its mention in ancient *Buddhist* and *Jaina* philosophies and only acquired the status of reverence after the commentary by Śankara in the 8th century CE.

It is this unique amalgam of varying concepts which the great scholars have discovered to be so fascinating that allowed them an infinite horizon for interpretations. Western writers since 1800 CE wrongly regarded *Brāhminism*, known now as *Hinduism*, as the *Vedic Religion* and decreed this as the scripture of the Hindus.[4]

Examples of a few frequently quoted verses from the *Gītā* are given below:

> Chapter 1. Arjuna gives his reasons for not wishing to fight.
>
> 1.41. O *Kṛṣṇa*! Due to lack of religion, women of the superior lineage will become immoral and corrupt, thus producing mixed race offspring.
>
> 1.43. The sins of men who corrupt the family producing half-castes will destroy the laws of the lineage and prescribed duties, [thus assuring hell

for all].

Chapter 2. *Kṛṣṇa* replies.

2.1. How do you get this despondency at this serious juncture? Your behaviour, unworthy of a superior person, will neither allow you heaven nor respect (on this earth).

2.16. The unreal does not exist; there is no non-existence for the real. The limits of these are recognised by the wise.

2.19. Neither knows the truth - the one who thinks this self as the killer and he who thinks it killed.

2.20. This soul is never born nor slain; nor will it perish after having come into existence. It is not killed when the body is killed - it is eternal, unborn, permanent, and unchanging.

2.23. No weapon can cut it and the fire cannot cook it; water can neither wet it nor wind can make it dry.

2.37. If you die, you shall go to heaven and enjoy this earth if you win. Hence you must surely fight.

2.47. You have a right to perform an action (ritual) but never for its results. Let not the fruits of the action be your purpose but do not be inactive.

2.55. When one relinquishes all desires and becomes content within oneself, then one becomes established in wisdom.

2.63. Anger produces confusion which leads to amnesia; this leads to dementia which causes the extermination of intelligence.

2.64. The man with self-control finds peace and calm when he wanders among material objects without wanting or hating them.

2.71. He achieves peace who gives up all desires, acts without any attachment or belonging or egoist mentality.

Chapter 3. Arjuna asks questions regarding action and *Kṛśṇa* explains the *Karma Yoga.*

3.1. If you think thoughts are superior to action, then why are you asking me to get on with this horrible work?

Kṛśṇa replies:

3.5. No one can stay even for a moment without action; all must perform actions according to the qualities ordained by nature.

3.6. He is a pretender who has controlled his organs of action but whose mind roams around sense object.

3.14. Rain produces food which produces living beings. Rain falls due to *Yagńa* which is the right action.

3.19. Therefore, always perform attentively the material action and the ritualistic action without attachment to achieve the Supreme.

3.23. If I were to stop performing action continually, men will stop too and imitate me.

3.42. Men say that mind is superior to the senses which are superior to the body; intelligence is superior to the mind but the most superior is the Self.

Chapter 4. *Kṛśṇa* explains *Yoga* and the science of Knowledge.

4.5. O Arjuna! We have been born very many times. I can remember them but you do not do so.

4.7.8. Arjuna! I reappear whenever there is a decline in the acts of righteousness and to save the faithful and destroy the evil doers.

4.18. One who understands action in inaction and vice versa is wise and remains in a transcendental position fully engaged in righteousness.

Chapter 5. Arjuna asks further:

5.1. First you ask me to renounce work and then again, to remain active. Kindly explain which will be the better option.

Kṛśṇa answers:

5.4,5. Only the simpletons separate philosophy from action. The wise see them as the same.

5.12. A firm devotee achieves peace because he offers the fruits of all activities to me. The person who does otherwise becomes entrapped in his desires.

5.16. Like the sun which makes everything visible, knowledge destroys the nescience and illuminates the mind.

Chapter 6. Arjuna asks:

6.34. Mind is impatient, turbulent, and obstinate. It is more difficult to control than a storm.

Kṛśṇa answers:

6.35,36. Yes, it is difficult but perfectly possible by constant practice and detachment.

6.47. He who is devoted to me with greatest faith gets most intimately united with me in *Yoga*.

Kṛṣṇa then goes on to show the *Viśvarūpa,* the macrocosm, which has the most frightening appearance.[5] [6] When Arjuna begs him to reveal himself as he really is, *Kṛṣṇa* shows him the benevolent form. Eventually, *Kṛṣṇa* had to order him to fight by firmly reminding him that he had no choice in the matter.

BG is certainly an exquisite panacea for a confused man who is unable to decide a right course of action. He gets reassured that "all will be well as long as you think it is God's doing; just do what you are told; do not complain that you are not getting your just wages or fruits of your service; and have the utmost faith in your God. You have seen the frightening form as well as the benevolent form of God; be prepared to face the consequences if you do not come to Me for refuge, after giving up all other religions". The purpose appears clear: support *Brāhminism*; even God says so!

A dispassionate analysis of *BG* suggests that this must be a modified or corrupt version of the original sermon given by

Vyāsa which has remained hidden, but we get the indication of this being present in the ancient past by the mention of *Vyāsa* by Sanjaya.[3] Of all the commentaries, I find the commentary by Swāmi Yogānanda, who obviously did not believe in the legend but interpreted the whole text in a presumed metaphysical-psychological battlefield, most plausible; he makes this a summary of available courses for a man to choose at times of internal conflict. He has named this method *Kriya Yoga.*[7]

The reason for the great popularity of *BG* is the spread of the *Bhakti* cult which received a great boost from the V*aiṣnavaites,* and the re-emergence of Hinduism, which was actively promoted by *Śankarcārya.* His commentary of *BG* certainly points to this fact. The British colonials had also shown great favour to the Indians of the *Brāhmin* caste**.[8] The praise by famous Western scholars also helped to enhance its fame as a source of profound philosophy from India. *BG* did not present any new philosophy but moulded the existent doctrines and focused them on *Kṛṣṇa,* the legendary incarnation of *Viśṇu.*

References:

1. Yogananda, S. (2002). *Bhagavad Gita. God Talks with Arjuna. Vol I.* (pp 30-34). Kolkata. Yogoda Satsanga Society of India.
2. *BG.* 18.75.
3. Rādhākṛṣṇan, S; Moore, C. A. (1957). *A Source Book in Indian Philosophy* (p. 101). New Jersey: Princeton University Press.

4. Miller, B. S. (1986). *The Bhagavad-Gita: Krishna's Counsel in Time of War* (pp. 147–154). Bantam Classic. New York.

5. *BG.* 11. 10-30.

6. *Ṛg Veda*. 10.90.

7. Yogananda, S. *Bhagavad Gita. God Talks with Arjuna. Vol I* (pp 569–78 Kolkata. Yogoda Satsanga Society of India.

8. Tharoor, S. (2016). *An Era of Darkness. The British Empire in India* (p. 127). New Delhi: Aleph Book Company.

❖

"Not believing in the glory of our own soul is what vedanta calls aethism".

Swamy Vivekananda

CHAPTER 19

Political Philosophy: Kautilya

Background:

A little historical information is essential to comprehend the political philosophy of one of the greatest thinkers of India in that era.

Manu Smriti was the orthodox manual for social organisation, rules and regulations, and effective control of the society in *Brahminism* until the era of *Mahāvīra Bardhamāna* (*Jainism*). There is no evidence of a well-developed modern concept of nationalism or patriotism until that time. According to *Ashtādhyāyi* of *Pāṇinī*, the Indian subcontinent was divided into probably sixty-nine *janapada*, i.e. principalities or townships of varying sizes, circa 800 BCE. They had begun to be amalgamated into sixteen *Mahājanapada*, (*mahā*, big; *janapada*, principalities). By this period, eleven of these sixteen *Mahājanapads* were identified in the Indo-Gangetic plains. By the sixth century BCE, the subcontinent was loosely divided into five regions, known as *Madhyadeśa* (Central), *Prācya* (western), *Uttarāpatha* (northern), *Prāticya* (eastern) and *Dakshina-patha* (southern). Monarchy had become firmly established, although some sort of republicanism or democracy was being practised in smaller *Janapads* which were showing dissent with the well- established orthodox *Brahminism*. According to Avari*, the greatest of these kingdoms was *Magadha*, which was spread over most of *Madhyadeśa*, the central region, from 550–529 BCE. The western region, *Prāticya*, was under the Syrian Achaemenid dynasty until usurped by the Macedonian Philip II in 336 BCE. His son Alexander marched eastward until 327 BCE.

The empire of *Magadha* had been first established by King Bimbisāra in 550 BCE. This was most prosperous, wealthy and always in danger of attack from the neighbouring northern mountainous *Janapads* and smaller kingdoms of the east and south. He successfully established a dynasty; his grandson Aśoka became very famous. He took up non-violence in remorse after decimating the southern kingdom of Kalinga and converted to *Buddhism*. This dynasty was replaced by the Nandā dynasty. By this time, the mighty empire had begun to suffer from internal feuds, poor administration and extravagance. This paved the way for the establishment of the *Mauryan* empire, which was founded by Candragupta Maurya. Scholars and moralists view him differently: as a soulless materialist who used whatever was to his advantage, or a wise pragmatist who recognised the need to engage in shady acts in order to achieve greater good.

The *Arthaśāstra*: The Principles of economics.

Pandit Viśṇu Gupta, better known as or *Cāṇakya Kautilya*, is the author of this treatise. There are many unproven anecdotes about *Cāṇakya*. He was most probably an accomplished *Tāntrik* who was trained at Nālanda University, Pātaliputra (now Patna, Bihar). He produced a treatise known as *Arthaśāstra,* circa 321–297 BCE, in Sanskrit. There is no doubt that this has been the most influential manual for government, politics and capitalism since that time in India. The original manuscript lay in oblivion after the fall of the

Mauryan empire, until rediscovered in 1905 by Rudrapatna. It has received much attention since 1909 AD, when the English translation by him was published. Later scholars have found that Niccolo Machiavelli's *The Prince* was similar to this treatise. A few have claimed a similarity with Plato's *Republic* and *The Art of War* by Sun Tzu.

Kautilya denies any original ownership of his ideas in the very first sentence, declaring this to be a compendium of the aphorisms of the ancient seers**. At the end, he demonstrates his vain nature by declaring that it was he who had rescued the science of weaponry, the scriptures, and indeed the earth from the unworthy Nanda king. He is regarded as the mentor, advisor and the prime minister of Emperor Candragupta Maurya.

Kautilya asserts that it is "*Artha*", the wealth and wealth alone, that is important in as much as the charity and desire depend upon wealth for their realisation. *Artha* determines the existence of state and its people.

He prefers monarchy to democracy. "The king who is well educated and disciplined in sciences, devoted to the good government of his subjects, and is bent on doing good to all people will enjoy the earth unopposed".

Duṇda nīti, the science of government, is the science of control, which must be done appropriately - leniency leads to anarchy, excessive punishment leads to revolution; appropriate and just punishment keeps the state stable. The state must protect the weak from the strong.

** *Kautilya* has quoted several philosophers, who could be his contemporaries, or before his time, in his treatise. Some are little known. Their names are: *Brihaspati, Bhāradvāja, Parāşhara, Pişuṇa, Kauṇapadanta, Vātavyādhi.*

He suggests four methods of negotiation with another hostile agent or state. These are *Sāma*, as equal; *Dāna*, by bribery; *Daṇda*, by punishment; and *Bheda*, by cunning.

Some extracts from the book of English translation by *Shāmaśāstry* (Biblio) are presented below***. This is to provide some indication of the vast spectrum of philosophy during the early Common Era in the Indian subcontinent.

Book 1. Concerning discipline:

Chapter 2. The end [purposes] of sciences.

Anvikşiki (science of logic), the three *Vedas, Vārtā* (agriculture, cattle breeding and trade), and *Danḍanīti* (science of government) are called the four sciences.

The School of *Manu* holds that there are only three sciences: the three *Vedas, Vārtā,* and the science of government, in as much as the science of *Anvikşiki* is nothing but a special branch of the *Vedas.*

The School of *Brihaspati* says that there are only two sciences: *Vārtā* and the science of the government, in as much as the three *Vedas* are merely an abridgement for a man experienced in affairs temporal.

The School of *Uşana* declare there is only one science, and that is the science of government; for, they say, it is in that science that all other sciences have their origin and end.

But *Kautilya* holds that four, and only four, are the sciences; it is from these sciences that all that concerns righteousness and wealth is learned, therefore they are so called. *Anvikşiki* comprises the philosophy of *Sāmkhya, Yoga*

*** [Non-copyright material]

and *Lokāyata.*

Righteousness and unrighteousness acts are learned from the *Vedas*; wealth and non-wealth from *Vārtā*; the expedient and the non-expedient, as well as potency and impotency, from the science of government.

When seen in the light of these sciences, the science of *Anvikşiki* is the most beneficial to the world, keeps the mind steady and firm in weal and woe alike, and bestows excellent foresight, speech and action.

Book 2. The duties of government superintendents:

Chapter 13.

"... having set up spies over his prime ministers, the king shall proceed to espy both citizens and country people.

Classmate spies formed as opposing factions shall carry on disputations in places of pilgrimage, in assemblies, houses, corporations, and amid congregations of people.

... Thus, in his own state a wise king shall guard factions among his people, friendly or hostile, powerful or powerless, against the intrigue of foreign kings".

Book 3. Concerning law:

Chapter 2.

"It is power and power alone which only when exercised by the king with impartiality and in proportion to guilt, either over his son or enemy, maintains both this world and the next.

Sacred law, evidence, history, and edicts of kings are the four legs of law. Whenever the sacred law conflicts with the rational law, then reason shall be held authoritative."

Chapter 3.

"Marriages are the basis of all disputes. Any kind of marriage is approvable, provided it pleases all those that are concerned in it".

Book 4. Removal of thorns:

This book deals with protection of artisans, merchants, detection of youths of criminal tendencies, examinations of sudden deaths, trial, and torture to elicit confessions, sexual intercourse with immature girls, and violation of justice.

Book 5. Conduct of courtiers:

This deals with measures to suppress treason against the king and his kingdom. The king in the interest of righteousness may inflict punishment in secret on those courtiers or confederacy of chiefs who are dangerous to the safety of the kingdom and who cannot be put down in open daylight.

Book 6. The source of sovereign states:

"The king, the minister, the country, the fort, the treasury, the army and the friend are the elements of sovereignty ...". "But a wise king, trained in politics, will, though he possesses a small territory, conquer the whole earth with the help of the best fitted elements of his sovereignty, and will never be defeated".

Book 7. The end of six-fold policy:

The circle of states is the source of the six-fold policy.

"... peace, war, observance of neutrality, marching, alliance, and making peace with one and waging war with another are the six forms of policy.

... that position in which neither progress nor retrogression is seen is stagnation.

... or if a king thinks (according to the above six options)

... thus, a king in the circle of sovereign states shall, by adopting the six-fold policy, endeavour to pass from the state of deterioration to that of stagnation, from the latter to that of progress".

Chapter 5.

"... by insulting the good and commending the wicked; by causing unnatural and unrighteous slaughter of life; by neglecting the observance of proper and righteous customs; by doing unrighteous acts and neglecting righteous ones; by doing what ought not to be done and not doing what ought to be done; by not paying what ought to be paid; and exacting what ought not to be taken; by not punishing the guilty and severely punishing the less guilty... the king causes impoverishment, greed, and disaffection to appear among his subjects; when people are impoverished, they become greedy; when they are greedy they become disaffected; when disaffected, they voluntary go to the side of the enemy or destroy their own master...".

"... ally of superior power should not be relied upon, for prosperity changes the mind. Even with little or no share in the spoils, an ally of superior power may go back, appearing contented; but sometime afterwards, he may not fail to sit on the lap of the conqueror and carry off twice the amount of share due to him...".

Book 8. Concerning vices and calamities:

"... ignorance and absence of discipline are the causes of a man's troubles".

Book 9. The work of an invader:

"... my teacher says that of enthusiasm and power, enthusiasm is better...

... powerful kings, whether young men, women, lame or blind, conquered the earth by winning over or purchasing the aid of enthusiastic persons...

... of power (money and army) and skill in intrigue, power is better...

... Thus, of the three acquirements viz. enthusiasm, power and intrigue, he who possess more of the quality mentioned later than the one mentioned first will be successful in over-reaching others...".

Chapter 7.

"... whether demoniacal troubles are absent, or are too many, or normal, the rites prescribed in the *Atharva Veda*, as well as the rites undertaken by accomplished ascetics, are to be performed for success.

... success can be achieved by securing the help of a friend and the enemy of the rear – enemy...

... as virtue is the basis of wealth, and enjoyment is the end of wealth, success in achieving that kind of wealth which promotes virtue, wealth, and enjoyment is termed success in all (*sarvārthasiddhi*, i.e. accomplishment of all objectives) ...".

Book 10. Relating to war:

Chapter 3.

"... may undertake open fight if he has secured the

favourable position to himself; otherwise, a treacherous fight...

... when a broken army, reckless of life, resumes its attack, its fury becomes irresistible; hence he should not harass a broken army (of the enemy)".

Book 11. Conduct of corporations:

"... The acquisition of the help of corporations is better than the acquisition of an army, a friend, or profits...

... The chief of corporations should endear himself to all the people by leading a virtuous life, by controlling his passions, and by pursuing that course of action which is liked by all those who are his followers...".

Book 12. Concerning a powerful enemy:

"... In order to escape from the danger from an immediate enemy, a king should frequently send to a *madhyama* or a neutral king (whatever would please him); or one may put one's whole property at the enemy's disposal...".

Book 13. Strategic means to capture a fortress:

"... when the conqueror is desirous of seizing an enemy's village, he should infuse enthusiastic spirit among his own men and frighten his enemy's people by giving publicity to his power of omniscience and close association with gods... him; for whoever fails to fulfil his promises becomes untrustworthy both to his own and his enemy's people.

... whoever acts against the will of the people will also become unreliable. He should adopt the same mode of life, the same dress, language, and customs as those of the people. He should follow the people in their faith with which they celebrate their national, religious and congregational festivals or amusements...".

Book 14. Secret means to conquer the enemy:

Chapter 1.

"... in order to protect the institution of the four castes, such measures as are treated of in secret science shall be applied against the wicked...".

This describes the manufacture and use of poisonous gases, and other forms of poisons".

Chapter 4.

"... having thus seized the territory of the enemy close to his country, the conqueror should direct his attention to that of the *madhyama* (the wavering) king; this being taken, he should catch hold of that of the neutral king. This is the first way to conquer the world...".

Chapter 5.

"... having acquired a new territory, he should cover the enemy's vices with his own virtues, and the enemy's virtues by doubling his own virtues, by strict observance of his own duties, by attending to his works, by bestowing rewards, by remitting taxes, by giving gifts, and by bestowing honours. He should follow the friends and leaders of the people...".

Book 15. Plan of a treatise:

Chapter 1.

Paragraphical divisions of this treatise. "... the subsistence of mankind is termed *artha*, wealth; the earth which contains mankind is also termed *artha*, wealth; that science which treats of the means of acquiring and maintaining the earth is the *Arthaśāstra*, Science of Polity. This *Arthaśāstra* or Science of Polity has been made as a compendium of all those 608 *Arthaśāstras* which have been written by ancient teachers as guidance to kings in acquiring and maintaining the earth".

It contains thirty-two paragraphical divisions: the book (*adhikāraṇa*), contents (*vidhāna*), suggestion of similar facts (*yoga*), the meaning of a word (*padārtha*), the purport of reason (*hetvārtha*), mention of a fact in brief (*uddeśya*), mention of a fact in detail (*nirdeśa*), guidance (*upadeśa*), quotation, (*apadeśa*), application (*atideśa*) the place of reference (*pradeśa*), simile (*upamāna*), implication (*arthapatti*), doubt (*samsaya*), reference to similar procedure (*presanga*), contrarity (*viparyaya*), ellipsis (*vākyaśeṣa*), acceptance (*anumata*), explanation (*vyākhyāyana*), derivation (*nirvacana*), illustration (*nidarśana*), exception (*apavarga*), the author's own technical terms (*svasañjá*), reference to a previous portion *(atikrāntávekṣaṇa),* command (*niyoga*), alternative (*vikalpa*), compounding together (*samuccaya*), and determinable fact (*úhya*).

"... this *Śāstra,* conforming to these paragraphic divisions, is composed as a guide to acquire and secure this and the other world. This is the one hundred and fiftieth chapter of the entire work. The fifteenth book, 'Plan of a Treatise, of the *Arthaśāstra* of *Kautilya*' is thus ended. In the light of this *Sāstra* one can not only set on foot righteous, economical, and aesthetical acts and maintain them, but also put down unrighteous, uneconomical and displeasing acts."

"... this *Śāstra* has been made by him who from intolerance (of misrule) quickly rescued the scriptures and the science of weapons and the earth which had passed to the Nanda king. Having seen discrepancies in many ways on the part of the writers of commentaries on the *Śāstras,* Viśṇu

Gupta himself has made (this) *Sūtra* and commentary".

Kautilya suggested a system of *Mandala* (federation) for the ambitious kings who wished to expand their kingdoms and assume greater political powers. This was to form a group of twelve states and take the leadership, accepting overall suzerainty. This was further refined by *Kamandak*i and produced as *Nītiśāstra.* This is the concept of the 'Federation of States'. This system was practised by the kings and emperors in India until she suffered pillaging and looting by the central Asian rulers, and colonisation by the British. The present political system of Federation of Indian Union is largely based on this principle.

❖

CHAPTER 20

Early Common Era

Background:

The beginning of the first millennium heralded many new influences in India. The *Maurya* dynasty had collapsed. According to Burjor Avari, most of India, except the far south, was under the three systems of authority: the central Asian *Kuśana*, the Deccan *Śatavāhana*, and the Western *Śakas*. Politically, the divine rights of the kings and the supremacy of priests including *Buddhist* abbots in all spiritual or religious matters had been firmly established. The western parts of the Indian subcontinent were in occupation by the powerful *Śaka* ruler Rudraman. The *Śatavāhana* dynasty was flourishing in the Deccan. Indo-Roman trade was at its height. Indian philosophers of this era were influenced by the Greek, central Asian (Chinese) and the Roman cultures. The prevalent philosophical concepts were modified, their corollaries were derived, and literary tradition along with architecture, fine arts, drama, and music developed. Great institutions of learning were established: abbeys, monasteries, temples, and colleges, resembling modern universities.

Expression of scientific concepts through mathematics: *Āryabhat*

Āryabhat was born in 476 CE at Patna, Bihar India. [His name probably should be spelled as Ārya Bhatta, i.e., *Ārya* belonging to the guild of *Bhat* or *Bhatta*; however, the error made by Bhāskara I, his pupil who spelled the name as

Āryabhat, has been continued over the years. *Bhat* means a singer, dancer, and entertainer and *Bhatta*, a head priest. We have no information about this.]

He was probably a scholar at *Nālandā* University. He was a mathematician, astronomer and a physicist. He had postulated the rotation of the Earth on its own axis, the spherical nature of the Earth and other planets. He correctly calculated the diameter of the Earth at the equator.

He also had calculated the value of π as 3.146. Although he used alphabets as numerals, his table of place values demonstrated that he had invented Zero; this was subsequently confirmed by George Ifrah and the Arab scholar Al Biruni. He explained the mechanism of the solar and lunar eclipses. He was the first to try to prove philosophical concepts with mathematics. His book *Āryabhātēya* is in 123 stanzas in four parts. These are:

Dasagītika Sūtra or Gītikapāda, dealing with astronomy.

Ganitpāda, dealing with mathematics – arithmetic, algebra, trigonometry, and the decimal system.

Kālakriyapāda, dealing with time and measurement.

Golāpāda, dealing with motion and spheres.

The first full translation and balanced commentary of this work was produced by Professor Walter Eugene Clark of Harvard University in 1930. This shows the extent of interest over this manuscript among mathematicians, both ancient and modern.

Varāhamihira, 505–87 CE

He wrote *Pancisiddhāntika*, which is a compendium of Egyptian, Greek, Roman and Indian mathematical concepts.

His main interest was in astrology, particularly on the effects of celestial bodies on human beings. He also corroborated the works of *Āryabhat*. Some believe that he had commented upon sex and sexuality, which was taken up in detail by *Vātsyāyana*.

Brahmagupta, 598–670 CE

People in India consider him to be the father of Indian mathematics. He used the *Brāhmi* digits as numerals and the alphabet 0 as Zero for place values. This Zero was subsequently developed by the Arab mathematicians as we understand it today. *Brahmagupta* wrote *Brahmasphutasiddhānṭa* and *Khaṇdākhandakya*. He mentions *Pancasiddhānta*, which shows that Indian scholars were aware of the Greek and Roman systems as well; however, this manuscript is not available now. *Brahmagupta* disagreed with several theories of *Āryabhat* but did not produce evidence for his criticisms.

Bhāskara I, 7 CE. It was he who spelled the name of his inspiration as *Āryabhāt*. He was also a great astronomer of his time who disseminated the mathematical work of Āryabhāta. He was the first to write in the decimal system and used 0. His works, *Mahābhāskariya* and *Laghubhāskaria*, are astronomical works in verse and *Āryabhātiyabhāshya* is the commentary on *Āryabhātiya*. The famous Indologist Henry Thomas Colebrooke wrote his acclaimed book *Algebra with Arithmetic and Mensuration*, from the Sanskrit of *Brahmagupta* and *Bhāskara* in 1817, bringing these scholars to the West.

There were many more philosophers in the first millennium CE. It was not only in the fields of mathematics and astronomy that philosophical thoughts flourished in that subcontinent. Although they discussed existing concepts, their interference resulted in significant changes and included new additions to the original concepts. Scholastic pursuits also continued. The following philosophers are well known.

Nagarjuna, 2 CE. He wrote *Mūlamadhyamakārikā* and has been credited as the founder of the *Madhyamaka* school of *Buddhism*.

Iśvarakṛśṇa, 2 CE. Wrote *Sāmkhyakārikā*, which was his explanation of *Sāmkhya*.

Vasubandhu and *Asańga*, 4 CE. They produced *Abhidharmakośa*, espousing *Madhyamaka* philosophy.[2]

Diṇāga, 5 CE, was the author of *Pramānasamuccaya*, and *Dharmakīrti* who, in 7 CE, wrote *Pramāṇavārttika*. These two philosophers greatly influenced *Buddhist* logic and epistemology in that period. *Diṇāga* produced his treatise systematising *Buddhist* logic, particularly dealing with Inference, *Anumāna*. He asserted that *Anumāna* for oneself is distinct from the *Inference* for others: *Svārthānumāna*, inference for oneself and *Parārthānumāna*, inference for others. This is so because it has to be much more robust to be able to convince others than oneself. Next he wanted to be specific regarding *Hetu*, i.e. the purpose of an optimum inference. He suggested that a subject had three forms, *Trairupiya*: it should exist in that subject, in a similar subject and should not occur in any other or dissimilar case. He presented this as a wheel of reasoning, or *hetucakra*. Similar logic is accepted in scientific circles and is known as positive, negative, false positive or false negative, or indeterminate results. *Dharmakirti* built upon this work and came up with the solution for removing all doubts. Examples: 'this is a pear tree because pear is on it'. This is the correct identification of a tree and a pear and there is no doubt. Also, 'there is not a bathtub here because it is incompatible with it being in this kitchen'. This qualified absence is similar to the *abhāva* as in the six accepted *Pramānas.*

Praśastapāda, 5 CE, wrote *Padārthadharmasaṅgraha*; explaining *Vaiśeṣika* philosophy.

Vātsāyayana, 6 CE, wrote *Nyāyabhāṣya,* explaining *Nyāya* philosophy. He also wrote a treatise on love and sex, called the *Kāmasūtra (Philosophy of Sexuality).*

"I am what thou art

Thou art what I am.

I am the psalm,

And thou art the verse.

I am the heaven,

And thou art the earth."

Atharva Veda 14.2.71. Translated by S Vidyalankar.

Nothing more explicit can be the ideal relationship between a man and a woman than depicted in this very ancient, beautiful verse. The wide spectrum of sex and sexuality has been deliberated in ancient Indian literature. The *Vedic* mantras imply the physical as well as the psychological or metaphysical aspects of sexuality. The *Chāndogya Upaniṣad* describes the vagina as "the fire that seeks the oblation of semen from which arises the foetus".[1] The *Ṛg Veda*[2] states the importance of this subject. The mantra that was worthy to give at the betrothal of the bride

Sūryā and the advice that "the knowledge was the pillow, the eye was the decoration, the heaven and earth were the treasures" clearly indicate that sexual awareness and its importance were essential to enjoy life in heaven and earth. The early scriptures stated "the marriage of a desiring woman with a desiring man, though without religious ceremonies, is the best marriage".[3] Rituals should be performed only in the case of a virgin[4]. The three main purposes of life were considered to be the *Dharma,* doing the right activity, *Artha,* earning sufficient resources to do so, and *Kāma,* to experience or enjoy the pleasures of doing so. The third purpose, i.e., the enjoyment, included the sensual pleasures, including sexual activities. Successful performance or achievements of these three purposes were regarded as being essential for achieving the ultimate bliss at the end.

Marriage was considered essential for a householder in the *Vedic* period; but neither the man nor the wife, specifically the *Patni,* was expected to be physically faithful to one another. They were lifelong spiritual partners in the conduct of duty, as ordained by the *Varṇāṣrama.* In the *Ṛg Veda,* we find a wife being called the *Patni, Bhāryā* or *Jaya.* Some suggest this to mean that *Patni* was the *Ardhāngini,* i.e., the other half, who was essential to become complete as one individual to perform all the religious rites together. Thē *Bhāryā* was the physical partner and *Jayā* was someone specially designated to produce offspring for a specific purpose.[5] However, incest and marrying someone outside the clan was forbidden.[6] The subsequent *Brāhminical* scriptures have made this very rigid and described eight types of marriages, fidelity for the women only, polygamy, rights of the husband, etc. They established strict rules for the break-up of marriage and care of children from lovers, besides many other related issues. There was also the concept of a marriage contract for a specific period. The *Ṛg Veda* suggests that the husband should be loved as the eleventh son, implying that the relationship between a man and a woman is not merely physical.[7]

Vatsyayana Kāma Sūtra:

Most of the physical aspects of this topic have been compiled by *Vātsyāyaṇa* around 600 BCE. *Vātsayana* begins by informing us that the sacred aphorisms for *Dharma* were given by Manu; for *Artha* by Bṛhaspati and for *Kāma* by the Sage Nandi. Nandi had given 1000 chapters which were abridged by Śvetaketu [son of Uddalaka in the Upaniṣads] to 500 in seven chapters, which in turn were commented on by seven different scholars.

Vātsayana claims that he has merely summarised these commentaries in his book, which is also in seven parts. Sir Richard Burton has translated this book into English. Apart from mentioning seduction, foreplay and acts of sexual union of different kinds, this has highlighted the subtle aspects of interpersonal relationship between a man and women. This also has described the need for the groom to instil confidence or faith in his new bride.[8] He reinforces the aphorism from the scripture by stating *"a girl forcibly enjoyed by one who does not understand hearts of the girls becomes nervous, uneasy, and dejected and suddenly begins to hate the man who has taken advantage of her"*[9]. Subsequent scholars have dealt with sexual philosophy in depth. Another well-known book is *Rati Rahasya* by Kokkoko, produced around 1000 CE. There are several other philosophers mentioned in this book, which is available in the Archaeology Library of India. There have been several philosophers in the past who have dealt with this subject in India.

It is interesting to note the contrasting philosophies of restraint in sex, as encouraged by *Yoga*, *Buddha* and *Jinas* versus enhancement of sexual prowess as advocated by the *Tāntriks*. To add to this is the philosophy attributed to *Āyurveda* that sex is both an invigorating, life force-enhancing activity and the source of intractable afflictions.

The erotic wall carvings, imagery and sculptures from India and fanciful paintings in the pornographic literature written in Sanskrit have shrouded the in-depth deliberations on the symbolism and many aspects of sex and sexuality. It is obvious that these ancient seers had taken marriage as the central or pivotal point from which all other aspects of sexuality* and related issues in terms of relationships and social conducts were assessed.

The following mantras from the *Vedas* give an indication of the perceived man-woman relationships during the ancient times:

May we always look at each other with love and compassion!

May our lives together be happy without any wickedness!

May the same spirit dwell in both of us!
Atharva Veda 7.36.1.

---

* The *Brahminical* manual known as *Paraskara Ṣruti*, for a part of the *Śukla Yajur Veda*, suggests abstinence for three days and nights after completion of the wedding ceremony. This was to be observed as an act of austerity, named as *Trirātravrata*, in order to develop self-discipline in matters of sex, in the belief that true love was not passion or passion-born, but was based on perfect self-restraint.[10]

O man! Do not be scared to perform your marital duties. Follow the path of Dharma; have courage and conviction. Endowed with strength, honour and valour, may you conform to the duties given to you by God and be happy. Yajur Veda 3.41.

Accept my gifts just as I accept yours; it is on this equilibrium of give and take that the world functions, making life a joyous living. Yajur Veda 3.50

May we live together to produce offspring.
Atharva Veda 14.2.71.

We find that sex and sexuality has not been taken up by most of the Western scholars dealing with Indian Philosophy. Perhaps it is the Victorian reticence and the double standards in all matters of sex that made the British and the latter Indian philosophers shy away from deliberating this important aspect. However, the ancient Indian mind had a flair for the free pursuit of any branch of knowledge without any hindrance or inhibition, as we can see from the *Vedic* times, until the beginning of the second millennium CE.

***Kumārila Bhatta,* 7 CE *and Prabhākara,* 8 CE.**

These two philosophers, teacher and pupil, differed in their understanding of "liberation" [salvation or *Mokshya].* For *Prabhākara,* it was the "absolute cessation of the body caused by the disappearance of all *dharma* and *adharma* (good and bad)" whereas *Kumārila* postulated this as "the state of self being free from pain". These two established their separate schools of philosophy to explain *Pūrva Mimāmsā.* Both had objected to God not being mentioned directly in the *Jaimini Sūtra*; thus, qualifying this as an atheist doctrine like the *Lokāyata.* This is absurd because the whole point of *Pūrva Mimāmsā* was to correctly perform what the *Brāhmaṇa* books and the later *Śastrās* had decreed.

Śankarācarya, 8 CE.

He propounded the 'non-dual' principle known as *Advaita Siddhānta,* also known as the *Viśṇu* Monism. He taught that "the relationship between *Brahma* and the individual *Ātmā* is *Advaita* (non-dual)".[11] He elaborated this by producing an extensive commentary on *Brahma Sūtra* in his *Brahmasūtrabhāṣya,*** as already discussed. The Western scholars like Wilson, Max Muller, Colebrooke, etc. have also given great credibility and support to *Śankarācarya's* commentary as the essence of the *Vedas* or the *Vedānta,* possibly because *Brāhminism* has been conducive for the feudal system of ruling over ignorant masses. This would be extensively debated and modified in the next millennium. A critical study of his commentary reveals that this aimed to refute the multiple philosophical thoughts and religious cults proliferating during that era of renaissance. He was a great scholar, debater and a prolific poet with the most melodious pen who obviously also believed in the myths and mythologies and orthodox *Brāhminism.* His command over Sanskrit is second to none. He arrived around the time when *Buddhism* was beginning its decline and *Brāhmanism* was seeking to be re-established. He commented and gave the explanation of the *Brahmasūtra.* He decided to quell the remaining doubters, i.e., the scholars who were following the doctrine of *Brahma* of the *Upaniṣads* and wrote the commentary in which he interpreted everything according to his theory of monism. There is no doubt that this

** Some examples of the *Brahmasutra* are given with their translation in Appendix 3.

commentary had been designed to support the orthodoxy of *Brāhmanism* and to re-establish that as the dominant religion in India.

This philosopher has had a profound influence on the Indian psyche which has continued for the past 1200 years. Being a *Sanyāsi* [one who has renounced the society and social norms], he himself was not obliged to pursue the rituals of *Karmakānda*, but he was a great believer in the ritualistic aspects of the *Vedas*. He travelled the length and breadth of the country and established four centres of *Brāhminic* ritualist learning at Sringeri, Puri, Dwāraka and Kanchi. He was totally against *Buddhism*, *Jainas* and *Carwākas*.

He wrote several important literary marvels, including a commentary on the *Gītā*. This too has been interpreted to support the *Brahmanic* doctrine. There are many legends about him which suggest that he had accomplished superior powers, or accomplishments, and was equally devoted to *Śiva, Śakti and Viśṇu* and *Laxmi.*

References:

1. *Chandogya Upaniṣad 5.8.2.*
2. *Ṛg Veda. 10.85.6,7.*
3. *Pūraskara Gṛhya Sūtra 1.4.16.*
4. *Manu Smriti. 3.27.*
5. Dixit, M. M. (2009). 1989. *Tyo Yuga* (pp. 103–5). Canada: Deva Group International.
6. *Ṛg Veda.10.* I0.1-14; 109.1-7
7. *Ṛg Veda 10.95.1-18*
8. Burton R. (2009). *Kama Sutra of Vatsyayana*. (p.50-52). Digireads.com Publishing.UK.
9. *Pāraskara Grihya Sūtra. 1.8.21.*

10. Pandey, R. (1969). *Hindu Samskāras. Motilal Banarsidass* (p. 223). Delhi.

11. Sarma, D. (2011). *Classical Indian Philosophy* (p. 204). New York: Columbia University Press.

❖

"A good wife always forgives her husband when she is wrong".

Barrack Obama

CHAPTER 21

The early second Millennium CE

Background:

The early part of this period recorded repeated looting and pillages of temples and universities, and bloodshed carried out by the central Asian hordes of horsemen, who were far stronger than the Indian military personnel. The political system too was undergoing repeated changes. Internal wars and expansion of territories from all sides were commonplace. However, the land was rich, and scholars were able to pursue their studies. Many remarkable achievements were seen in the fields of medicine, surgery, trade, astronomy, shipbuilding, mathematics, architecture etc. Fine arts and music, dance and drama became more established. This was recognised as *Rasa Śāstra.* The following three well-known scholars expanded the depths of understanding in mathematics, astronomy, and ancient literature. These were:

Bhāskara II, aka *Bhāskaracārya,* 1114 CE. He is the author of *Siddhāntaśiromani,* which is his first full work in mathematics, algebra, and the decimal system.

Mādhava, 1340 CE. He founded the Kerala School of Astronomy and Mathematics. He had been given the title of *Golavid* (the Master of Spheres). His main works are *Golavāda, Madhyāmanayanaprakāra, Vanvaroha, Sphutacandrāpti.*

Neelakantha Somayaji, 1501 CE. He was a renowned astronomer of his time and also wrote epicyclic and eccentric models of the planetary system. His treatises are: *Tantrasamgraha golasāra, Siddhāntadarpaṇa.*

This period also witnessed the preponderance of many devotional groups for *Viṣṇu, Śiva* and *Śakti,* which had started a few hundred years earlier. Those who worshipped *Viṣṇu* became known as *Vaiṣṇavas* and regarded him as *Brahma.* This is also known as the *Bhakti* cult.

The Islamic influence:

Central Asian horsemen, like Bin Qasim and Ghazni, had continued to attack the northern Indian territories and convert some forcefully to Islam. However, Islam had already arrived peacefully to the ports in Gujarat, Tamilnadu and Kerala in the 7th CE, brought by Arab traders who had themselves been recently converted to Islam. The Muslim Sultanet had been established by Sultan Iltumish in Delhi and then in Bengal and Deccan. Shah Mir had become the first Muslim ruler of Kashmir in 1339. These prevented further assaults from the north-west. Further references are included in Chapter 22. Sufi evangelism began to flourish in India.

Sufism in India: The Sufi cult flourished, and further subsects developed; notable among these were Chistia, Qadiriya, Suhrawardia, Naqshbandi (Syariah, Thariaqah, Haquiqah and Wallaya). The Chisti order developed from the Wallah. The Chisti order of Sufis had been established in Chisti near Herat in Afghanistan in 930 CE. This is famous for its emphasis on love, tolerance and openness.[1] The Sufi saint Moinuddin Chisti settled in Ajmere around the middle of the 12th century CE and directed social welfare activities in India. Ajmer was dubbed the "nucleus for the Islamisation of central and southern India". The fall of the Abbasid dynasty early in the 13th century CE resulted in hordes of Muslim Sufi poets and philosophers going to India and settling there. This helped a great deal to spread this doctrine in India.

Sufism widely flourished along with devotional music, and a benevolent syncretism was established between the Hindus and the Muslims. This corresponded well with the Bhakti cult that was developing in India; the Sufi 'Sama', the twirling dance of the *dervish,* with music and devotional songs, was similar to the *Sāma* chants of the *Vedas.* It has been widely accepted that the downtrodden, uneducated masses of lower castes in India readily took to conversion to Islam. Significantly, a few people of the higher and privileged castes too were attracted to Islam. Sufism is similar to the *advaita* Monism of *Śankara* in the sense of believing in the 'oneness with Allah', the Ultimate. Many Sufi poets like Moinuddin Chisti, Baba Farid and Rumi, are well read. Prince Dara Sikoh translated several *Upaniṣads* into Persian, from which they were later translated into Latin. India remains a stronghold of Sufism even today. The World Sufi Conference was organised by India in 2016 to counterbalance ISIS extremism.

The *Bhakti* movement

The philosophical deliberations regarding self, the ultimate bliss, liberation, purpose of life, the universe, etc. continued. The *Advaita Siddhānta* of *Śankara* was not acceptable for many philosophers. *Śankara* had mostly used those *Upaniṣads* which supported the theistic philosophy of the *Brāhmaṇas* and ignored the original *Ṛg Vedic* mantras. His theory of monism became modified several times during this half of the millennium. This has again found an extraordinarily strong continuation among the *Swami*

Narayana followers; this movement was established by *Swami Sahajānanda,* who became *Bhagavan Swaminarayan* in 1801. He died at the age of forty-nine. He had simplified this philosophy by stating, "In the *dvaita* philosophy, a devotee worships God while remaining separate from him, while in *advaita* the devotee feels oneness with God".[2] There are more than 1000 *Swaminarayan* temples and a few million followers worldwide. They have taken the vows of vegetarianism, abstinence from drugs and alcohol, sexual fidelity, and to keep the purity of body and mind.

Rāmānuja, 1000–1100 CE. Established *Viśistādwaita Siddhānta.*

Nimbārka, 1200 CE. Established *Dwaitādaita siddhānta.*

Mādhvācārya, 1300 CE. Established *Dwaita siddhānta.*

Ballavācārya, 1500 CE. Established *Śuddhādwaita siddhānta.*

A short synopsis of these different groups is given here:

Rāmānuja asserts that it was *Brahma* and its manifestation which brought out the universe. *Brahma* is formless, undefinable and is *Viśṇu*. The three characteristics, i.e. the *sat (truth), cit (*consciousness) and *jada,* (the inert) which are inherent within *Brahma,* created the entire universe composed of six types of materials. Hence, faith in this form leads one to the ultimate release or salvation. This doctrine is also congruent with *Pancarātra* doctrine. *Rāmānuja* has a very large following in southern and central India. He is known as a metaphysical and epistemological realist, who believes in the reality of *Brahma* as well as the physical world.

Nimbārka proposed that *Brahma* is dual and no single, but both are really the same without a second! This is to appease the debate between *Brahma,* who has no attributes (*Nirguna Brahma*), and *Brahma,* who has attributes (*Saguna Brahma*). *Viśṇu* is either one or both. This belief is followed by the Kumāra group of *Viśṇu* worshippers. This is also known as *Vedāveda* (apparently different but not so in reality).

According to *Mādhvācārya,* there is a profound relationship as well as difference between *Brahma* and *Ātmā* (the Ultimate Entity and the Soul). He expanded this concept to be universally applicable, stating that there were five main inter-relational differences in this universe. These are: i. *Jeeva* (a living being with soul); ii. *Viśṇu* (the Ultimate, the *Brahma*); iii. *Visṇu* and the inert or non-living (*Jaḍa*); iv. *Jīva* and *Jīva*; and v. *Jada* and *Jada.* This philosophy is also known as *Tatwovāda* (elementalism).

The fifth doctrine of pure monism propounded by *Ballavācārya* has Lord *Kṛśṇa* as the ultimate entity in whom one can find salvation or *mukti.* His theory of pure monism is illustrated by his example of a spark and aflame. He asserts that both are fire and, hence, are the same.

The *Bhakti* cult was getting more widespread. There were several sects following *Buddhism, Jainism, Śaivāites, Vaiśṇavaites, Tāntriks, Upaniṣadists* and *Lokūyatikas* to the extent that the orthodox *Brāhmanism* was beginning to be threatened. This is particularly so because none of the cults were supporting the orthodoxy of the caste system and the fancy religious rituals. Other great scholars during this period were concentrating in the fields of mathematics, astronomy, music, literature, architecture, medicine and fine arts.

Sāyaṇācārya, CE 1400, was the younger brother of

Mādhvācārya and the royal priest to King Vira Bukka of the Vijinagara Empire in the northern Deccan. He too had excelled in the studies of the *Vedas, Brāhmaṇas, Āraṇyakas* and all the *Smritis.* He had many priests working under him. Probably this assisted him to produce voluminous commentaries on the scriptures which have remained as the gold standard until the present time. He gave the definition of *Devatā, Ṛṣi, Mantra,* etc.

His commentary on the *Ṛg Veda* shows great bias towards traditional *Brāhminism.* He has interpreted many *Ṛks* which give great importance to *Brāhmin* priests. These also serve to remind the kings to be generous in rewarding the priests for their services. His commentaries re-emphasised the importance of *Brāhminism.* Southern India was still largely following orthodox *Brahminism* except at the southern tip, which had a significant presence of Christianity, Judaism and Islam.

The *Sikh* Philosophy: Guru Nānak and Guru Govind Singh[3]

Guru Nānak 1469–1539 CE. He was born in that part of Punjab near Lahore which is now in Pakistan. From an early age, he had begun to show signs of disaffection against orthodox *Brāhminism.* Although married and working as an accountant, he left home and went in search of spiritual satisfaction. He is said to have travelled all over India, Afghanistan and the Middle East for thirty years, meeting learned seers, philosophers and religious leaders. Eventually he formulated his own opinions, which are as follows:

- The way to spiritual growth is through meditation.
- There is only one God.
- All human beings can have direct access to

God without any need for priests and rituals.

- Everyone is equal, irrespective of birth and gender.

He established a new following. He built the first Gurdwāra at Kartarpur. His followers were called *Sikhs.* They chose a spiritual teacher to explain his teachings after his death in 1539 and maintained this tradition until the tenth teacher.

Guru Govind Singh was the tenth teacher of the *Sikhs*. He established a unique cultural order called the *Khālsa* – the Pure – and preached an ethical way of life, also known as the soldier saints, in 1699.

This became a religion, although there is no priest, no formal religious ritual, and no named god. He made a compendium of lectures preached by Guru Nānak and the subsequent gurus. This is called *Guru Grantha Sāhib* (the venerated tome of teaching). This compendium has been regarded as the spiritual guide of the *Sikhs* since his death in 1708. The *Sikhs,* who have taken initiation into the *Khālsa* sect, are known as *Amritdhāri Sikhs* and carry the *Khālsa* symbols, the five Ks, on their person.

K- keśa – preserved hair; signifies denial of pride in one's appearance.

K- kripāṇa – dagger; signifies protection of the weak and struggle against injustice.

K- kaṛā – bracelet; signifies restraint and gentility.

K- kacchā – a knee-length type of short; signifies chastity.

K- kanghā – a wooden comb; signifies a clean and organised mind and body.

Sevā is the mandatory service every *Sikh* must render to someone in the community. They do this through Gurdwāra (at the door of the Guru), which is like a temple without any deities, but where a copy of the *Guru Grantha Sāhib* is kept ceremoniously. Four doors – namely the door of Peace, the door of Livelihood, door of Learning and the door of Grace – lead to the interior sanctum of the Gurdwāra. Free food is prepared and served by volunteers to anyone who comes to pray and meditate in the Gurdwāra. This is part of the mandatory rendition of service to the needy.

Although the Muslim attacks and rule had not greatly affected the Indian intellectual world, apart from the destruction of their universities and libraries, there was no denying the cultural destruction incurred by India. Many believe that the *Sikhism* established by Guru Nānak was modified by the last Guru Govind Singh to counter these undesirable effects. This was an aesthetic attempt at protecting the Punjab from the relentless Muslim attacks from its eastern and western borders. The 'purity' emphasised by *Khālsa* was to signify the preservation of their culture and the protection of women from the defiling acts of these invaders.

References:

1. Smith, P. (2012). *Anthology of Poetry of the Chisti Sufi Order* (p. 183). Australia: New Humanity Books.

2. *Swaminarayan Darshan*, as quoted by APJ Abdul Kalam in *Transcendence (p. 22)*, 2015. India: Harper Collins.

3. bbc.co.uk/religion/religions/sikhism; accessed 24/12/2020.

CHAPTER 22

1500–1999 CE

Background:

The Delhi Sultanet was overcome in 1526 CE by Babur, a descendant of Cengis Khān, who established the Mughal Empire. By the time he died in 1530 CE this stretched from the Himalayas to Gwalior and the Indus to the Ganges in the east. The period of the Mughal dynasty in India saw great developments in architecture, trade and commerce. India had become very prosperous. This empire lasted until 1870, when India became a colony of the British, although the East India Company had already become a major influence in life there by 1670 CE. Babur's grandson, Emperor Akabar, was known as agreat patron of arts, music and literature. He respected all religions in India and did not encourage any interference in their practices. His great grandson, Prince Dara Sikoh, was a Sufi scholar, who learned Sanskrit and translated several *Upanişads* into Persian. However, his brother Aurangazeb (1658-1707) was a cruel ruler, intolerant of all other religions, and persecuted many groups indiscriminately all over the empire. The Deccan kingdoms and most of the rest of India were under his domain. This destabilised the empire by changing the existing political alliance among the Rajahs of several smaller vassal states.

Along with this, the political upheaval and the religious discontent among the masses presented great opportunities to The British East India Company, who had landed on the western port of Gujarat in 1609 with two ships bringing luxury goods for trade. At that time India, under the Mogul

Emperor Shah Jahan, was probably the wealthiest nation; this was estimated to be 23% of the wealth of the entire world[1]. These conditions were ruthlessly exploited by the British. The British not only colonised the huge geographical area but, more importantly, the minds of several generations of Indians, who actually began to believe that the Indians needed to be educated, to be civilised and accept Western supremacy. They had been indoctrinated sufficiently to believe that the Western culture and ethical values were far superior to their Indian heritage. This notion is still being entertained by many. It is worth quoting Thomas Macaulay. He was instrumental in establishing the British education system in India and, in 1835, said:

> "... We must at present do our best to form a class who may be interpreters between us and the millions whom we govern; a class of persons, Indian in blood and colour, but English in taste, in opinions, morals and in intellect ...".[2]

The result of this education, in a most unpredictable manner, also ignited the spark of patriotism in India, which was not the intended purpose. This heralded the search for a new order of thinking, which could perhaps assimilate the newer Christian values and the traditional Indian philosophy, which would help in removing colonial rule in India. The practical application of religion to foster nationalism had begun, probably for the first time. The social reformers also became disgusted with the great favouritism shown by the British colonials to the privileged people belonging to Brahmin caste. This had encouraged the creation of a social system worse than the most severe type of apartheid ever seen in this world. Hence the rise of *Aryasamaja* and *Brahmasamaja*.

References:

1. Tharoor, S. (2016). *An Era of Darkness* (p. 4). New Delhi: Rupa Publications.
2. Ibid (pp. 215–238).

❖

The *Brahmasamāja*: Ram Mohan Roy, 1772–1833 CE.

Born in a *Brāhmin* family, he had studied Sanskrit and sought answers to his queries on spirituality and religion in the *Vedas* and the *Upaniṣads*. He continued his spiritual pursuits by translating the *Veda* Mantras and *Upaniṣads* into Bengali and English. He was honoured for this work by the French.

As a social reformer, he became a journalist and the founder and editor of two newspapers to try to dispel the morass of superstition and ugly tenets of *Brāhminism* present during his time. He saw the necessity of creating a focus group to propagate his values and put pressure on the British for reforms. So a *Brahma Samaj* was established in 1815 CE, which reconverted the Christians and Moslems who were originally Hindu followers back into Hinduism. This cult did not accept the caste system, the *Sati* (suttee) custom, and promoted the pure *Upaniṣadic* concepts of monotheism, the monism of *Brahma*. He had a good following among the progressive Bengali intelligentsia but was loathed by the orthodox *Brāhmins* and accused of being a renegade.[1]

He founded the Vedanta College in 1822 to teach the true *Vedic* concepts and monotheism. He had opposed the establishment of a Sanskrit College at Calcutta because that would have reinforced the corrupt *Brāhminism*. He wrote and published a book, *Precepts of Jesus, the Guide to Peace and Happiness*, to remind the Christian missionaries of the true meaning of the Gospel so that their practice of coerced conversion into Christianity would be stopped.

He became the first political activist protesting for freedom of speech, religion and also against the British systems of tax and revenue collections. He was given the Title of 'Raja' by the Muslim ruler of Bengal and sent as his emissary to London. He died in Leicester in 1833 before he could return to continue his political and social activism. He was the second philosopher after *Kautilya* to suggest religion and patriotism as the tools for political purposes.

Swami Dayānanda Saraswati, 1825–1883 CE.

Born in a *Brahmin* family in Gujarat, Mūla Śānkara was a thoughtful and devout boy until he became disillusioned by the death of his young sister. He ran away from home at the age of fourteen in search of the true knowledge. After twenty years of meeting many scholars, saints and wise men all over India, he eventually met his guru at Mathura, who directed him to study the *Vedas*, which he did. His guru renamed him Dayānanda Saraswati. He became satisfied with the knowledge imparted by the *Vedas*. He began to re-establish the true *Vedic* philosophy and renounce the orthodoxy of *Brāhminism*.

He believed in the spirituality as propounded in the *Ṛks* of the *Ṛg Veda*. Preservation of the purity of faith in the *Vedas* was of utmost importance to him. He strongly advocated the concepts of *Dharma*, which he believed to be free from any bias and as was the embodiment of righteousness; it was not the performance of any *Yagńa. Adharma* was falsehood and everything that was in opposition to the true teachings of the *Vedas.*

He disowned the practice of priesthood, idol worship, sacrificing an animal and the caste system.*

He established a new order in society, known as the *Ārya Samāj*, on 7th April 1875, which was founded on the following philosophy.[2]

1. *God is the efficient cause of all true knowledge.*
2. *He is existent, blissful, formless, omnipotent, immanent, and eternal without any beginning or end. He alone is worthy of worship.*
3. *The four Vedas are the only true scriptures.*
4. *One should be forever ready to accept the truth and to reject falsehood.*
5. *All acts should be performed according to Dharma.*
6. *The main purpose of the Ārya Samāja is to do good to people in society.*
7. *Our conduct in life should be guided by righteousness and love.*
8. *We should promote Vidyā and dispel Avidyā.*
9. *We must not be content with our own welfare but should be equally conscious for others also.*
10. *One should restrain oneself to the rules to promote the well-being of all but should be free to pursue the rules for one's own Dharma.*

Dayānanda encouraged people to go back to the *Vedas* and

---

* The relevant original works, which are free of copyright restrictions, are given in italics.

its uncorrupted spiritual teaching. He tried to advocate various social issues – women's rights, education, widows' welfare and remarriage. He was the first philosopher to lead a political movement – the freedom fighters of India – against British rule. He created a social reform group – the Arya Samaj – before declaring "India is for Indians" the following year in Bombay. He was the first philosopher to demonstrate two principles:

i. The establishment of a righteous foundation first is essential to achieve a political gain.

ii. A combination of religion and patriotism becomes a powerful political tool.

This second concept was subsequently used very effectively by Lokamānya Tilak, Subāś Bose, Sāvarkar, Lājapat Roy and later by Gāndhi to spread and strengthen the freedom movement in India. Rebellious socialism was added to this movement by the spiritualist Swāmi Vivekānanda.

References:

1. Raja Ram Mohan Rao. Wikipedia; accessed 05/11/2020.

2. *www.arya-samaj.org, accessed 03/11/2020.*

❖

Vivekānanda, 1863–1902 CE.

"Feel like Christ and you will be a Christ; feel like Buddha and you will be a Buddha".

"My ideal indeed can be put into a few words and that is: to preach unto mankind their divinity and how to make it manifest in every movement of life". Vivekānanda

He was born as Narendranāth Ghose in Kolkatā. He had a

good voice and would often be invited to sing classical and devotional songs at social gatherings, thus supplementing his modest resources while studying at the Presidency College. He believed in the recently established *Brahma Samāj* and used to be associated with its activities. He became a graduate but did not get any regular employment. He became Swāmi Vivekānanda after being initiated as a *Sanyāsi* by his spiritual mentor, *Sri Rāmakṛśṇa Paramhamsa,* the most benevolent *Tāntrik* sage who was the priest at the temple of *Kāli* at Dakśineśwor near Kolkatā.

Vivekānanda preached the fundamentals of the doctrines of the *Upaniṣads,* did not accept the traditional *Brāhmin* orthodoxy, and believed *Brahma* manifested in everything. He believed in universal oneness - meaning all were ultimately the same *Brahma,* the Spirit. He was the first of the holy men from India to ever leave the Indian subcontinent - the holy land of the *Brāhmins* - and to travel to the lands of *Mlechhas,* the non-believers. Swāmi Vivekānanda was the first Indian philosopher, mystic and a spiritualist to preach *Brahma* of the *Upaniṣads* as accurately and authoritatively as possible to the West. He spoke at the Parliament of Religions in Chicago in 1893, addressing the 7000 delegates as "Brothers and Sisters of America", thus espousing the concept of the 'world brotherhood'. He explained the difference between religion and spiritualism. Religious differences were many, but the spiritualism was the same. He illustrated the essence of this philosophy through the story of a frog living in a well. He quoted his spiritual leader who had experienced this oneness with the Spirit in all religions by practising meditation as a Hindu, a Muslim, and a Christian.

Swāmi Vivekānanda gave credit for all his actions to his

guru. He believed in a healthy body for a healthy mind and that service and love to all brought true happiness to one. Mokśha was achieved in the current life and not after death. He believed in the eternal nature of *Brahma* and all his manifestations, thus differing from the traditional belief in a creator who had created this world. He died aged thirty-nine but managed to preach the universal values of love, compassion and service to all. His call for the emancipation of unprivileged classes was also a veiled warning to the ruling British of the revolt that would ensue against them if they did not mend their ways.

I quote his original statements from 'All power is within you' in the following paragraphs:

Socialism with a spiritual basis:

"Each individual has to work out his own solution; there is no other way, and so also with nations. ... everything goes to show that Socialism or some form of rule by the people, call it what you will, is coming on the boards. The people will certainly want the satisfaction of their material needs, less work, no oppression, no war, more food. What guarantee have we that this or any civilisation will last unless it is based on religion, on the goodness of man?

... human society is governed by four castes – the priests, the soldiers, the traders and the labourers ... last will come the labourer (Śūdra) rule. All the members of society ought to have the same opportunity for obtaining wealth, education or knowledge ... Freedom in all matters i.e., advance towards Mukti, is the worthiest gain of man ... Those social rules which come in the way of unfoldment of freedom are injurious; and steps should be taken to destroy them speedily. Those institutions should be encouraged by which men advance in the path of freedom.

Remember the nation lives in a cottage. The peasant, the shoemaker, the sweeper, and such other lower classes of India have much greater capacity for work and self-reliance than you. They have been silently working through ages and producing the entire wealth of the land without a word of complaint. Very soon they will get above you in position. Gradually capital is drifting into their hands, and they are not so much in trouble with wants as you are. Modern education has changed your fashion, but new avenues of wealth lie yet undiscovered for want of the inventive genius. You have so long oppressed these forbearing masses; now is the time for their retribution. And you will become extinct in your vain search for employment, making it the be-all and end-all of your life!

If the labourers stop work, your supply of food and clothes also stops. And you regard them as low-class people and flaunt about your own culture! Engrossed in the struggle for existence, they had not the opportunity for awakening of knowledge. They have worked so long uniformly like machines guided by human intelligence, and the clever educated sections have taken the substantial part of the fruit of their labour. In every country this has been the case. But times have changed. The lower classes are awakening to this fact and making a united front against this, determined to exact their legitimate dues...The upper classes will no longer be able to repress the lower, try they ever so much. The well-being of the higher classes now lies in helping the lower to get their legitimate rights.

When the masses will wake up, they will come to understand your oppression on them, and by a puff of their mouth you will be entirely blown off! It is they who have introduced civilisation amongst you; and it is they who will pull it down... Therefore, I say, try to rouse these lower classes from slumber by imparting learning and culture to them. When they will awaken – and awaken one day they must – they will also not forget your good services to them and will remain grateful to you...

Before flooding India with socialistic* or political ideas, first deluge the land with spiritual ideas. The first work that demands our attention is, that the most wonderful truths confined in our *Upaniṣads,* in our scriptures, in *Purānas* – must be brought out from the books; brought out from the monasteries, brought out from forests, brought out from the possession of selected bodies of people, and scattered broadcast all over the land... Make them understand their real condition and say, "O ye brothers all Arise! Awake! How much longer will you remain asleep?"

"All philosophy and scriptures have come from the plane of relative knowledge of subject and object. But no thought or language of the human mind can fully express the Reality which lies beyond the plane of relative knowledge! Science, philosophy etc. are only the partial truths. So they can never be adequate channels of expression for the transcendent Reality. Hence viewed from the transcendent standpoint, everything appears to be unreal – the religious creeds, and works and, I and thou, and the universe – everything is unreal. Then only it is perceived: "I am the only reality; I am the all-pervading *Ātmā* and I am the proof of my own

---

* Karl Marx, 1818–1883; *The Communist Manifesto* was published in 1848. Vivekānanda could have had access to it during his visit to England in 1893.

existence." Where is the room for a separate proof to establish the reality of my existence? I am as the scriptures say, '*nityam asmat prasiddham*' – always known to myself as the eternal subject I have seen that state, realised it."

His main contribution remains the explanation of the sublime philosophy of *Brahma* and propagation of this sublime truth to the rest of the world. After a profound meditation under a peepul tree in August 1890, he declared.

"Here under this peepul tree one of the greatest problems of my life has been solved: I have found the oneness of the macrocosm with the microcosm. In this microcosm of the body everything that is there [in the macrocosm] exists. I have seen the whole universe within an atom.

I have experienced even in my insignificant life that good motives, sincerity, and infinite love can conquer the world. One single soul possessed of these virtues can destroy the dark designs of millions of hypocrites and brutes.

Man is constituted of the will, emotion and cognition. These qualities can be harnessed and sublimated to the divine level. *Karma Yoga* and *Raja Yoga* are the paths both to vitalise and spiritualise the will in man. *Bhakti Yoga* purifies and divinizes emotion and raises man to Godhead. *Jňana Yoga* sharpens the intellect and transforms it into intuition. These paths are not exclusive of one another, but they blend into a wholesome self-culture. The message of Swāmi Vivekānanda is to evolve superman by inculcating the practice of these time honoured *Yogas*.

Death is inevitable, let the body fall in serving a noble cause. ... The highest truth is this: There is no other God to seek. He alone serves God who serves all beings.

The *Vedānta* teaches man to have faith in themselves first. As certain religions of the world say that a man who does not believe in a personal God outside of himself is an atheist, so the *Vedānta* says a man who does not believe in himself is an atheist. Not believing in the glory of our own Soul is what *Vedānta* calls atheism. To many this is no doubt a terrible idea; and most of us think that this ideal can never be reached; but the *Vedānta* insists that it can be realised by everyone.

As soon as you say, 'I am a little mortal being', you are saying something which is not true. You are giving the lie to yourselves; you are hypnotising yourselves into something vile and weak and wretched.

The greatest error, says the *Vedānta*, is to say that you are weak, that you are a sinner, a miserable creature, and that you have no power, and you cannot do this and that. Every time you think in that way, you, as it were, rivet one more link in the chain that binds you down, and add one more layer of hypnotism on to your own soul ... No man becomes purer and purer, it is a matter of great manifestation. The veil drops away, and the native purity of the soul begins to manifest itself.

The ideal of faith in ourselves is of the greatest help to us. If faith in ourselves had been more extensively taught and practised, I am sure a large portion of the evils and miseries that we have would have vanished.

Do you feel for others? If you do, you are growing in oneness. If you do not feel for others, you may be the most intellectual giant ever born, but you will be nothing; you are but dry intellect and you will remain so. And if you feel, even if you cannot read any book and do not know any language, you are in the right way ... Feel like Christ and you will be a Christ; feel like Buddha and you will be a Buddha. It is the feeling that is the life, the strength.

Vedanta formulates not universal brotherhood but universal oneness. I am the same as any other man, as any animal – good or bad, anything. It is one body, one mind, one soul throughout. Spirit never dies. How can even the body die? One leaf may fall – does the tree die? The universe is my body. See how it continues. All minds are mine; with all feet I walk; through all mouths I speak. In everybody I reside.

Silly fools tell you that you are sinners, and you sit down in a corner and weep. It is foolishness, wickedness, downright rascality to say that you are sinners! You are all God. See you not God and call Him man?

The *Vedānta* says, there is nothing that is not God. It may frighten many of you, but you will understand by degrees. The living God is within you, and yet you are building churches and temples and believing all sorts of imaginary nonsense. The only God to worship is the human soul, in the human body. Of course, all animals are temples too, but man is the highest, the Taj Mahal of temples.

None can teach you; none can make a spiritual man of you; you have to teach yourself; your growth must come from inside. What can an external teacher do? He can remove the obstruction a little, and there his duty ends.

The ideal of *Vedānta* is to know man as he really is, and this is its message, that if you cannot worship your brother man, the manifested God, how can you worship a God who is unmanifested?... but I have the same God in me, as you have in you. And that is what we want, no privilege for anyone, equal chances for all; let everyone be taught that the Divine is within him, and everyone will work out his own salvation.

Gift of political knowledge can be made with the blast of trumpets and the march of cohorts, gifts of secular knowledge with fire or sword. But spiritual knowledge can only be given in silence like the dew that falls unseen and unheard yet bringing into blossom masses of roses. This has been the gift of India to the world again and again.

Do not care for dogmas, or sects, or churches or temples; they count for little compared with the essence of existence in each man, which is spirituality, and the more this is developed in a man, the more powerful is he for good.

What I want to propagate is a religion that will be equally acceptable to all minds; it must be equally philosophic, equally emotional, equally mystic, and equally conducive to action ... And this combination will be the ideal, the nearest approach to a universal religion. Would to God that all men were so constituted that in their minds all these elements of philosophy, mysticism and work were equally present in full. That is the ideal, my ideal of a perfect man. Everyone who has only one or two of these elements of character, I consider 'one-sided'; and this world is almost full of such one-sided men with knowledge of that one road only in which they move; and everything else is dangerous and horrible to them. To become harmoniously balanced in all these four directions is my ideal of religion.

What is the watchword of all ethical codes? "Not I, but thou". The happiest moments we ever know are when we entirely forget ourselves."**

❖

Sri Aurobindo, 1872–1950 CE.

Born as Arabinda Ghosh in an Anglophile Bengali family, he was educated at St Paul's School in London and then at Cambridge University. Professor Aurobindo was a scholar, a linguist, with mastery over Sanskrit, English, Greek and Latin, and native Indian languages.

Political philosophy:

Sri Aurobindo became a political activist at first, taking up the editorship of the magazine *Bande Mātaram*. Sri Aurobindo's political philosophy was inspired by two predecessors: Swāmi Dayānanda Saraswati and Rām Mohan Roy. He was prepared for armed struggle to achieve independence from the British and had a large following, including Subash Chandra Bose. He had been supporting the Indian Nationalist movement from Baroda from 1893–1900. He became well known as a freedom fighter when he came out in the open as the editor of a political journal advocating Indian independence. As an activist, he was imprisoned three times but released due to lack of evidence. He is credited with being the first to demand total independence from the British. He declared in *Bande Mātaram:*

"Political freedom is the life-breath of a nation; to attempt social reform, educational reform, industrial expansion, the moral improvement of the race without aiming first and foremost at political freedom, is the very height of ignorance and futility. ... The primary requisite national progress,

---

** From: Swāmi Vivekānanda on Himself.

national reform, is the free habit of free and healthy national thought and action which is impossible in a state of servitude."

He sought asylum in Pondicherry, which was under French control, to escape continuing persecution by the British. Soon after this he became interested in philosophy and mysticism and began to write prodigiously. He established an Āśrama there in 1926, with the help of a French lady known as the Mother, who became his spiritual collaborator****. He died in 1950, but the Mother became his spiritual successor and continued to preach his ideas. He wrote for *Ārya* regularly. His well-known works are published as *The Life Divine, Synthesis of Yoga, The Secret of the Veda* and *Essays on the Gitā and Sāvitri.* The Āśrama is active but the Auroville is currently under Government of India administration and, sadly, not able to inspire and enthuse the ideals of its founder.

Supermind and mysticism:

He suggests that there is a continuous involution and evolution of the Supreme, variously known as the Primal Energy, *Brahma,* God, *Parameśwara* or *Puruṣa.* Just as life from matter evolves into a being, a mind, an intellect, a soul and *Brahma,* the reverse process is also equally true. He personally experienced the state of oneness with the divine being during his meditation and began to speak with conviction. He left political activities after this experience.

*** Auroville continues to propagate his teachings. The Mother established the Auroville, a Utopian infrastructure, to help people reach this higher level of mental development, i.e., to achieve the Supermind. Sadly, a casual visitor to *Mātrimandir* – their central hub of the whole philosophical concepts – gets the impression of this being another new cult in the making, which is way out of its intended objective.

He made no apology for the interwoven religion and esoteric concepts in Indian philosophy and declared, "Philosophy is the intellectual search for the fundamental truth of things. Religion is the attempt to make the truth dynamic in the soul of man. They are essential to each other. A religion that is not the expression of philosophic truth degenerates into superstition and obscurantism, a philosophy which does not dynamise itself with the religious spirit is a barren light, for it cannot get itself practised".[1]

He differed greatly from Śankarācārya's monism and proposed that the world was real.

He wrote:

"We speak of the evolution of Life in Matter, the evolution of Mind in Matter; but evolution is a word which merely states the phenomenon without explaining it. For there seems to be no reason why Life should evolve out of material elements or mind out of the living form, unless we accept the Vedantic solution that Life is already involved in Matter and Mind in Life, because in essence Matter is a form of veiled Life, Life a form of veiled Consciousness.[2]

"A certain kind of Agnosticism is the final truth of all knowledge. For when we come to the end of whatever path, the universe appears as only a symbol or an appearance of an unknowable Reality which translates here into different systems, physical values, vital and sensational values, intellectual, ideal and spiritual values.[3]

"It is *Vidyā,* the knowledge of oneness that we know as God; without it *Avidyā,* the relative and multiple consciousnesses, is a night of darkness and a disorder of ignorance. Yet if we exclude that field of ignorance, if we get rid of *Avidya,* as if it were a thing non-existent and unreal, then knowledge itself becomes a sort of obscurity and a source of imperfection. We become as men blinded by light so that we can no longer see the field which that illumines."[4]

Sri Aurobindo suggests that this kind of mental awareness does not come without effort. It is necessary for man to prepare himself for this leap into super-mind by an elaborate discipline of *Yoga* which he calls the *Integral Yoga* – the comprehensive and all-inclusive transformation of the mind and the life of the individual. The essence of his teaching is that a super-mind exists between the manifest world and the Spirit which is the dynamic manifestation of the Absolute.

References:

1. Radhakrishnan, S; Moore, C. A. (1973). *A Source Book in Indian Philosophy* (p. 578). New Jersey: Princeton University Press.
2. Aurobindo, S. (2017). *The Life Divine.* (p. 55) Pondicherry: Sri Aurobindo Āśram Trust.
3. Ibid, (pp. 710–15).
4. Ibid, (p. 879).

❖

Mohandas Karamchand Gandhi [*Mahātmā Gāndhi].*

Mohandas Gandhi was born in Gujarat in 1869. He was the son of a very high-ranking officer, *Diwān,* in that province which was also under British rule. He read law at London and became a barrister before returning with a view to eventually succeeding his father. However, he could not succeed as a lawyer there and went to South Africa, where he became a successful barrister and a civil rights leader of the expat Indians. He had developed a unique system of political and moral philosophy which became highly effective. His biographer, Louis Fischer, describes this transformation as "a remarkable case of second birth in one lifetime". He had been greatly influenced by Leo Tolstoy and John Ruskin.

He returned to India with this experience. He established Sabarmati Āśram and began undertaking the creation of an ideal community. He practised celibacy [began to regard his wife as mother], self-discipline and the highest standard of austerity and morality. Because of his pious values, service to the downtrodden, his stand against man's inhumanity to man and renunciation of all worldly possessions, he was revered as *Mahātmā* and was regarded as the Father of the Nation.

He also led India into independence, did not hold any office but was the most influential and powerful political leader of Indians. India became independent on 16 August 1947. He was shot dead by Nathuram Godse, a Hindu bigot, while MG was going to take part in the evening prayer meeting at Delhi. One and a half million people marched behind his cortège and a further million watched his funeral. Prime Minister Jawaharlal Nehru, wiping his tears and choked with emotion, informed the nation:

"... the light that has illumined this country for these many years will illumine this country for many more years, and a thousand years later that light will still be seen in this country, and the world will see it and it will give solace to innumerable hearts. For that light represented the living truth, and the eternal man was with us with his eternal truth reminding us of the right path, dawning us from error, taking this ancient country to freedom ... A madman has put an end to his life." All India Radio broadcast.

And the whole nation wept with him. Millions more in the world mourned his death.

The Gāndhian philosophy:

Gandhi began by infusing a sense of self-confidence and ethical values among the expat Indians in South Africa. He advised them to disregard caste and religious differences and to speak the truth, even in business. To his Christian friends who wished him to convert to Christianity, his answer was, "I do not seek redemption from the consequences of sin but from the sin itself". He developed his political philosophy, *Satyāgraha,* while in Durban. It has been said that MG took the concept of civil disobedience from Thoreau, the famous American who opposed black slavery. MG has denied this in a letter and explained that civil disobedience failed to convey the full meaning of the struggle and hence he had coined *Satyāgraha* [*Satya* = truth which gives power, strength, love; *āgraha* = persuade, request, entreat, enthuse, induce] to his philosophy. Powerful persuasion conducted peacefully was *Satyāgraha.* This was not 'passive resistance' but a most powerful and dynamic tool to a political activist. He illustrated this in his own words: "... it is to obey the law of final supremacy of spirit over matter; of liberty and love over brute force". He explained that it was not part of the tactics to humiliate or embitter the opponent by taking advantage of his adverse conditions, but to hope by sincerity, chivalry and self-suffering to convince his brain and conquer his heart. "A *satyāgrahi* should have no fear, therefore he never becomes afraid to trust the opponent – implicit trust in human nature is the very essence of his creed". He further emphasised saying "the physical force is nothing compared to moral force and that moral force never fails."[1]

He was another believer in the religious and cultural syncretism among the diverse ethnic groups of Indians. He was equally supported by the Muslims and the Christians in his struggle for Indian independence. This was resented by the ruling British administration. Hence this cooperation and brotherhood among the political activists of different faiths in India was significantly weakened by the British, who were instrumental in establishing a political party to orchestrate the partition of India. The Muslim League was established in 1906. Its leaders could be manipulated to suit the British interests. Its staunch leader, Jinnah, switched to the Muslim League from the Indian National Congress and eventually became the founding father of Pakistan. However, two thirds of the Muslims in India chose to remain in India and only about seven million migrated to Pakistan. Thirteen million Indians were displaced.[2]

What did he give to India and to the world?

MG's philosophy of non-violent activism, *Satyāgraha*, and cultural syncretism, has been adopted worldwide, not only for political activism but also for social reforms. Martin Luther King Jr used this effectively in the USA against social discrimination and racism. Nelson Mandela used this doctrine to develop the post-apartheid South Africa as a 'rainbow nation'. Gandhi had been nominated for the Nobel Peace Prize five times but never received the award. The UN has made 2nd October, his date of birth, the International Day of Non-Violence. He is a well-known name all over the world.

Albert Einstein, Lord Mountbatten, and many more distinguished people from all over the world praised him. I find the most poignant comment was from General Douglas MacArthur, the victor of Japan in WW2, who said, "In the evolution of civilisation, if it is to survive, all men cannot fail eventually to adopt Gandhi's belief that the process of mass application of force to resolve contentious issues is fundamentally not only wrong but contains within itself the germs of self-destruction".[3]

Many, however, accuse him of precipitating the severe consequences of the partition of India which saw nearly 15 million migrate and the tragic Hindu Muslim riots which killed millions of Indians. They might ask: 'would armed struggle for Indian independence have resulted in so many deaths and the partition of a nation'? We shall never know, of course, but all we can say is that there was an Indian who sacrificed his life to uphold the values of humility, selfless love and service to fellow humans. He was as much of a Sufi saint as a Hindu Mahatma.

References:

1. Fischer, L. (1997). *The Life of Mahatma Gandhi* (p. 227). Harper Collins.
2. Tharoor, S. (2016). *An Era of Darkness* (p. 174). Aleph Book Company.
3. Fischer, L. (1997). *The Life of Mahatma Gandhi* (p. 21). Harper Collins.

❖

Dr Sarvepalli Rādhākṛṣṇan, 1888–1975.

Dr Rādhākṛṣṇan is the most quoted and famous Indian philosopher of the last millennium. Born in a humble Telugu *Brāhmin* family, he won a scholarship to study at the Madras Christian College, Tamilnadu, India, where he subsequently became a professor. After several prestigious professorships in India, he was appointed the Spalding Professor of Eastern Religion and Ethics at Oxford University and was knighted by King George V in 1931. He became the Indian ambassador to USSR in 1949, Vice-President of India in 1952 and the second President of India in 1957. He preferred Doctor rather than Sir as prefix to his name after Indian independence, although we have no definite knowledge if he ever relinquished the British Knighthood. He was a world-renowned scholar, statesman and teacher. His birthday, 5th September, is celebrated in India as Teachers' Day. He also received many prestigious national and international awards and honorary titles, the last being the 'The Knight of the Golden Army of Angels', conferred by Pope Paul in 1964. He was also nominated for the Nobel Prize for Literature sixteen times.

Philosophy of Dr Rādhākṛśnan

His co-author, C. A. Moore, summarises his philosophy thus: "In essence, his philosophy is absolute idealism, but in a form and with a dynamic character which, instead of nullifying the great richness of many facets of life and experience in terms of a wholly transcendental Absolute, recognises the reality and the meaning of the many aspects and grades of experience". I am tempted to paraphrase this sentence as 'he was a pragmatist'. He interpreted the *Advaita* philosophy of *Śankara* in a way which would make it acceptable to many. He was deeply impressed by his earlier exposure to Christianity and freely admitted, "I was not able to confine philosophy to logic and epistemology". However, he accepted that, "When the Vedas are regarded as the highest authority, all that is meant is that the most exacting of all authorities is the authority of facts".[1]

He was also a deep scholar of the Bible along with the *Vedas*, the *Upaniṣads* and the *Smritis*. His suggestions that human beings were banished from heaven and that they became ignorant by drinking the waters of the Leth, and his complete faith in the *Puraṇic* characters, would suggest his belief in Greek mythology, the Bible and the *Puraṇas.*[2] He had profound knowledge of the *Vedas*, *Gītā* and the *Upaniṣads.* However, he followed traditional *Brāhminism* in his translations of the *Gītā* and his commentary on Indian philosophy so comprehensively presented in two volumes. Dr Rādhakrṣṇan did not propound a novel concept himself.

He had a unique style of comparative expositions of the *Upaniṣads* and *Smritis* with Biblical anecdotes, Christian saints, and scholars. He was deeply impressed by the Western philosophers like Kant, Muirhead, Whitehead, Plato and Hegel, and agreed with many ideas put forward by the liberal Italian philosopher Benedito Croce. He is thus known as the bridge between the Indian and the Western philosophies. Several examples of this are seen in his book *An Idealist View of Life*, e.g., "The unity of man and God is the fundamental thesis of the great philosophic tradition which has come down to us from the *Upaniṣads* and Plato. Aristotle, Plotinus, Śankara, Spinoza, Bradley and a host of others are witnesses to it."[3]

References:

1. Rādhakrṣṇan, S; Moore, C. A. *A Source Book in*

Indian Philosophy (p. 616). New Jersey: Princeton University Press.

2. Ibid, (p. 628).
3. Ibid, (p. 631).

❖

APJ Abdul Kalam, 1931–2015.

A most charismatic personality, a physicist, scientist, spiritualist, poet, and a dreamer, APJ Abdul Kalam is probably the most influential philosopher who has been able to ignite the minds of 700 million people of India under the age of thirty-five. He was also known as the Rocket Man of India. He was the eleventh President of India, 2002–07. He also became known as the People's President. He was born in a poor, devout family of a Muslim boat man who was highly respected in the pilgrim town of Rameshwaram. Kalam studied in the local school and then physics at St Joseph's College, Trichi. He read Aeronautical Engineering at MIT Madras. He was subsequently trained by some of the most eminent scientists in India, viz. Dr Vikram Sārābhāi and Professor S. Dhavan, and by working in advanced space research, rocket science and nuclear laboratories. He was the dIrector who successfully developed the missile programme and the nuclear bombs in India. He was elected by a large consensus to be the President of India after his retirement as a scientist. He declined to accept a second term, preferring to teach young people of India and inspiring them to attain great heights. His purpose in making India nuclear and missile-capable was to make her a 'developed' nation which would restore the pride and confidence of the Indians who had been subject to English rule and humiliation for more than 200 years.

Philosophy of APJ Abdul Kalam.

He had been deeply impressed by Hindu, Christian, and Muslim faiths since early childhood.[1] Along with the Quran, he was equally well versed in the Srutis, the Smritis and the Bible. He wrote, "the example of those inter-religious meetings at my family home is most worthy of emulation. Because now, throughout the nation and the world, the need for such frank and general dialogue among cultures, religions and civilisations is more urgent than ever". His spiritual guru was the Pramukh Swamiji of the Swaminarayan Sect, Akshardham, Ahmedabad. He declared in the parliament during his acceptance speech as the newly elected President of India, "I would like to endeavour to bring about unity of minds among the divergent traditions of our country".[2]

He said, "for great men, religion is a way of making friends; small people make religion a fighting tool".[3]

He initiated the famous 'What Can I Give' movement among the youths in India, encouraging them to excel in their vocation and in service to the community and the mother land.

He ended his book *Transcendence* with the following:

"All of us – bright atheists and committed religionists – need to awaken now and hear the earth's call ... The only thing that will redeem humankind is cooperation ... and working towards a planet transformed by our care".[4] He died of a sudden heart attack when he was giving a talk to university students in Guwahati, Assam, on the preservation of the earth.

His legacy is this syncretism that he embodied in appreciating various elements of the many spiritual and cultural traditions of India. He began his autobiography by quoting from the *Atharva Veda*:[5]

"This earth is His, to Him belong those vast and boundless skies

Both seas within Him rest, and yet in that small pool He lies".

He was the first philosopher, scientist, poet, and simple man who was able to demonstrate by his life the symbiotic relationship between science and spirituality.

References:

1. Kalam, A. P. J. (2015). *Transcendence* (p. ix). New Delhi: Harper Collins.
2. *Ṛg Veda* 10.191.4.
3. Kalam, A. P. J. *Ignited Minds* (p. 108). India: Penguin books.
4. Kalam, A. P. J. (2015). *Transcendence* (p. 225). New Delhi: Harper Collins.
5. *Atharva Veda*, 4, 16.

❖

The Dalai Lama, 1931-

The current most famous, yellow-hatted Lama is believed to be the 14th Dalai Lama. Born in a farming family in north-east Tibet, he was known as *Lhamo Dhondup*. At two years of age, he was recognised by the monks as the incarnation of the 13th Dalai Lama, *Thubten Ghyatso*. He was then educated until the age of twenty-three and subjected to the highest examination. He assumed the office of the Dalai Lama in 1954. He lives in exile in northern India and received the Nobel Peace Prize in 1989.

He is regarded as the *Avalokiteshwara* by his sect, the *Dugpas,* but claims to represent all Tibetan people. He has relinquished his executive power as the head of Tibetan State in Exile. His books and several interviews reiterate Buddha's view, which are more like the *Theravādin* than the *Mahāyāna* School of Buddhism. He is more of a spiritual teacher of the people of the world than a philosopher. According to H. C. Cutler, "he applies the principles of Buddhism to everyday problems and reveals how one can find balance and mental and spiritual freedom".

❖

CHAPTER 23

Conclusion

The time-travels as described in the foregoing chapters compel us to ask, "What is the relevance of all those ancient philosophical concepts in modern times?" Strange as it may seem, the quest of humanity even today is still the same search for that bliss or happiness, which had started in prehistoric times. This search has been the objective of Indian philosophy.

This brings us to the second question: "What have we learned so far?"

I find that the *Vedic* mantras freely and honestly admitted the various uncertainties and conjectures about creation and other esoteric issues. They had, however, succeeded in establishing a Utopian social system, the *Satya Yuga,* with moral and ethical values which have lasted until the present time.

The *Brahmins* were aware that the Ultimate *Brahma* did not vocalise – hence they created the 'Creator *Brahmā' and* many gods and mythological characters to persuade people into their fold. We can see that the rigidly administered theosophy, which was totally incompatible with the idealistic *Ṛg Veda*, began to prosper under the guise of *Brahminism.* This evolved into what is known as religion in modern parlance. This religion, named by the English as Hinduism, although described by Megasthenes as the 'religion of the Indus', despite being based on myths, fantasies, truthfulness, superstitions and faith, had become very successful in establishing a sophisticated culture, which produced advancement in music, dance, literature, astronomy, medicine and mathematics. *Brahminism*, although very draconian in its implementation, nevertheless encouraged security, further advancement of knowledge, arts and crafts and literature. But this has become an example today of how a system could degenerate into abhorrent social decadence. Paradoxically, this also led on to higher philosophical thinking and its manuals produced the *Upaniṣads*, heralding the era of Renaissance, the era of doubts, the *Dwāpara Yuga*. The *Vedāntīs*, i.e., the *Upaniṣadists*, were divided into two groups, one supporting traditional *Brahminism* and the other presenting a separate doctrine headed by *Brahmā*.

The great reformers during the renaissance tried to re-emphasise the ethical and moral values by using superstition as a means to do so. The Vaiśeṣika of Kaṇāda and Nyāya of Gotama established the foundations of acceptable epistemology which has been the hallmark of Indian philosophy. We are advised that the validity of an argument, a proposition or a concept must be corroborated by irrefutable evidence. Kaṇāda and Gotama have gone even further and established the essential requirement for any entity to qualify as valid evidence. *Samkhya* has proposed the best possible theory of spontaneous creation (evolution) of the universe. No other philosophy has been able to postulate an alternative explanation of the formation and dissolution, as *Samkhya* does. *Yoga* and *Tantra* have focussed on metaphysical aspects and shown the methods of how the physical and the non-physical entities can be harnessed for the achievement of the ultimate bliss.

In order to shake off the undesirable draconian system of

Brahminism which was being justified as the divine order, the atheist schools of *Cārbāka, Mahāvīra* and *Buddha* initiated new orders, promoting equality, nonviolence, love, and universal brotherhood which were the original *Vedic* concepts. Although partially successful until the 7th CE, they have also gone into decline, promoting rituals and semblance of *Brahminism* in their ministrations. *Brahminism* rebounded with vehemence after the advent of Kautilya and Śankarācārya which led to a number of different cults, social and religious orders. It is interesting to observe that the whole of the Indian subcontinent is filled with all these different doctrines and their devout followers who at times violently cross the limits of mutual tolerance.

We can see that the nihilistic philosophy of *Buddha* and *Mahāvīra* and the atheism of Cārbāka could not provide lasting opposition to the concept of feudalism which included imperialism, capitalism, and Machiavellian style of governance. This led to the demise of the greatest Maurya Empire and heralded the foreign invasion of India and her disintegration. This system was continued by the kings and princes of small kingdoms, to succumb to the Mughal and British rule, which also eventually faced the same extinction.

These nine schools of classical Indian philosophy shaped the Indian society over the next two millennia. The simultaneous development in several different fields which occurred in the Common Era has been well recorded in history. Their interpretation and the effects over the Indian society, however, have been either deliberately ignored or misrepresented.

We can clearly see that the ancient way of learning, earning, reforming, and renouncing, guided by a monotheistic faith without a name, gender or a temple, church, mosque or a *Vihāra,* was the most successful time in the history of India. They called that era the *Satya Yuga* or Utopia. Mental and physical purity, uplifting thoughts, charitable actions along with enjoyment in life were common aspirations for most people. We can see that a slow decline of higher moral and idealistic principles had begun with the organised ritualistic practices, which were acknowledged in the ancient literature as the *Treta Yuga*, the era of the thrice daily rituals. Despite this recognition, Indian minds continued to pursue material self-interest at the cost of everything – fellow humans, nature, and spiritual advancement. By deviating from the concepts of 'live and let live', human selfishness began to produce great suffering for many, as subsequent events and philosophical concepts would show.

The tremendous developments in science, technology, and personal acquisition of wealth in the world today have done little to enhance the power within oneself which is essential for us to survive with equanimity, dignity, self-confidence, and contentment. The fact that modern preachers of spirituality and religion have been popular with even the educated masses demonstrates that man needs a religion to look up to, not because he needs a god to cling to, but as a prop for holding on to something at times of distress and to absolve personal responsibility. This is illustrated by deification of Lord Kṛśṇa, Bhagavān Mahāvīra, Lord Buddha, Lord Jesus and Prophet Mohammad by their followers and the rejection of *Lokāyata* and other atheistic concepts. The current gurus and preachers are enjoying their multimillion-pound business empires by exploiting the mental weakness and superstition among their followings.

The Indian *Brāhminism* is the oldest prototype for all the existing religions today. This has proliferated to the extent that the United Nations has officially recognised twenty religions in the world. This makes me wonder whether man really wishes to know the truth! Human society still has the same four castes - the leaders, soldiers, businessmen, with the workers at the bottom of the heap in any nation, as before.

The Indian philosophers resisted, and many revolted, against the evolved rigid religious system of *Brāhminism* which they did not think was conducive to intellectual and spiritual fulfilment. Their attempts failed. The *Upaniṣadists*, the social reformists, the followers of *Sāṁkhya, Nyāya, Vaiśeṣika, Mahāvīra, Buddha, Lokāyata, Āryabhat, Nānak, Rām Mohan Roy, Dayānanda, Vivekānanda, Rāmakṛṣṇa, Aurobindo* and many more suggested that *Brāhminism* was not the answer for inner peace, equitability, and universal brotherhood. Directly or indirectly, they wished to revert to the earlier *Vedic* philosophy which had assured individual freedom, enforced duty to the community and to oneself, encouraged introspection, continuous education, and preservation of nature.

The rampant rivalry among the religions, nations, leaders, businessmen and the common man is generating an atmosphere of hatred, violence, and greed. The fanatic followers of organised religions have created unpardonable and cruel divisions within humanity which we can see in our daily lives. The religious wars waged by man against his fellow man and the futility of it are obvious to all. The current concepts inherent in any of the dogmas of secularism, interfaith movements, atheism, agnosticism, and religious fanaticism have clearly not become sufficient and effective enough for everyone to feel safe and empowered to seek and realise one's own spirituality.

The way forward:

It is the challenge of our time that we find a mechanism where our individuality is enhanced along with the emancipation of the whole human community and preservation of natural resources.

The study of the evolution of Indian philosophy shows how humanity at large has also accepted its idealism. The world has acknowledged the concepts of universal brotherhood and an equitable society with dignity of labour at all levels. This was propagated by the seven *Ṛṣis* in the *Rg Veda*. Similarly, the world peace by *Buddha*, the nonviolence by Gandhi, the preservation of nature by Mahāvīra, the spiritualism with social justice and responsibility by *Vivekānanda*, and the syncretism of the *Sufis* and APJ Abdul Kalam have been very well received. That the human beings can develop a Super-mind was demonstrated by Sri Aurobindo. These are just a few examples. Imperialism had been denounced by the Emperor Asoka more than two millennia earlier. Indian philosophers have continued to deliberate on the means to enhance the internal strength within man, whether by *Yoga, Tantra, Bhakti, Sufism, Sikhism* or *Knowledge*. These are as relevant and of value as before.

We have created a very unequal society in trying to improve our personal lifestyles. Although the imperialistic political adventures have largely ceased, the quest for economic domination is not any less threatening to the world today. As a result, we can see the great divide between the rich and poor, and the sickening hoard of the earth's resources among the relative few. The latest pandemic continues to demonstrate the unbelievable levels of destitution even in the wealthy nations. Unless we begin to realise and act, believing that it is immoral to control excessive wealth for personal greed and that there must be equitability in the use of the earth's resources, we are unlikely to achieve this ideal in this century. Sadly, until the limits are defined at both ends, i.e., the minimum vs maximum wages (wealth), this imbalance will continue unabated.

This wide gap will continue to escalate the conflicts too. We can overcome this by adopting a modified social order of *Vedic* times when a man had to go through four stages in life - i.e., learning, earning, retirement (further learning, introspection, and mentoring), and eventual renouncing. The idea then was to earn as much as possible with honest means and use the wealth for enjoyment and observing social responsibilities until retirement at fifty years. This provided an automatic ceiling to the acquisition of further wealth, for social norm did not encourage earning after reaching that age. However, the experience and skill of the retiree were still utilised in preparing the next generation. Another way could be for any society to voluntarily agree to put a ceiling on the acquisition of personal wealth of its members to a specified upper limit, perhaps twenty to forty times higher than the average. The challenge for an individual will be to succeed in one's enterprise and gain the satisfaction that that will ensue. Once that egoistic goal is achieved, the surplus should be given back to the community, not as an act of charity for tax benefits, but as a moral duty towards humanity at large. This will help in spreading the resources, i.e., the natural wealth, and reduce inequality. The ancient

Indian philosophers had shown the way but, sadly, they could not overcome the human weakness of avarice and selfishness for material wealth due to mass illiteracy, ignorance, and superstition.

The history of Indian philosophy has also demonstrated that even the atheists need some sort of a religion! If an organised religion is a must for our society, let this be the Religion of Compassion, which was preached by Buddha, Jesus, and Mohammad and *Veda Vyasa*. This is the greatest usefulness of the *Vedic* philosophy in the present time. Hence a man should be encouraged to adopt a special, very personal and secret 'designer religion'. This should neither have a visible intermediary between one and his or her faith nor a common place for worship. This is essential because the plethora of religions has divided human beings and driven them apart into adversarial camps controlled by the religious leaders. This has done little to strengthen universal brotherhood. We all love to celebrate life events, our successes and good news. Let these ritualistic practices be nondenominational and truly joyous occasions so that all can join in without being conscious of belonging to different faiths.

The existing religious leaders would benefit by adapting to the changed times. They could be the champions for the poor, the disadvantaged and the disabled by utilising their huge resources for setting up social enterprise schemes, not-for-profit sharing businesses and banks to alleviate the poverty and gross inequality, and by opening their institutions as museums, schools, rehabilitation centres, and for a variety of other services. This millennium in its infancy has already suffered from three pandemics of increasing severity and the resultant destitution and depravity, even in the developed affluent nations.

A multi-faceted lifestyle which enhances our minds, self-confidence, and enjoyment without depleting the earth's resources could be the way forward.

❖

"A certain kind of agnosticism is the final truth of all knowledge".

Sri Aurobindo

Appendix - 1

Examples from the *Vedas*

Note: The translated excerpts of the Vedic mantras and the Upaniṣads are offered as evidence of the above narration. These are literal and word-for-word translations. No commentary is given. It is presented in the style of the original mantras, as far as possible; hence may appear as incorrect English.

On the beginning:

Ṛg 10.90.1. Having thousands of heads, eyes, feet, that *Puruṣa,* covering the earth from all sides, exists beyond the place measurable by ten fingers.

Ṛg 90.4. The *Puruṣa*, existing in three portions, ascended up. This one portion became the creation again. Then that *Puruṣa* pervaded all over the living and non-living beings.

Ṛg 10.129.1. At that time, the existent was not, the non-existent was not; the Space was not, that splendid sky was not; what, where and under whose dependence was the desirable object? Was there the dense unfathomable water?

Ṛg 10.129.4. That cause, the first seed, which was at the beginning produced the desire to create in the mind of the creator. The learned, after contemplation through knowledge, discovered in heart the relationship of that which exists with that which does not.

Ṛg 10.129.6. Who really knows by what reason and from where this creation has been produced and who shall explain here well? The gods have been later than the creation of this universe. Who knows from which this creation was produced?

Ṛg 10.129.7. He either holds or does not hold to this creation from whom this creation was made. He too, the master of this universe, who is the excellent sky knows or does not know this creation.

Atharva 9.9.14. The wisdom of God joined with energy governs the universal wheel which is revolving eternally in the Space drawn towards the full extent of this world by ten. All the constellations and regions depend on the source of this energy.

Atharva 10.53.6. *Kāla* produced the reality and wealth of creation and shines as the sun. All truly find their existence within the *kāla* who makes these visible to the eyes.

Ṛg 6.48.22. The heaven originated only once. The earth originated only once. The milk of *Prişni* originates only once. Any other matter like that milk does not exist.

On society:

Ṛg 10.191.3. O (performers of good deed)! May the *Mantras*, the group, the heart with minds of you all become similar. I recite similar *Mantra*. I perform the offering in fire through your similar oblation.

Ṛg 10.191.4. O (performers of good deed)! As your common actions can be performed, like that your resolve too may become similar indeed. May your hearts and minds become similar.

Atharva 5.2. 26/27. O friends! Let us work hard together, have the strength to cross this turbulent stream full of upheavals and discard the sins; standing firm and erect, enjoy the fruits of our endeavours.

On God:

Ṛg 1.154.4. Alone, who upheld the earth of three elements, the heaven and the entire regions, filled his three regions with everlasting sweetness and delight by sustenance.

Ṛg 1.154.5. The source of sweet ambrosia is in the excellent abode of *Viśṇu* having many brave exploits. The men, fond of God, become happy there. Surely *Viśṇu* like this is our relative. May I attain that dear divine region.

Ṛg 1.1.1. I praise the leader of *Yagńa,* the performer of the *Yagńa,* the invoker of the gods, the giver of the superior wealth, the God *Agni.*

Atharva 13.5.14-21. He who knows God is one neither two, three, four, five, six, seven, eight, nine or ten. God oversees all, the living and the non-living. He has the supreme power. He is one and one alone. All the powers of divinity becomes Him, the one and only.

Ṛg 1.164.46. He is the divine fine winged *Sūrya,* (God, the righteous). The learned describe the same one *Sūrya* by many forms. He has been called *Agni, Mitra, Indra* and *Varuna*. Similarly, he has been called *Yama, Mātariśwa,* and *Agni.*

Yajur 32.1. God. You are the fire, the sun, the moon, the life breath, the seed, the water, the universe and also the creator *Prajapati.*

Ṛg 4.1.8. Those excellent real births of the three forms of this *Agni* are liked by all. Pervaded inside the boundless Space, may the master *Agni,* pure, bright and very white, come to our *Yagńa.*

The right path to salvation:

Yajur 31.18. The only, no other, way for the devotee to ultimate liberation is to know the destroyer of darkness of ignorance, the *Puruṣa* who has the greatest effulgence of the sun.

Atharva 43. 3.1. O effulgent enlightened guide, lead me on that path in which the knowers of the *Vedas* attain the highest state.

Sāma 782. Intellect and pillar are surely the two oars which carry men safely across the tumultuous sea of life where the fools drown themselves.

Ṛg 1.36.14. O pillar! Tall, you save us from sin through knowledge. Burn the robbers of our intellect. Raise us for progress and long life. Take our prayers to the gods.

Ṛg 5.51.15. May we move on the beneficial paths like the sun and the moon and be united with the wise non-violent God, who repeatedly gives us the desired boon.

Yajur 40.5. He who realises that The One contains all the living and non-living within One-self can comprehend that The One is within all as well. Therefore, he does not get confused.

The true light:

Ṛg 4.13.3. Seven great horses carry that *Sūrya,* the observer of all the regions, to whom the stable gods, without quitting own work, serve from all sides to remove darkness.

Ṛg 4.14.5. Why does this *Sūrya,* baseless, unbound, turned up, facing down,not fall? The pillar of Space, the all pervading *Sūrya* nurtures the heaven. Who has understood all that?

Ṛg 3.62.3. We contemplate on that exquisite luminosity of the god *Sabitā.* May he encourage our intelligence. (The earth, heaven and sky were added to this as the *Gāyatri Mantra*).

Ṛg 3.57.6. The giver of shelter, the omniscient, O God *Agni*! That unique wisdom of yours getting unattached as the stream of the cloud enhances us; give us that fine intellect benefiting all.

Ṛg 5.44.9. Among these hymns, the foremost remains resounding in Space. That phase of *Yagńa* does not perish in which extensive prayer is done. Where the hymns are bound with pure words, the desires of the hymn singer do not shake there.

Soma:

Ṛg 9.66.2. O The Flowing *Soma!* You become the king of all by your two radiances which exist facing the opposite directions.

Ṛg 9.66.17. We praise *Soma* who is braver than the brave, stronger than the strong, and greater giver than the generous.

Ṛg 10.117.8. He, having one portion of wealth crosses the path of the man having two portions by much time to secure riches; the man having two portions follows the man with three portions; the man having four portions goes forward and observing the rows of men with two portions, remains close.

Speech, Word:

Ṛg 10.71.2. As by the strainer to the barley flour, where the learned men purifying the speech by mind pronounce, there the hymn singers know the friendship; the beneficial prosperity lies within the speech of these learned.

Ṛg 10.125.1. I (*Vāgāmbhriṇī*) roam with the *Vasus*, and the *Rudras*. I roam with the *Ādityas* and all the gods. I hold both *Mitra* and *Varuna*. I hold both the *Āświns.*

Ṛg 10.125.3. I am the mistress of the kingdom. I am the procurer of the riches. Am the chief among the gods and very wise. Entering into many, protecting many, the same me is kept around by the gods.

Ṛg 10.125.4. He who sees, breathes and hears this word well eats *annam* (sustenance) by me. The men who are the non-believers in me, they perish. O famous man! I tell you things worthy of respect; listen to that.

The soul after death:

Ṛg 10.14.7-8. O father! You too go nicely to the same place by the ancient path to which our ancestors had reached; go nicely and see the kings, the gods, *Yama* and *Varuna* pleased by food grains.

O father! Assemble with the ancestors in the superior Space. Become together with *Yama,* the fulfiller of boons. Relinquishing the sin, come to the house again and become one with the bright superior body.

Ṛg 10. 135.1-7*.

1. As in the shade of a leafy tree in which place *Yama* with other gods drinks *Soma*; there the lord of people, our father, likes the ancient hymn singers.

2. Finding fault, I looked by that sinner mind to the father, roaming the heaven, and fond of the ancient hymn singers. Again, I desired to receive him.

3. O *Kumāra*! Without looking, you climb into that wheel-less chariot, having one post, going all over; the new chariot which you made by mind.

4. O *Kumāra*! The chariot which you, hearing the comforting words and leaving the learned, have driven, that has brought you in this region, well placed in the boat of wisdom.

5. Who produced this *Kumāra*? Who drives the chariot? As this *Kumāra* become worthy to be returned like that. Who shall say to us that matter today?

6. As *Kumāra* became worthy to return, then the great debate* occurred. Thereafter, the job of getting out from the front of the main place of *Yama* was done.

7. The house which is of *Yama* that is said to have been built by gods. This musical instrument is played for this *Yama*. *Yama* is adorned by the hymns. Y.

Caste is not a birthright:

Rg 1.18.1. O *Brahmanaspati!* Make me, the *Soma*-maker, famous as to the *Ṛṣi Kakshivān*, who is the son of (the slave) *Usijā*.

Rg 1.116.3. O *Āświns*! Like any dying man forsaking wealth, *Tugra* really let go *Bhujyu* in the ocean. You two delivered that *Bhujyu* by your own boats, by going to the Space and above the water. [This

---

* This debate is the basis of *Kathopaniṣad.*

probably refers to the river Tigris.]

Additional mantras are given below from the *Ṛg Veda*:

Ṛg 1.115.1. *Sūrya*, the face of the gods and the unique eyes of *Mitra, Varuṇa* and *Agni* rose. The soul of the ambulant beings and also of the static materials, *Sūrya* pervaded the heaven, the earth and the Space.

Ṛg 1.115.5. *Sūrya* makes that form upon the lap of the sky for the sight of *Mitra* and *Varuṇa*. His golden horses produce limitless bright power and another dark power too, nicely.

Ṛg 3.35.11. We invoke *Indra,* the listener of hymns, the giver of happiness, winner of the riches, killer of the Vritras in the battles, rich, the superior leader, terrific for our protection in the battle conducted for securing the food grains.

Ṛg 3.56.3. The powerful three breasted *Sūrya* wanders having three kinds of brightness, many forms, three seasons, and many kinds of offsprings. He, the sprinkler, is the holder of water in many types of vegetations.

Ṛg 4.17.19. The gods and men cannot stop the hymn singer living under whose shelter he becomes his favourite, when the praised, rich, *Indra* singly indeed, kills the un-retreating *Vritras*.

Ṛg 4.18.19. I without recourse cooked the entrails of a dog. I did not know the giver of happiness among the gods. I saw the wife insulted. Thereafter the hawk brought sweet *Soma* for me.

Ṛg 4.23.8. There are many strengths of truth. Indeed, the hymn for truth surely destroys the sins. The bright hymn of truth filled with knowledge violates the deaf ears of man.

Ṛg 4.23.9. The bodies bearing truth for beauty are firm and delightful. The hymn singers want many food grains through truth. The cows enter into the *Yagńa* bearing the truth.

Ṛg 4.26.1. I am *Manu* and *Sūrya.* I am the learned *Ṛṣi Kakshivān*. I had decorated the learned *Uşāṇa.* O men! Look at me. *[Vāmadeva].*

Ṛg 4.27.1. I knew of the births of all these gods while in the womb. One hundred strong female bodies protected me. Thereafter I emerged fast, becoming a hawk.

Ṛg 4.33.2. When the *Ribhus* made the parents able through service, nurture, and by deeds, then (they) received friendship of the gods. The learned *Ribhus* held the prosperity for the hymn singer.

Ṛg 4.33.5. The eldest *Ribhu* said 'let us make this one *Camas* into two'. The second said 'let us make three *Camas*'. And the youngest said 'let us make four *Camas*'. O Ribhus! *Tvastā* praised your words (resolve). [*Camas,* a special bowl for drinking *Soma*.]

Ṛg 4.43.1. Among the revered gods which god surely indeed listens to the praise and who accepts the praiseworthy hymn? For the heart of which god among the immortals shall we recite this dear and luminous superior hymn along with oblation?

Ṛg 4.43.2. Who comes very swiftly among the gods? Who is the great benefactor? Who gives happiness? That chariot having fast horses which the daughter of *Sūrya* chose is said to be fast.

Ṛg 5.43.16. May this hymn nicely receive the earth, the Space, and also the vegetations, crops and food grains for riches. May every god become easily invoked for me. May the mother earth not keep us in stupidity.

Ṛg 5.18.4. They place food grain on the *Kuşa* strewn in *Yagńa* who protect the hymn in the mouth or among whom the unique radiance exists.

Ṛg 6.6.2. That *Agni* is praised who, the giver of shelter to whom the cows come to give milk, to whom the fast horses and the well born learned, come. O *Agni*! Provide sustenance to the hymn singers.

Ṛg 6.52.16. We go on that faultless beneficial way through which man destroys all the enemies and also receives the riches.

Ṛg 6.75.6. A skilled charioteer seated in the chariot carries the horses forward wherever he wishes. The reins control the minds of the horses. The reins control the minds of the horses from the rear. O hymn singer! Praise the importance of the reins.

Ṛg 7.1.1. O *Agni*! May we not have to live in a house without people. May we not become without bravery. O the benefactor of the house! May we live serving you in the houses with people.

Ṛg 7.18.5. The praiseworthy *Indra* made the widely spread rivers fordable and also easily crossable for the King *Sudāsa*. He made the curse of the wicked violator of the hymn singer and the river contemptible.

Ṛg 7.35.3. May the creator become provider of peace for us! May the guardian surely become the provider of peace for us! May the earth expanded with food grain become provider of peace for us! May the heaven and earth become the providers of peace for us! May the mountain become the provider of peace for us! May the fine hymns of the gods become the providers of peace for us!

Ṛg 7.66.16. Kept by the gods, the clear effulgence of *Sūrya* rises; may we see that hundred years. May we live for a hundred years.

Ṛg 8.1.5. O holder of *Vajra, Indra*! Let me not sell you for a great price. Having hundreds of riches, the holder of *Vajra, O Indra!* Let me not sell you for a hundred, thousand and ten thousand also.

Ṛg 8.3.23. Like the ambulant horses delivering the son of *Tugra* to his house, that horse whose axle is carried by ten others was given to me.

Ṛg 8.4.19. We, among the men, received the enormous wealth with hundreds of horses in the donations performed by the bright king *Kurunga* to secure a place in heaven.

Ṛg 8.5.22. O two *Āświn*! When did the son of *Tugra,* left in the ocean, serve you both whose chariot had gone to the ocean by the ambulant horses?

Ṛg 8.101.15. The mother of the sons of *Rudra*, daughter of the *Vasus,* the sister of the *Ādityas*, the cow is the centre of ambrosia. I surely say to the learned men, O men! Do not kill the sinless cow.

Ṛg 8.101.16. Only the man with little knowledge rejects the cow, praised by hymns, the imparter of speech, recitor of the word, coming towards me for the gods.

Ṛg 9.66.19. O *Soma* as *Agni*! Make long lives available for us and provide power and food grain also. Destroy the malevolent from afar.

Ṛg 9.73.3. The pure rays sit near the hymn. *Soma*, the ancient father of these, protects the duty. *Soma,* the covering of all, hides the enormous Space. The learned indeed are able to secure *Soma,* the roamer in the waters.

Ṛg 9.112.1. Our hymns and actions of men, too, are of many varieties. The carpenter desires the wood, the physician wishes for the disease, and the performer of the *Yagńa* wishes for the host, the preparator of *Soma*. O *Soma*! You flow all around for *Indra.*

Ṛg 9.112.7. O *Soma!* Keep me in that immortal, imperishable region where there is imperishable radiance and in which region, the happiness exists. O *Soma*! You flow all around for *Indra.*

Ṛg 10.151.5. We invoke the goddess of devotion in the morning, at midday and at sunset. O Goddess *Śraddhā*! Make us devout here.

Ṛg 10.155.1. The non-giver, the harsh speaker, ugly, O shrew! Go towards the mountain. We, by those actions of *Śirimbītha*, destroy you.

Ṛg 10.155.3. Having an ugly chin, O misfortune! Make that lifeless drift wood which flows there by the bank of river your support and go by that to the other side.

Ṛg 10.164.1. O lord of the mind! Go far. Step away far. Roam far away. Observe the distant *Nirritī.* The mind of living man dwells in many objects.

Ṛg 10.164.3. Many bad deeds which we have committed while awake and asleep by hope, ambitions or despairs, may *Agni* take all those unpleasant and bad deeds far from us.

Ṛg 10.166.2. Unviolated and unscathed like *Indra,* I am the destroyer of enemy. May all these enemies become living under my feet.

Ṛg 10.166.5. O wicked persons! I, the performer of all duty, the overcomer by radiance, came. I take your mind, deeds and group under control.

Ṛg 10.169.4. Being the life breath of gods, embryo of living beings, this god *Vāyu* roams as wished. The sounds of this *Vāyu* are heard, and not seen in the form. We, for that *Vāyu*, serve by donations.

Ṛg 10.174.2. O King! Defeat those who are our enemies. Defeat him who is hostile to us. Defeat the enemy, fond of battle, by surrounding him.

Ṛg10.184.1. O woman! May *Viśṇu* make your womb. May *Prajāpati* sprinkle semen. May *Tvaṣṭā* vary the forms. May the creator nourish the embryo.

Ṛg 10.190.1. The light was born by the radiant rigorous asceticism of the creator and then the Truth was also born. Then the night was born. Then was born the sky, the possessor of water.

Ṛg 10.190.2. The year was produced from the sky full of water; the year became the lord of all moments of time making the days and nights.

Ṛg 10.190.3. The creator, as before, made the sun and the moon and also the delightful heaven, the earth and the Space.

Ṛg 10.191.2. O Men! You all assemble. Talk. May your minds know similar like, the ancient gods having similar knowledge who accept the portion of the oblation of the *Yagńa.*

Notes: *There is a curious legend about a pupil who was unable to pay the fees asked by his guru. He had to vomit out the Mantras which he had memorised and the partridres (tittries) ate that vomitus. Their chirpings were* presented as the divine revelations and called the *'Taittaria Samhitā of the Yajurveda'*. The purists, however, did not accept this recension of *Yajurveda* and dubbed it the *Kṛśṇa Yajurveda* (the black *Yajur Veda).*

***Brāhmin* priests had begun to quote the *Smriti* also as *Śruti or Śabda*, and deliberately added *Brāhmaṇa* rituals within the corpus of the *mantras* of the *Yajurveda*.

❖

Appendix - 2

The *Upanişads*

The following *Upanişads* are presented in brief to illustrate the variety of philosophical concepts deliberated in them.

1. *Iśābhāşya Upanişad, or Iśā Upanişad.*

This is placed first among the *Upanişads.* This is the last chapter in *Śukla Yajur Veda Mādhyāndinī Samhitā* compiled by the sage *Yāgńabalkya.* It has eighteen verses. This *Upanişad* is a commentary (*Iśa,* the God; *Bhāşya,* commentary) on God. This *Upanişad* has the maximum number of learned commentaries, probably because the later verses appear to contradict the ones in the first half. The question of *Vidyā,* the true knowledge; *Avidyā,* ritualistic practices; *Sambhuti,* the Ultimate; *Asambhuti,* destruction or *Vināsa* are the main issues of contention. My own view is that some of the contentious verses were later additions and did not belong to the original mantras of the *Yajur Veda.*

"Giving up selfish and desire-motivated actions, performing acts of charity and service, devotion to God and considering human life more as a blessing than as a curse, are the central messages of this small but beautiful *Upanişad.*

2. *Katha Upanişad. (Kathopanişd)*

This has 119 verses in six sections. This is the imagined dialogue between Kumāra (*Nāciketās*) and *Yama* developed in *Taittiria Brāhmaṇa,* originally based on the *Rg Veda. Brahma* is likened to the root of an upside-down tree – which has its roots in the space and the branches in nature – and is immortal. The roots are not visible. Hence every suggestion is discarded as *ney ti, ney ti,* [not that, not (even) that], arguing 'how can any thing describe the undescribable?' How can a something that is formless be identified when it has no form? But this *Upanişad* tries to define *Brahma*. All the *Mantras* of the *Ṛg*

Veda which are the foundation of this philosophy are given in Appendix 1, Ṛg Veda 10.135.1-7.

3. *Kena Upaniṣad.*

This is an ancient *Upaniṣad* which is attributed to the *Talabkāra Brāhmaṇa* of the *Sāma Veda.* It is a small compilation of thirty-five verses, although the last two sections are in prose. *Kena,* by whom? The answer is, of course, *Brahma!* It also gives two fables to explain that *Brahma* is more powerful than all the gods and also that it is through Him that Indra became victorious.

1.1 Begins with a question: 'Directed by whom does the mind function? By whom does the life-breath begin its work? By whom does the speech is made able to speak? Who makes the eyes see and the ears hear?' (Clarity is found in the next verse.)

1.2 Those wise men, who know that It is the eye of the eyes, mind of the mind, speech of the speech, life of the life, become immortal when they depart from this world.

4. *Praśna Upaniṣad.*

This is the discourse between six great philosophers who went to an enlightened *Ṛṣi Pippalāda* to ask the following questions:

i. How is this world created?

Answer: By the matter and the life-breath, *the Prāṇa.*

ii. How many entities support the body?

Answer: Just one, the *Prāṇa.*

iii. Whence is the *Prāṇa* born?

Answer: From the *Ātmā*, the soul.

iv. What sleeps and what is awake? In whom are all united and dissolved?

Answer: When sense organs merge with the mind, the body sleeps; when *Ātmā* merges with the Supreme Spirit, the *Brahma*, all get united and get dissolved into 'That'.

v. What is achieved by meditating on *Āum?*

Answer: *Āum* has three sounds, (also three units of time) a; meditation for one unit of time or on A, he achieves a human birth; if he concentrates on the first A and the second U, i.e. two unit time or on AU, he attains the celestial (lunar) regions after death until born again, and if he concentratedly meditates on all three, AUM or three unit time, he achieves the region of *Brahma* – the *Brahmaloka* – from which there is no return.

vi. Who is this sixteen attributed *Purusha*?

Answer: He is the *Puruṣa* in you. He created *Prāṇa* which created the faith, the Space, air, fire, water, earth, organs, mind and food which created dynamism, discipline, mantras, the worlds and the names of the worlds, all of which are like the spokes in a wheel (where these spokes are not known separately from the wheel); just like the ocean where the rivers merge but only the ocean is known. The wise who know this are beyond life and death. There is nothing beyond!

5. *Muṇḍaka Upaniṣad.*

Literally, *Muṇḍaka* means shaved head. This could also suggest that this was taught to the shaven-headed ascetics who must have compulsorily completed the special rites of *Śirovrata.* This is attributed to *Ṛṣi Atharvan*, who is said to have received the *Atharva Veda.* There are three chapters with two sections in each having sixty-five verses in all.

Question: What is that which, if known, everything becomes known?

Answer. There are two kinds of knowledge – the higher, *Parā* and the lower, the *Aparā*. The *Vedas* and the *Vedaṅgas* give you the lower knowledge, the higher knowledge is received by *Akṣara,* the Imperishable. *(Akṣara* also means the alphabet).

2.6.6. By the higher knowledge, the wise comprehend that which cannot be seen, grasped; which is formless, without source or features, all pervasive and eternal, never diminishing and extremely subtle.

3.1. The two friends with beautiful plumes sit on a branch of the same tree; one eats the delicious fruit, the other merely keeps looking.

3.3.9. He who knows *Brahma* becomes *Brahma.*

6. *Aitareya Upaniṣad:*

Sage *Mahidāsa Aitereya* who compiled the *Aitereya Āraṇyaka* is attributed to this *Upaniṣad.* This is composed of the last two chapters with thirty-three verses of the *Āranyaka.*

1.1.1. *Āum*! In the beginning, this was but the absolute Self alone. There was nothing else whatsoever that blinked. It thought 'let me create the worlds'.

1.2. Then he created the following four worlds:

i. *Ambholoka,* the world of celestial waters,

ii. *Marichiloka,* the world of the world with celestial lights,

iii. *Maraloka,* the earth with mortals, and;

iv. *Āpoloka,* the subterranean world of water.

1.3 This is *Brahma*; *Indra, Prajāpati,* all these gods, the five elements, the big and the small who procreate through eggs, wombs, moisture and soil and those that fly and those that are static are all impelled by *Brahma*. These have consciousness which affords them their reality. Consciousness is the eye of this cosmos and this is *Brahma*.

7. *Taittirīa Upanişad:*

This comprises three parts which belong to the chapters 7, 8, and 9 of the *Taittirīa Āraṇyaka,* a manual of *Kṛśṇa Yajurveda*. The parts are known as *Sikśāvalli, Brahmāṇandavalli* and *Bhṛguvalli.* The first part deals with the science of intonation, pronunciation, the meaning, the joining of the alphabets, of words and the intent of the words. The part ends with important commands to the pupil at the completion of the studies.

"Speak the truth. There must not be any inconsistency about your statements, or deviation from your path of righteousness. You must always protect yourself and do not be careless about learning, teaching and conducting propitious activities. Give pleasing gifts to your preceptor. Go and continue your lineage".

The second part deals with the concept of *Brahma*: 'One who knows *Brahma* achieves the Infinite'. '*Brahma* created this universe out of Himself and to Himself will this merge'. 'He entered into this universe as *Ātmā* and hence all that exists is *Brahma*.'

The happiness attained by the realisation of *Brahma* imparts an aspirant the absolute bliss, calculated by *Śankarācarya* to be $20^{4\times5}$ times more than the ideal human happiness. The third part is an account of the sage *Bhrigu* who is taught by his father *Varuna* the facts about *Brahma.*

8. *Mahānārāyaṇa Upanişad:*

This is regarded as a minor *Upanişad*, although it is of considerable size. It has three recensions containing eighty, sixty-four and twenty-five chapters attributed to *Sāma Veda*, the *Kṛśṇa Yajurveda* and the

Atharva Veda respectively. This is considered a relatively late compilation because it has reference to *Rāma* and *Hanumana.* This regards both *Narayana or Vişnu* and *Rudra or Śiva* as the supreme *Brahma.*

It asserts that the highest principles of human endeavour are truth, austerity, self-restraint, quietude, charity, duty, procreation, *Agni* worship, meditation, and renunciation.

9. *Brihadāranyaka Upanişad:*

This is part of *Śatapatha Brāhmana of Śukla Yajurveda* and is both, an *Āranyaka* and an *Upaniśad,* containing a manual of religious rites and philosophical concepts. It was the sage *Yāgńavalkya* who was the compiler of this *Madhyandini* recension of *Śukla Yajurveda.*

The *Upanişad* is divided into three parts: *Madhukānda, Munikānda* and *Khilakānda* respectively.

Madhukānda: This begins with a special process of meditation, translated literally as the ritual slaying of a horse, the Aśvamedha Yagńa. This ritual of thanksgiving to *Brahma,* in which a horse represents *Brahma,* is conducted by priests and hosted by the kings when they succeed in annexing other kingdoms and all the assembled guests celebrate by feasting on horse meat. However, in this *Upanişad,* this is a symbolic representation of a special method of meditation known as 'superimposition' where one assumes the subject of contemplation to be superimposed upon a familiar object or upon oneself. Here an aspirant is taught to superimpose the *Prajāpati,* the *Kāla* and the *Devatās* [the Creator, Time and the deities] onto himself to achieve the supreme state of bliss, the *Brahma.*

"It is the desire that binds an individual and it is meditation on the Self, *Ātmā,* that liberates him from this bondage." "In the ultimate analysis, it is the man that is *Brahma,* the Supreme Self".

Munikānda: This consists of six *Brāhmaņas* which are really the accounts of the debates between Yāgńavalkya and six other great philosophers at the famous conference organised by King Janaka of Mithila. King Janaka had invited all the learned scholars, philosophers and teachers. The one who would be accepted by all as the greatest scholar would receive the prize of a thousand cows whose horns were tied with nuggets of gold.

This also has the legends of Bālāki and the King Ajātśatru. It is curious to note that a *Brahmin* was being imparted the brahmavidyā by a Kshetriya. Bālāki had only known about the *Saguṇa Brahma*, and so the king taught him about the *Brahma* without any attributes, i.e. the *Nirguṇa Brahma*.

There is the famous debate between Yagńavalkya and Gārgi, the nudist *Ṛṣikā* (female Ṛṣi). Yāgńavalkya becomes accepted as the greatest scholar where he silences all his opponents and finally establishes that the *'Ākāśa*, the unmanifested Space or Ether, is the indestructible which pervades 'that' which is above the heaven and below the earth as well as between them and which is, was and will always be. This is *Brahma*. He describes this as not big, not minute, neither short nor long, not dark, not Space, without eyesight, without life-breath, without mind and without any attribute at all, hence indescribable. This is the famous aphorism, "neti, neti"– not that, not even that.

Yāgńavalkya explains the profound truth to his wife Maitreyi that "one holds being dear not out of love for beings, but out of love for oneself". The corollary to this teaching is that we feel happy or sad by ourselves and not by what others do to us. We grieve for ourselves when we apparently grieve the dead.

Eventually, he leaves the conference hall by saying that a man was like a huge tree. Like a tree which sprouts another from its root even when it dies, so does the man who comes from *Brahma*, the root of all.

This also has the famous dialogue between Yagńvalkya and his wife Maitreyi before he renounces his wealth to go to become a *Sannyāsi*.

He teaches her the theory of monism, saying the perception of duality has been due to Avidyā, the false knowledge. This is a complete transformation of a priest from being a vain, wealth-seeking practitioner of *Brahminism* to openly accepting that the physical aspects of the rituals were false.

The *Khilakānda*: This introduces supplementary austerities. This begins with the famous aphorism which states that if a thing is complete in its real nature, it remains complete irrespective of where it is, what is taken out of it, or added to it. It remains unchanged. That is the Truth. That is *Brahma*.

The chapter ends with the declaration that "*Brahma* is self existent. Salutations to *Brahma*."

10. *Chāndogya Upaniṣad:*

This is related to the Tāndya recension of the *Sāma Veda*. It has 628 mantras compiled in eight chapters which are divided into 154 sections. This *Upaniṣad* is mainly a manual of a number of *Vidyā* or methods of meditation (austerities) for an aspirant to realise the *Brahma*.

The novice is encouraged to begin by contemplation on *Aum,* which is the principal part of a *Sāman* chant, also known as *Udgītha*. Next come a series of instructions for meditation on the sun. These are also known as the *Madhu Vidyā*. *Gāyatṛ* metre is used to concentrate on the *Brahma*. Then the aspirant progresses to practise the *Sāndilya Vidyā,* which focuses on *Ātmā*. In this manner, several complex meditations *viz. Ṣoḍaśakala Vidya, Saṁvarga Vidyā, Upakosala Vidyā, etc.* are taught in succession.

The famous dictum "*tat tvam asi*" [that, you are!], meaning "the realised man is the *Brahma*", is stated in this *Upaniṣad*. It defines three routes for the soul of the dead person:

i. *Arcirādimārga* – the path of no return, i.e., to *Brahma loka* for a devout person who has practised the various *Vidyas*.

ii. *Dhūmādimārga,* the path of the smoke, for a devout person performing rites without realising their importance to the world of ancestors from which it eventually returns to the earth and.

iii. *Samsara* - cycle for the atheist, the recurring cycle of repeated births and deaths.

There is a nice story of the father *Uddālaka Āruṇi* who notices the vanity in his son *Śvetaketu*, who had just returned after completing his studies. He asks him "what is that by knowing which everything becomes known"? *Svetaketu* did not know that it was the knowledge of *Brahma* which made everything known. This is similar to the question in *Brihadāraṇyaka Upaniṣad,* "who or what sees the eye, if the eye sees everything?"

There is another legend of a discourse between *Nārada Sanatkumāra* about the nature of the Infinite, the *Bhūman*. Another story of importance is that of *Indra,* the king of the gods and *Virocana,* the king of the demons, who go to learn about *Brahma* from *Prajāpati* who told them that the *Brahma* was the seer (the one who perceives) behind the eyes. *Virocana* understood that it was the man who was the supreme and went away satisfied with this knowledge. But *Indra* was not satisfied. He insisted on knowing the Truth. Eventually *Prajapati* instructed him that *Ātmā* perceived from behind the eyes and all sense organs and was the immortal entity which was separate from the physical body.

11. *Kauşītaki Upanişad:*

This is a part of *Kauşītaki Āraṇyaka* which is the modified *Brāhmaṇa* attributed to the *Ṛg Veda*. Its contents are similar to *Aitereya Upanişad,* although some doubts have been expressed by scholars on some of the texts as not being part of the original compilation.

The *Upanişad* begins with the discourse of *Citra Gangyanāni* to

Gotama Āruṇi where he postulates the paths available for the souls to follow after the death of the physical body.

He describes the route in succession as being the world of the moon, the world of fire, world of wind, world of *Varuna*, world of *Indra*, world of *Prajāpati* and finally the destination, i.e., the world of the *Brahma*. The souls from the ordinary and ignorant mortals fall down to earth as rain from the first world of the moon. The souls climb up to different levels according to the achievements made while alive in the physical body and return eventually to the earth again except when it reaches the world of *Brahma*, from where there is no return to a physical body ever again.

There are interesting discourses between *Indra* and *Pratardana* where the former reveals his true nature. The discourse between the king Ajātaśatru and Bālākī reveals that the essence of everything is *Brahma*. There is a poignant and emotional ritual to be followed at the time of imminent death of the father, when the son becomes the continuation of the former.

12. *Māṇḍūkya Upaniṣad:*

This is the shortest *Upaniṣad* which is attributed to the *Atharva Veda*. This deals with *Aum* or *Om*, which is regarded as the symbol of the World, the *Ātmā* and the *Brahma*. Sage Gaudapāda, the teacher of Śankarācārya, wrote a commentary, a kārikā, on this *Upaniṣad*, which is succinct and focused.

A free translation of all its verses is given below.

1. *Om* is all – the past, the present, the future and beyond.

2. *Om* is *Brahma*. It has four parts:

1. The first part is waking, the *Vaiśvānara* who has seven appendages and nineteen facets and experiences external objects.

2. The second part, the *Taijasa*, is the dream state which recognises

the internal entities; it also has seven appendages and nineteen facets.

3. The third part is the dreamless sleep. This is *Prajńa,* the pure mass of bliss, cognition, and enjoyment. This is the beginning and the end of all – the master of all, the internal controller and knower of everything.

4. This is *Turia,* the fourth part. This is unique, indescribable, aware of all, and beyond knowledge. He needs to be realised.

3. *Ātmā is Aum – a, u, m.*

4. *A* is the first *Vaiśvanara,* the awake state; the knower of this achieves all his wishes.

5. *U* is *Taijasa,* the second syllable. Its knowers are all knowledgeable of *Brahma.*

6. M is the third syllable; the knower of this knows everything and gets merged with *Brahma.*

7. The fourth part is indescribable – it has no attributes; he who knows this knows *Brahma* and attains his own real self.

13. *Śvetāśvatara Upaniṣad:*

This is attributed to the *Kṛṣṇa Yajurveda*. This repeats many mantras from the *Vedas* and does not appear to come up with additional ideas.

It is in six chapters.

The first chapter tries to present *Brahma* in the usual manner as done by the other *Upaniṣads*. The second chapter pays homage to *Sābitṛ*. The third chapter elaborates the *Puruṣa* of the *Ṛg Veda*. The fourth chapter offers prayers to *Rudra* and gives some indication on *Tantric* practices; it also brings about the concept of *māyā*, the illusion and God, the illusionist. Chapter 5 tries to define *Ātmā*, being the minutest to the infinite. It goes further and says that it has no beginning nor an end, and neither existence nor non-existence. Chapter 6 confirms that this *Upaniṣad* was composed by Śvetāśvatara (man with a white horse) who knew *Brahma* and passed this on to the *Sanyāsis*.

14. *Jabala Upanisad:*

This is also known as *Jabala Darśana Upaniṣad*. This is attributed to the *Sāma Veda*. *Ṛṣī Dattatreya*, who is regarded as the giver of this *Upaniṣad*.

This is one of the twenty or so *Upaniṣads* on *Yoga*. This is earlier than *Patanjali Yoga Sutra*. Although this is also an eight-limbed, *astānga* practice of *Yoga*, it differs from *Patanjali Yoga Sūtra* in many aspects.

15. *Amritbindupaniṣad:*

1. The mind is mainly considered to be of two kinds – the pure and impure; the former possesses lust and the latter is devoid of any desire.

2. It is the mind of man that is the cause of bondage and emancipation. If attached to sense objects, it leads to bondage and, if free of this attachment, it leads to liberation – this is the teaching of the great sages.

16. *Tejabindūpaniṣad:*

8. *Brahma* is bliss itself beyond the causality of happiness. Difficult to be perceived, unborn, eternal, indestructible and constant, it is free from all the functions of the mind.

9. The Extreme, the supreme refuge, the knowledge beyond and independent of mind, the *Ātmā*, the Space and established in all that is action, that is *Brahma*.

17. *Brahmanopanişad:*

17. Like the oil in the mustard, butter in the yoghurt, water in the waves, fire in the timber, so is *Brahma*, the soul within the soul.

18. *Kaivalyopanişad: 8, 9, 19*

I am that one and only *Brahma* into which everything is born, where everything remains, and in which everything dissolves.

Appendix - 3

*Brahmasūtra**

The following texts are examples to illustrate the most abstruse nature of this compilation. It is practically impossible to make a reasonable interpretation from only one *Sūtra*. However, grouping several *Sūtras* together makes the overall interpretation plausible.

Śānkarbhāşya had been presented in four parts, each with four chapters. Each chapter has four sub-chapters containing a number of topics in each. This format has been followed by subsequent authors. I have maintained the same format so as to assist the readers in comparing this presentation with earlier works. The first thirty-one *Sutras* are presented to illustrate the difficulty in correct interpretation by literal translations, vaguely implied references to the *Upanişads*, questions and answers, doubts and beliefs, and opinions apparently contradicting earlier assertions.

Part one:

General introduction: This part tries to bring together various aphorisms from the *Upanişads*, the *Vedas, Āraṇyaks* and the *Brāhmaṇa* books to try to achieve a consensual view of *Brahma* and *Ātmā*. The Vedantins have come up with the concept of *Brahma* being the one and only source of everything. They do not see the concept of *Ātmā* and the material world as separate valid entities. Many other schools of philosophy have been proposing various concepts of the *Atmā* and the material world too. The *Brahmasūtras* attempt to bring all these concepts together, refute them of their uniqueness and explain in such a way as to make all their views acceptable and conforming eventually to the *Brahminic* views, which they equated as the *Vedic* views.

Chapter 1. Known as *Samanvāya.*

Topics under discussion:

Introduction to *Brahma* and congruence of the views supported by evidence. *Sūtra* 1–4.

Athāto brahmajigńāsā: *athāto,* now here, hence; *Brahma, Brahma; jigńāsa,* reflection, enquiries.

Janmādyasya yatah: *yatah,* for this; *janmādi,* birth etc.; *asya,* its, of this universe.

Śāstrayonitvāt: *śastra,* scriptures; *yonitvāt,* because the womb, the birthplace.

Tattu samannavyāt: *tu,* but; *tat,* that; *samannavyāt*, by congruence, consensus.

Translation:

Therefore, we should now reflect here on *Brahma*. Its birth, etc. occurs in here. *But, is that a consensus of opinion*? This has been taught by the scriptures.

Comment:

There has been much speculation on 'therefore' *(atah)* by the commentators. *Śankara* does not explain the reason. We might care to remember that pupils had to memorise all the *Sūtras* without first understanding their meaning. The *Sūtras* were not usually explained to the pupils until they embarked on higher studies. The author might have been telling his students that it was now the time to learn their meanings. Max Muller says that since *Pūrva Mimāmsā* had been studied, the *Uttar Mimāmsā* could now be studied. Deussen thinks it wise to concur with *Śankara*. However, if the scriptures had been studied already, there would be no need to reflect or speculate on the *Brahma.* 'It' denotes life, soul or *Ātmā*. Bādarāyana is accepting the challenge from the doubter (the *Upanişadist*) and is inviting a debate on *Brahma.* The relevant references are found in: Tai S. 3.1; RV 10.18.1-7; Bri.3.4.5; Cha 7.1.5.

Topic under discussion:

Deliberation on the First Cause of creation, *Sūtras* 5–11

5. *Īkśyateyrnārśabdam: Ikshate,* from the points of view; *na*; no; *aśabdam*; not Word.

6. *Gaudascennātmaśabdāt: cet,* if understood; *gaudah,* state of being subordinate; *ātmaśabdāt,* due to the word *Ātmā.*

7. *Tanniṣthasya mokshopadeyśāt:* liberation, as taught; for the one devoted to it.

8. *Heyatvāvacanacca: heytwa-avacanat,* too derogatory, not said; *ca*, also.

9. *Swapyayāt: swa,* self; *apyayat,* due to merging into.

10. *Gatisāmānyāt:* due being similar knowledge.

11. *Śrutatwācca; Śruti*, Śruti; *tat,* that; *ca*, also.

Translation:

From various points of views due to the word *Ātmā,* this is a state of being subordinate. Also, on account of it merging into itself, it cannot be depended to lead to liberation. But due to absence of contradiction by the Word (*Śruti*), *Brahma* is the First Cause. So is declared by the *Śrūti*, too.

Comment:

Brahma and *Ātmā* are not the same; *Ātmā* merges into *Brahma* and is subordinate to the latter. This discussion is based on the following: Ai 1.1.1-2; Ch 6.2.1,3-4; Ch 6.3.2; Ch 6.7.8; Ch 8.3.3; Mu 1.1.9; SV 3.19.

Topic under discussion:

Blissful *Brahma*, *Sūtra* 12–19

12. Ānandamayoabhyāsāt: Anandamayah, full of bliss*; abhyāsāt,* due to having been repeated.

13. Vikaraśabdānneti cenna prāchuryāt: vikār-śabdāt, by the altered Word; *na,* no; *iti cet,* if understood like this*; na,* no*; prācuryāt,* by reason of being abundant.

14. Tattdhetubyapadeśacca: ca, and; *tattdhetubyapadeśāt,* by the declaration as the Cause.

15. Māntravarnikameba ca gīyete: ca, and*; māntravarnikam,* that one mantra described by*; evaonly; gīyate,* is declared.

16. Neteroynapapatteh: na, no; *itarah,* the other*; anupapattah,* being illogical.

17. *Vedabyapadeśācca*: *ca,* and*; veda-byapadeśat,* due to proved difference.

18. Kāmācca nānumānāpekshyā: ca, and; *kāmāt,* as by desire; *na*, no*; anumāna apekshya,* inference, expectation.

19. Asminnasya ca tadyogam śāsti: asmin, in this*; ca,* and*; śāsti,* traditional education, *yasya,* its; *tad yogam,* that merger.

Translation:

Brahma is full of abundant bliss. This has been repeatedly declared. This has been accepted as the Cause. What if it is understood that the difference exists by inference? No, it is proved another illogical desire, due to the altered Word. The traditional education confirms this.

Comment:

Reference is found in TU.1-4; TU 2.5, TU 2.7.

Topic under discussion:

Brahma is different from all; *Sūtra* 20, 21.

20. *Anantastaddharmopadeśāt: antah,* within the deepest interior; *tat-dharma- upadeśāt,* its quality according to the teaching.

21. *Vedabyapadeśāccānyah: ca,* and; *veda-byapadeśāt,* difference explained, by others.

Translation:

Brahma in its deepest form is different from all others; and this difference has been explained by others.

Comment:

BU 3.7.9; ChU 1.6. 6-8; ChU 1.7.5-8. Interpret *anthasta* as the orb of the sun, although called differently, e.g. *Sāman, Uktha, Yajus, Brahma;* they declare all these to mean the same *Brahma.*

Topic under discussion:

Identity of *Brahma, Sūtra* 22–27.

22. *Ākāśstallingāt*: *Ākaśah,* (*Brahma* is) the Space; *tat-lingāt,* that, due to that sign.

23. *Ata eva prānah: atah eva,* hence; *prānah,* it is *prāna* (the life-breath).

24. *Jyotiścaraṇābhidhānāt*: *Jyotih*, effulgence; *abhidhanat*, due to the mention of; *carana*, foot (feet).

25. *Chandoabhidhānānneti cenna tathā cetoarpaṇanigadāttathā hi darśanam: chandoabhidhānāt,* due to reference to the metre; *cet*, if understood; *na,* is not like that; *cetoarpaṇanigadāta,* the application of concentration of the mind; *tatha hi, (*and) in that way; *darśanam,* it is seen. (in other texts).

26. *Bhūtādipādabyapadeśopapatteścaibam: ca,* and; *bhuta-ādi-pāda-byapadeśa-upa-patte* representation of things or beings, etc. offered as feet for the understanding; *evam,* it is like that.

27. *Upadeśabhedānneti cennobhayasminnapyavirodhāt: upadeśabhedāt,* due to the difference in the stated specificics; *iti cet,* if thus understood, then; *na,* not; *avirodhāt,* been objected by; *ubhayasmin api,* under both circumstances.

Translation:

Brahma is the Space due to that sign; it is *Prāṇa* the life-breath; it is that effulgence. If understood as feet, it is not so; it is fragment of the (*Gāyatri*) metre understood as such in other philosophies. This has not been objected under both circumstances.

Comment:

The *Gāyatri* metre may be indicating The Effulgent, signifying *Brahma*. See ChU 1.9.1-2; 8.14.1; 1.11.4-5; 3.13.7 and 3.12.6-7 for reference to the above *Sūtras*.

28. *Prāṇastathānugamāt: prāṇah,* the life-breath; *tathā,* like that; *anugamāt,* comprehended.

29. *Na vakturātmopadeśāditi cedadhyātmasambandhabhūma hyasmin: na,* it is not so; *atma-upadeśāt,* having been taught for oneself; *vaktuh,* of the teacher; *iti cet,* if understood like this; *adhyātma-sambandha- bhūma,* has plenty of relationship for self; *hi, asmin,* because, in this.

30. *Śāstradṛṣṭyā tūpadeśo vāmadevavat: tu,* but; *upa deśah,* the teaching; *Śāstradṛṣṭyā,* from the scriptural point of view, *vāmadevavat:* as by *Vāmadeva.*

31. *Jīvamukhyaprāṇalingānneti cennopāsātraividhyādāśṛtatvādiha tadyogāt : jīva-mukhyaprāṇa-lingāt,* on account of the symbolism of the Self and the Chief *Prāṇa; na,* not so; *iti cet,* if thus understood; *na,* not so; *upāsā-trai-vidyāt,* will lead to three-fold meditations; *aśṛtatvāt,* due to the acceptance; *iha,* here; *tad- yogāt,* because that is joined with the (*Prāṇa*).

Translation:

Prāṇa is comprehended like that but this is not so; (although) there is plenty of relationship in this between the *Brahma* and the Self, as taught by the teacher. This is supported by the scriptural points of view, as in the teaching of the *Ṛṣi Vāmadeva*. If on account of the symbolism of the Self and the Chief *Prāṇa*, it is understood thus, it is not so because this acceptance will lead to three-fold meditations, since *Prāna* is joined here with *Brahma*.

Comment:

The reference here is to *Ṛṣi Vāmadeva* where he says that he had to eat the entrails of a dog to keep his *Prana* alive, but *Brahma* is immortal. Hence although mentioned loosely together, the self and *Brahma* are very different. The details are in the *Ṛg Veda,* Mandala 4.

* Excerpts from my translation, in preparation from the original compiled by Bādarāyaṇa.

❖

Appendix - 4

Dhammapada: The *Buddha's* path of wisdom

Buddhists believe that this collection of *Buddha*'s teachings should be used as a manual for daily contemplation. There are 423 aphorisms collected in twenty-six chapters. A few (nearly 11%) are selected as examples to show the spectrum of the subjects which are covered. Only the essence within these aphorisms is presented, based upon the English translations by Eknath Easwaran and Acharya Buddharakkita. It is interesting to note the mention of *Yama,* the god of death and *Mara* equivalent to *Nirṛtī,* as well as the characteristics of a true *Brāhmaṇa* of the *Ṛg Veda* in these aphorisms. There is also mention of the fire worship, rebirth and the *Purāṇic* concept of hell!

Essence of the aphorisms:

1. Mind makes us what we are.

11. Mistaking the essential and believing in the nonessential, a man can never realise the truth of anything.

14. Passion cannot penetrate into a well-controlled mind.

15-17. Evil doers suffer and torment themselves with remorse but the doers of good delight, here and elsewhere.

24. Righteousness, watchfulness, discipline and doing benevolent deeds enhances your glory.

27. Do not adopt careless attitudes. Indulging in sensual pleasures leads to heedlessness. Meditate to attain happiness.

35. Hard to achieve, but a disciplined mind brings happiness.

40. Our body is like a delicate container, but the mind is a fort and wisdom is our weapon which guards against *Mara*.

44. One's own focused mind does more good to one than even one's own parents.

50. Find your own done and undone actions – do not find fault with what others have done or undone.

55. The fragrance of virtue is the sweetest of all.

58. A fragrant and beautiful lotus blooms on the rubbish heap.

62. When one is not his own, to whom does his wealth and sons belong?

81. The wise are not shaken by praise or blame, like the rock which does not move in a storm.

98. The *Arhats* (the enlightened *Buddhists*) make a place inspiring for all, no matter whether it is a village, wilderness, a valley or a hill.

100. One useful word which provides peace is better than a thousand words which do not do so.

104. Self-conquest is superior to any other conquest – nothing can turn this into defeat.

111. Live for one day as wise and meditative rather than a hundred years as immoral and unrestrained.

112. Make haste to do good, lest your minds delight in evil.

128. There is no place to hide from the results of an evil deed.

160. You become your only protector – if you can control yourself fully.

177. The wise rejoices in giving and that makes him happy for ever.

183. The teachings of *Buddha* are: avoid all evil deeds, cultivate good and clean your mind.

201. Discard victory and defeat if you wish to live happy.

202–3. Our worst affliction is hunger. The worst crime is hate. No bliss is higher than the *Nirvāna*.

209–16. Intimacy, attachment, endearment, affection, all these generate grief and fear. Remain unattached.

221–3. Check your anger. Overcome the liar by the truth, the miser by generosity, and the wicked by goodness.

237. The time to depart has come; there is no resting place in your final journey, yet you have made no preparations for departure!

238. Make an island for yourself.

248. Remember. Evil things like greed and wickedness are not easy to control. These drag you into misery.

251. There is no furnace like lust, no bond like hatred, no trap like deluding yourself and no stream like infatuation.

256. The wise search for both, the right and the wrong, before passing any judgement.

270. Noble is one who is harmless to all.

284. If a man harbours desire, however subtle, for a woman, his mind remains in bondage like a calf to the mother cow.

290. Renounce lesser happiness for a greater happiness.

301. Delight in the practice of meditation whether during the day or night.

308. The alms given by the devout becomes like a red hot ball of fire when swallowed by a corrupt and uncontrolled monk.

329. Do not seek any company if you cannot find a wise and prudent friend who leads a good life.

333. Good is: avoidance of evil, acquisition of wisdom, resoluteness in faith and service to all.

339. The thirty-six currents of cravings sweep an undisciplined man towards grief by rousing sensual passions in him.

356–59. Lust, hatred, delusion and desire are the banes of mankind like the weeds in a field.

370. Cut off the five: self-illusion, doubt, beliefs in rites and rituals, lust and ill-will. Abandon the five: craving for divinity with or without a form, conceit, impatience and ignorance. Cultivate the five: faith, energy, mindfulness, concentration and wisdom. Overcome the five bonds: greed, hatred, delusion, false views, and conceit; a monk then become an *Arhat*.

385. He is a *Brāhmaṇa* who has no "I" nor "mine".

393. In whom does the truth and righteousness exist is a *Brāhmaṇa*.

❖

Appendix - 5

Sanskrit words with equivalent English meaning

Āchārya:	A head priest, a preceptor, an enlightened teacher, a degree or qualification.
Adhikarī:	Rightful owner, authority, an authorised person, an entitled person, an officer.
Adhyāsa:	Superimposition, mixing up.
Ahamkāra:	Pride, Ego, Self-consciousness, Conceptions of one's individuality.
Ākaśa:	Sky, Ether, Space, Ocean, Atmosphere, *Brahma*, an open space.
Ākhyāna:	Communication, story, tale, account, narrative.
Akhyāti:	There is no such thing as erroneous knowledge [the thing is there but its interpretation or identification is done by the intellect].
Amrita:	Immortal, elixir of life, undead, and a priest.
Anyathākhyāti:	The Theory of Error – the perception of *ātmakhyati* is negated by previously available additional information.
Apavarga:	Completion, release, emancipation, end, intermediate region.
Araṇya:	Forest, wilderness, desert, a foreign place, a distant land.
Āsana:	Seat, a posture, a technique.
Āśrama:	A stage in life, a hermitage, a dwelling place of a

sage, a college or a school, a thicket.

Ātmakhyāti: The first vague awareness of something being present or experienced.

Avidyā: Nescience, pseudo-knowledge, ignorance, unwise.

Bodhisatwa: An enlightened *Buddhist* monk at the penultimate stage of Buddhahood; a teaching *Buddha*, an *Arhat*.

Brahma: *The Ultimate,* a Mantra, A special priest. [All English literature spells this as *Brahman,* for which I see no justification. The Sanskrit word is best transliterated as *Brahma.* Hence, I have maintained *Brahma* throughout the book.] *Brahma* has been accepted as *being of two kinds: Saguṇa and Nirguṇa Brahma*, the first with attributes and the latter without any attribute, i.e., The void of the void.

Brahmacārī: A celibate, unmarried. A true Brahmačarī is without any physical and mental experience of sexual intercourse.

Brahmarandhra: A spot on the scalp believed to be over Lambda, the point of junction of the occipital and parietal sutures in the skull. This is symbolically protected by the *Brāhmaṇas* by preserving the tuft of hair (*Śikhā*) over this area.

Brata: A vow, an austere practice, a form of penance, a religious ritual or fast.

Chanda: Metre, Prosody.

Chitta, Buddhi: Consciousness, Supermind, some similarity with intelligence or perception.

Devatā, Deva: A god, a respected individual, a respectful form of addressing someone, God.

Devi:	The feminine of Deva.
Dharma:	Characteristic, nature of a substance or an individual, responsibility, duty, moral law, prescriptions, or sanctions of a religion.
Dhyāna:	Meditation, Contemplation, concentration.
Dukkha, Pāpa:	Misery, pain, unhappiness, sin.
Dvāra:	Door, gateway, entrance, exit.
Grantha:	Tome, treatise, a religious book.
Guṇa:	Quality, character, nature.
Guru:	A teacher, preacher, spiritual teacher, God.
Hita:	Beneficial, advantageous, suitable, proper, kind.
Hitā:	Arterioles in the heart, small blood vessels, fine nerves.
Huṅkāra:	Grunt, growl, shout, challenge, roar.
Iśwara (Iśa):	God, master, ruler, king, capable of, liable, lord, the Supreme spirit, Rudra, to be valid.
Japa:	Repetition of a holy name or an aphorism or a mantra.
Kafa:	One of the three primary causes of disease according to *Āyurveda*. (*Kafa*: respiratory and circulatory systems: *Vāta*: joints and immunology and *Pitta*: digestive system and endocrinology).
Kaivalya:	A state of oneness with nothing, the Ultimate void, the Mokshya, mastery in a subject.

Karma:	Action, job, fate, performance.
Karmakānda:	Ritualistic practices.
Krathana:	Sudden interruption of breath, apnoea during sleep, danger of suffocation.
Mānas:	Mind, sentiment, feeling, heart.
Manḍana:	Ornaments, make-up.
Mimāmsā:	Separation of components, analyses.
Mokshya:	As *Kaivalya*, the state of true Bliss, the final liberation.
Nirbikalpa:	Without any alternative, without any attributes, the extreme stage of meditation.
Nirukta:	Etymological interpretation of words, expressed, defined.
Nirvanā:	*syn* Kaivalya.
Nishreyas:	as *Kaivalya* above, also a state where nothing remains.
Padārtha:	Matter, signifying any physical as well as metaphysical and psychological entity.
Pancatan mātra:	The five primal continuous particles in the formation of matter (subatomic).
Prakṛti:	Nature, quality, kinds.
Pralāpa:	Speaking gibberish, lamentation.
Pratignā:	Resolve, promise, dẹtermination.
Raja, Rājā:	Shining, one of the three primordial *Guṇas*, King.

Ṛk.	A mantra from the *Rg Veda*.
Ṛtwija:	A performer of the prescribed religious *Yagña* according to the seasons; any performer of a good deed, a righteous person.
Sabikalpa:	With alternatives or with attributes, often referred to deep meditation which focuses on a divine form.
Sādhanā:	Practice, meditation, austere contemplation.
Samādhi:	Trance-like state, burial place of saints.
Sāmaṇ:	The mantra from the *Sāma Veda*.
Samkhya (Sānkhya):	One of the schools of Indian philosophy; numbered.
Sankalpa:	Pledge, also synonym of *Pratigña*.
Sanyāsi:	A hermit, someone who has renounced worldly possessions, an abbot.
Śāstra:	Scripture, a holy book, manual, science, technique, teaching, direction, advice, any religious or scientific treatise, law book, rules, as attached after the word denoting a subject.
Śāstra:	Scripture, a holy book, manual, science, technique, teaching, direction, advice, any religious or scientific treatise, law book, rules, as attached after the word denoting a subject.
Satya:	The truth, real, God. The eternal.
Siddhi:	Accomplishment, prowess, capability.
Sūtra:	A thread, a complex aphorism, a system of composing a verse, a formula.

Tama, (tamas): Darkness, one of three primal qualities, demonic characteristic, ignorance.

Tāpa: Heat, burning, warming.

Tapa: Performing austerity, consumed by heat, to suffer pain, to torment oneself.

Tapasyā: Synonymous to *Sādhanā* accompanied by self-torture or torment.

The words in Sanskrit are transliterated from Devanagari into Roman script in the text. The various key words which have surfaced among these schools of philosophy are the following:

Vajra: A powerful weapon, specially made by *Twaştā* from the live skeleton of a *Ŗşī*, to help Indra so that he could kill an enemy, commonly identified as *Vritra.*

Varṇa: Colour, caste, kind, race, form, aspect, manner of theatrical dress, a syllable (alphabet).

Vāta: Flatulence, wind-god, one of the three humours of the body.

Vidhātā: The maker, the fate.

Vidhi: Statute, method, procedure, direction.

Vidyā: The mantras of the *Vedas*, true knowledge, science.

Vināśa: Annihilation, destruction.

Vritra: A legendary enemy of Indra, any enemy, a wicked person, a sorcerer.

Yagña: A religious performance, a righteous action, any benevolent activity. According to Moniere Wilson, this means 'worship, devotion, prayer, praise; act of worship or, devotion, offering, oblation, sacrifice; the former meaning prevailing in the *Vedas*, the llatter in post-*Vedic* literature'. [The word 'sacrifice' is being inappropriately and universally used even when the rituals do not offer any animal sacrifice. Animal sacrifice during a few special rituals was often a symbolic activity during the *Vedic* period, as in the concept of superimposition.]

Yajamāna: A client, the householder who is asking a priest to perform a ritual on his behalf.

Yuddha: War, battle, conflict, insurgence, wrestling.

Yupa: Post or a pillar, a stake, a column erected in honour of a victory.

❖

BIBLIOGRAPHY

(as printed with or without diacritic marks).

1. Abdul Kalam, A. P. J. (1999). *Wings of Fire. An Autobiography*. University Press Private Ltd.
2. Abdul Kalam, A. P. J. (2002). *Ignited Minds*. Penguin Books.
3. Abdul Kalam, A. P. J. (2015). *Transcendence*. Harper Element.
4. Adamson, P., Ganeri, J. (2020). *Classical Indian Philosophy*. Oxford University Press.
5. Arnold, D. (1965). *Buddhists, Brahmins, and Belief*. Columbia University Press.
6. Aurobindo, S. (2017). *The Life Divine*. Sri Aurobindo Ashram (4th impression).
7. Aurobindo, Sri. (1998). *Essays in Philosophy and Yoga*. Sri Aurobindo Ashram (4th impression).
8. Aurobindo, Sri. (1956). *The Secret of the Veda*. Sri Aurobindo Ashram.
9. Avari, B. (2016). *India: The Ancient Past*. Routledge.
10. Bartley, C. J. (2002). *The Theology of Ramanuja*. Routledge Curzon.
11. Bharat, G. (2016). *Nāṭya Śāstra – Revisited*. Bharatiya Vidya Vhavan.
12. Bhattarāi V. *(1960) Srimadbhāgavat Mahāpurāṇa Vol 1–2*. Sajha Prakashans. (Nepali).
13. Buddharakkita, A. (1985). *Dhammapada. The Buddha's Path of Wisdom*. Buddha Dharma Association Inc.
14. Burton, R. translator. (2009). *The Kama Sutra of Vatsyana*. Digireads.com. Publishing.
15. Chand D. *Atharva Veda*. Munshiram Manoharlal Publishers Pvt. Ltd. (*Sanskrit-English)*.
16. Cowell, E. B., and Gough, A. E. (1858). *The Sarva Darshan Samgraha of Madhavacharya*. Translation; Keegan Paul Trench and Trubner & Co, London.

17. Dalai Lama, Cutler, C. W. (1998). *The Art of Happiness*. Coronet Books. Hodder and Stoughton.

18. Deussen, P. (1912). *The System of the Vedanta*. Translated by Johnson C. Open Court Publishing Company.

19. Easwaran, E. (2007). *Dhammapada*. Blue Mountain Centre of Meditation.

20. Fadiman, J., Frager R. ed. (1997). *Essential Sufism*. Harper Collins Publishers.

21. Fischer, L. (1951). *The Life of Mahatma Gandhi*. Harper Collins Publishers.

22. Gandhi, M. K., translated from Gujerati by Madhav Desai. (2017). *An Autobiography or the Story of My Experiments with Truth*. Navjivan Publishing House.

23. Ganeri, J. (2020). *The Oxford Handbook of Indian Philosophy*. Edited. OUP.

24. Gautam, K. C. (2016). *Tulasikrit Ramayana: Bhasa Tika Sahita*. Ratna Pustak Bhandar.

25. Gautam, P. C. (2014). *Modern English Translation of the Rig Veda Samhitaa*. Book University, Bharatiya Vidya Bhawan. *(Sanskrit-English)*.

26. Gautam, P. C. (2018). *Reflections on Contemporary Values, Beliefs and Behaviours. Adventures of an enquiring mind.* Cambridge Scholars Publishing.

27. Goyandaka, G. (1947). *Śrimadbhagavadgītā*. Gita Press. *(Sanskrit)*.

28. Goyandaka, H. K. (2074) *Srimanmaharshi Veda Vyasa Praneeta Vedanta Sutra*. Gita Press, Gorakhpur. 2074. *(Sanskrit-Hindi)*.

29. Helwa, A. (2020). *Secrets of Divine Love*. Naulit Publishing.

30. Hill, J. (1817. Copyright-free ebook). *History of British India*.

31. Humphreys, C. (1951). *Buddhism*. Penguin Books.

32. Jayaram, V. *Chānodgya Upaniṣad,* Pure Life Vision. LLC. *(Sanskrit-English)*.

33. Joshi, K. L. (2006). *Sixteen Minor Smritis*. Parimal Publications.

34. Kak, S. (2016). *Matter and Mind: Vaiśeṣika Sūtra of Kaṇāda*.

Mount Meru Publishing. *(Sanskrit-English).*

35. Kakkar, S. (2004). *Mira and the Mahatma*. Penguin Books.
36. Kāmatā, D. (2013). *The Untold Story of the Bhagavad Gita*. createSpace.co.
37. Kamath, P. Isopanishad: (2020). *The Story of Brahmanism's Triumph*. Kindle edition.
38. Kanitkar, V. P., Cole, W. O. (1995*). Hinduism*. Hodder Headline Publishing.
39. Kashyap, R. L. (2005). *Taittiria Samhita.* Sri Aurobindo Kapali Sastry Institute of Vedic Culture. (*Sanskrit-English).*
40. Kumar B. (2004). *Vaidik Wāngmaya kā Itihās.*Parimal Publications. *(Hindi).*
41. Luitel T. (2008). *Sāma Veda.* Vidyarthi Publications. *(Sanskrit-Nepali).*
42. Luitel T.(2008). *Yajur Veda.* Vidyarthi Publications. *(Sanskrit-Nepali).*
43. Luitel T. (2008). *Yajur Veda.* Vidyarthi Publications. *(Sanskrit-Nepali).*
44. Luitel T. (2009). *Manusmriti.* Vidyarthi Publications. *(Sanskrit-Nepali).*
45. Macdonnel, A. (1900). *A History of Sanskrit Literature*. D Appleston and Co. Bibliolife.
46. Mahesh Yogi. website www.pdfdrive.com.transcendental; accessed 17/12/2020.
47. Majumdar, R. C. (1952). *Ancient India*. Motilal Banarsidass.
48. Mason, P. (1985). *The Men Who Ruled India*. Rupa Publications.
49. McGreor, R. C. (1993). *Oxford Hindi English Dictionary*. OUP.
50. Miller, B. S. (1998). *The Yoga Discipline of Freedom*. Yoga Sutra attributed to Patanjali. Translator. Bantam Books Inc.
51. Mohanty, J. N. (2000). *Classical Indian Philosophy*. Rowman & Littlefields Publishers.
52. Monier Williams, M. A. (2002). *Sanskrit English Dictionary*. Motilal Banarsidass.
53. Muller, F. M. (1993). *History of Ancient Sanskrit Literature So*

Far as it Illustrates the Primitive Religion Of The Brahmans. Asian Educational Services.

54. Muller, F. M. (2006). *Satpath Brahmana. The sacred book of the East Part 1.* Elibron Clasics Series One. Adamant Media Corporation.
55. Muller, F. M. (2006). *The Sacred Books of the East.* Adamant Media Corp.
56. Muller, F. M. (2003). *The Six Systems of Indian Philosophy.* University Press of the Pacific.
57. Muller, M. F. (1993). *A History of Ancient English Literature.* Asian Educational Services.
58. Olivelli, P. (1996). *Upanishads: A New Translation.* Oxford University Press.
59. Overy, R. (2003). *Complete History of the World.*Harper Collins.
60. Pandey, R. (1969). *Hindu Saṁskāras.* Motilal Banarsidass. *(Sanskrit-English).*
61. Pattanaik, D. Jaya. (2010). *An Illustrated Retelling of the Mahabharata.* Penguin Random House.
62. Radhakrishnan S., Moore, C. A. (1957). *A Source Book in Indian Philosophy.* Princeton University Press.
63. Radhakrishnan, S. (1948). *The Bhagavad Gītā.* George Allen and Unwin Ltd.
64. Rajanish. website www.britannica.co; biography, accessed 17/12/2020.
65. Rajagopalachari, C. (1951). *Ramayana.* Bharatiya Vidya Bhavan. Mumbai.
66. Rawson, P. (1973). *The Art of Tantra.* Thames and Hudson.
67. Robson, K. (2015). *The Usborne Encyclopedia of World Religions.* Usborne Publishing Limited.
68. Rochr, Rosane. *What life was like in the Jewel in the Crown. British India 1600-1905.* Time Life Books.
69. Ruhe, P. (2001). *Gandhi.* Phaidon Press Inc.
70. Ruskin, J. (2006, originally 1862). *Unto This Last.* Cosima Inc.
71. Russel, B. (1946). *History of Western Philosophy.* Routledge.

72. Sarma, D. (1969). *Classical Indian Philosophy, A Reader*. Columbia University Press.

73. Sarma, S. (2018). *Sri Jabala Darsana Upanishad*. Panchawati Spiritual Foundation, Kindle edition. *(Sanskrit-English).*

74. *Sastri, D. N.* (1953). *Bharatiya Darshan Shastra*. Motilal Banarsidass. *(Hindi).*

75. Śarma, R; Śivaram, Tukaram.T. (Editors). (1898) *Sayanacharya virachita Pāda pāṭhutāca Rg Veda Samhitā*.Mumbai, Gaṇapati Kṛśṇji Mudrālaya. (Sanskit).

76. Shamashastri. (1915). *Arthashastra of Kautilya*. *(Sanskrit- English).* Government Press.

77. Singh, K. V. *Hindu Rites and Rituals*. Penguin Books. Ebooks.

78. Singh, U. (2009). *A History of Ancient and Early Medieval India*. Pearson India Educational services Noida.

79. Sinha, N. L; Vidyābhūşan, MMSC. (1930). *The Nÿaya Sūtras of Gotama*. Motilal Banarsidass. *(Sanskrit-English).*

80. Skinner, J. D. (2017). *Practical Zen. Meditation and Beyond*. Singing Dragon. Jessica Kingsley Publishers.

81. Smith, P. (2012). *Anthology of Poetry of The Chisti Sufi Order*. New Humanity Books.

82. Stoler Miller, B. (1986). *The Bhagavad-Gita*. Translator. Bantam Classic.

83. Suzuki, D. T. (1964). *An Introduction to Zen Buddhism*. Dead Authors Society.

84. Swami, A. (1907). *The Gospel of Ramakrishna*. Global Grey.

85. Swami, B. (2004). *Brahma Vidya*. Central Chinmaya Mission Trust. *(Sanskrit-English).*

86. Swami, C. (1954). *Prasnopanisad*. Central Chinmaya Mission Trust.

87. Swami, G. *Eight Upanishads with the Commentary of Śankārācārya. Vol 1–2*. Advaita Ashrama. (*Sanskrit-English).*

88. Swami, G. (1965). *Brahmasutra Bhashya of Sankaracharya*. Translated. Advaita Ashrama. *(Sanskrit-English).*

89. Swami, H. (1998). *The Ten Cardinal Upanishads, a brief study*.

Rama Krishna Matha.

90. Swami, P. (1968). *Bhagavad Gita as It Is*. Bhakti Vedanta Book Trust. International Society for Krishna Consciousness.

91. Swami, S. (2005). *Śānkarpancakam;* Śaradāpītha Prakāśanam, Sri Dwārakā, India. *(Sanskrit)*.

92. Swami, S. (2012). *Yoga Sutras of Patañjali*. Integral Yoga Publications. *(Sanskrit)*.

93. Swami, T. (1994) *Hindu Culture: An Introduction*. Central Chinmaya Mission Trust.

94. Swami, V. (2013). *All Power is Within You*. Vivekananda Kendra Prakashan Trust.

95. Swami, V. (2017). *Brahmasutras According to Śri Śaṅkara*. Advaita Ashrama. *(Sanskrit-English)*.

96. Swami, V. (2017). *Brahmasutras*. Advaita Ashrama. *(Sanskrit-English)*.

97. Swami, V. (2012). *Conflicts and Confusions in Indian Culture*. Central Chinmaya Mission Trust.

98. Swami, V. (1963). *On Himself*. Advaita Ashrama.

99. Swami, V. (2007). *The Yoga Sutras of Patanjali – The Essential Yoga Texts for Enlightenment*. Watkins Publishing.

100. Swami, Y. (2002). *God Talks with Arjuna. The Bhagvad Gita.* Vol1-2. Yogada Satsanga Society of India. (*Sanskrit-English)*.

101. Swami, Y. (1946). *Autobiography of a Yogi*. The Philosophical Library Inc.

102. Swami, M. (1980). *Minor Upaniṣads*. Advaita Ashrama. *(Sanskrit-English)*.

103. Tanahashi, K. Shneider, D. T. (1994). *Essential Zen*. Harper San Francisco.

104. Taylor, J. (1893). *Prabodh Chandrodaya or Rise of The Moon of Intellect*. Translation. Asiatic Society.

105. Thapar, R. (1992). *Interpreting Early India*. Oxford University Press.

106. Tharoor, S. (2016). *An era of Darkness*. Adelphi Book Company.

107. Aurobindo S. (1972). *The story of his life*. Sri Aurobindo Ashram.

Pondicherry.

108. Thoreau, H. D. (2015). *Civil Disobedience*. Xist Publishing.

109. Unknown. (1966). *The Teaching of Buddha*. Bukkyō Dendō Kyōkai.

110. Vaidya, C. V. (2001). *Epic India*. Asian Educational Services.

111. Verma, S. K., Sahai, R. N. (2015). *Oxford English Hindi Dictionary*. OUP.

112. Vidyalankar, S. (1983). *The Holy Vedas – A Golden Treasury*. Clarion Books.

113. Vivekananda, S. (2017). *All Power is Within You*. Swamy Jyotirmayananda Publisher.

114. Vivekananda, S. (1963). *On Himself*. Advaita Ashrama.

115. Woodroffe, J. (2001). *The Principles of Tantra Vol 1–2*. Sivalik Prakashan.

116. Woodroffe, J. (2010). *The Serpent Power*. Ganesh and Company.

117. Woods, J. H. (1914). *Yoga System of Patanjali*. Motilal Banarsidass.

118. https://en.wikipedia.org/wiki/Mahanarayana upanishad, accessed on 14/11/2020.

119. https:*//en.m.wikipedia.org/wiki/Zoroaster*, accessed on 27/12/2020.